LEADING, STRUCTURING AND FACILITATING TEAMS

A Field Guide for Club Managers

LEADING, STRUCTURING AND FACILITATING TEAMS

A Field Guide for Club Managers

EDWARD A. MERRITT, PHD

STATLER PRESS

Copyright © 2011 Edward A. Merritt,
First Edition

Without limiting the rights under copyright reserved above, no part of this publication may be reproduced, stored in or introduced into a retrieval system, or transmitted, in any form or by any means (electronic, mechanical, photocopying, recording, or otherwise), without the prior written permission of both the copyright owner and the publisher of this book.

Published by Statler Press

ISBN: 1-59330-734-9

Printed in the United States of America

ALL RIGHTS RESERVED

For Margaret, Lucy, and Ismo

Contents

Chapter 1: ... 1
   Goal Setting ... 1
   About This Topic ... 1
   Organization ... 2
   Competencies ... 2

Lesson 1 ... 4
   Introduction to Goal Setting ... 4
   Why Goal Setting? ... 5
   1.1. Mini Case: Managing Yourself ... 6
      Discussion Question ... 7

Lesson 2 ... 18
   Benefits of Goal Setting ... 18
   1.2. Mini Case: The Visionary Boss ... 19
      Discussion Question ... 20

Lesson 3 ... 30
   Steps in Establishing a Goal ... 30
   Step One: Identify the Problem ... 30
      Brainstorming ... 30
      Ranking ... 30
   Step Two: Map a Strategy ... 31
   1.3. Mini Case: Brainstorm, Rank, and Map ... 31
      Discussion Questions ... 32

Lesson 4 ... 42
   Step Three: Setting SMART Goals ... 42
      Specific ... 42
      Measurable ... 43

Acceptable	43
1.4. Mini Case: Setting a Specific Goal	46
Discussion Question	47
Lesson 5	**56**
Step Three: Setting SMART Goals (Continued)	56
Realistic	56
Timely	57
1.5. Mini Case: Realistic and Timely Goals	58
Discussion Questions	59
Lesson 6	**68**
Step Four: Identify Resources	68
Step Five: Recognize Risk, Contingencies, and Conflict	68
Risk	68
Contingencies	69
Conflict	69
1.6. Mini Case: Risk, Contingencies, and Conflict	69
Discussion Questions	71
Lesson 7	**84**
Step Six: Get Feedback	84
1.7. Mini Case: Feedback	86
Discussion Question	86
Lesson 8	**95**
The Goal Statement	95
1.8. Mini Case: The Goal Statement	96
Discussion Question	96
Lesson 9	**105**
Achieving the Goal	105
The Cognitive Approach: Visualization	105

Physical Approach: Setting Objectives	106
Recording Progress	107
Frequency Count	107
Time Duration	107
Reinforcing	107
Goal Aids	108
Goal Re-evaluation	108
1.9. Mini Case: Visualization	109
Discussion Question	110
Lesson 10	**116**
Managing Goal Achievement	116
1.10. Mini Case: Managing Goal Achievement	119
Discussion Question	121
Summary	128
Chapter 2	**133**
Why Teams Are Important	133
About This Topic	133
Organization	134
Competencies	134
Lesson 1	**136**
Why Teams are Important	136
Affiliation	136
The Urge to be an Individual	137
2.1. Mini Case: I Want to be a Star	138
Discussion Question	139
Lesson 2	**147**
Team or Individual?	147
Group Process Versus Individualism	147

Roots of Team Process	148
Lesson 3	**151**
Why People Join Teams	151
Teams can be More Effective Than Individuals	152
Characteristics of Effective Teams	153
Lesson 4	**155**
Learning Styles	155
2.4. Mini Case: The Wedding Cake Team	156
Discussion Question	157
Lesson 5	**163**
Team Success	163
Club Groups and Teams	164
Teams Differ From Groups	166
Developing Groups Into Teams	167
Team Values	168
Organizational Conditions	168
Skills	168
Team Roles	169
Work Preferences	170
2.5. Mini Case: The Club Menus	171
Discussion Question	171
Conclusion	179
Chapter 3	**182**
Phases in Team Development	182
About This Topic	182
Organization	183
Competencies	183

Lesson 1 — 185
- Introduction to Phases — 185
- Recurring Phases — 185
    - Therapy Groups — 185
    - Interaction Process Analysis — 186
- Sequential Stages — 186
    - The Four-Stage Process — 186
    - Life Cycle — 187
    - Phases — 188
    - Five Stages — 189
    - Forming — 189
    - Storming — 189
- 3.1. Mini Case: The Beginning — 190
    - Discussion Question — 194

Lesson 2 — 206
- The Middle — 206
    - Storming Begins to Calm — 206
    - Growth and Interaction Emerge — 207
    - Maturity Develops — 207
    - Norming — 208
    - Performing — 208
- 3.2. Mini Case: The Middle — 209
    - Discussion Questions — 212

Lesson 3 — 221
- Disengagement — 221
    - Disengagement — 222
- 3.3. Mini Case: The End — 222
    - Discussion Questions — 224

High-Performance Teams	230
Chapter 4	**233**
Decision Making	233
About This Topic	233
Organization	233
Competencies	234
Lesson 1	**237**
Team Decision Making	237
Advantages of Group Decision Making	237
The Process	238
Classical Theory	238
Assumptions	242
Assessment	243
4.1. Mini Case: Electric Ethics	245
Discussion Questions	247
Lesson 2	**261**
Behavioral Theory	261
4.2. Mini Case: Renata's Plan	265
Discussion Question	266
Lesson 3	**275**
Alternatives	275
The Interacting Group	275
The Nominal Group	278
The Delphi Technique	278
4.3. Mini Case: Use E-Mail	279
Discussion Question	280
Lesson 4	**285**
Structured Decision Making	285

Why Use Structure?	285
Dialectical Inquiry	285
The Stepladder	286
Voting	288
Lesson 5	**290**
Structured Decision Making (Continued)	290
Consensus Mapping	290
Procedural Rationality	291
4.4. Mini Case: Out Of Order	292
Discussion Question	293
Lesson 6	**302**
Unstructured Decision Making	302
Consensus	302
Leader Prerogative	302
Delegation, Referral, and Delay	303
Negotiation	304
4.5. Mini Case: The Swim Team	304
Discussion Question	305
Competing Motives	312
Lesson 7	**314**
Advantages of Team Decision Making	314
4.6. Mini Case: Sam's Scotches	316
Discussion Question	317
Lesson 8	**323**
Challenges in Team Decision Making	323
Groupthink	323
Vigilant Interaction	325
Emotions	325

Stress	325
4.7. Mini Case: Golf Spikes	327
Discussion Question	328
Lesson 9	**335**
Deciding Alone or Using a Team	335
Higher Quality Outcomes	337
4.8. Mini Case: The Wedding Cake	337
Discussion Question	338
Bibliography	**344**

Chapter 1:

Goal Setting

This is the first of four major topics in the course Organizational Behavior: Team Processes in Private Clubs. In this first topic we will discuss the importance of goal setting to one's success as a club manager. A complete listing in order of the four topics to be covered in this book:

1. Goal setting: managing yourself to manage others,
2. Why teams are important,
3. Phases in team development, and
4. Decision making.

About This Topic

The Goal-Setting Topic is divided into 10 lessons. Each lesson will take approximately 30-45 minutes to read and understand. Furthermore, each lesson will take another 30-45 minutes to envision ways in which one can apply the ideas presented in the text.

Note: I want to gratefully acknowledge the valuable contributions of Professor Florence Berger to this section.

Organization

The unifying and recurring stream used throughout this text is in providing readers with information that will allow them to become better and more effective managers in their positions. Each chapter topic begins with the introduction and discussion of theories, concepts, ideas, and best practices relative to the subject topic.

Following the presentation of theories and ideas, I have designed mini cases, which propose scenarios that can be solved, managed, and or mitigated using this new knowledge. The application exercises (the mini cases) are best solved using a combination of both new knowledge and past knowledge that has come from training, education, logic, and experience.

Finally, for each mini case, I have re-printed seven example answers from managers with whom I have worked in the past. I have found that readers benefit tremendously from having a variety of answer examples drawn from managers from all corners of the globe and each with different perspectives, educations, and backgrounds.

Competencies

1. Identify six benefits of goal setting and summarize their positive outcomes if managers implement them properly. Taxonomy of Measurable Variables: Bloom: Comprehension. ACPHA: Introduce.

2. Utilizing the six-step process for establishing a goal, construct a written goal statement that includes answers to the seven following points: Who, what, where, when, why, how, and who cares? Taxonomy of Measurable Variables: Bloom: Application. ACPHA: Reinforce.

3. Categorize the five components of a SMART performance goal and describe how each of these components

individually contributes to a thorough and well-developed goal. Taxonomy of Measurable Variables: Bloom: Analysis. ACPHA: Reinforce.

4. Examine the fundamental premise behind the cognitive approach of visualization in goal achievement. Appraise the four steps involved with visualization which will prove beneficial toward the final outcome. Taxonomy of Measurable Variables: Bloom: Analysis. ACPHA: Reinforce.

5. Compare and contrast the differences between the orientations of the physical approach of setting objectives and the cognitive approach of visualization. Appraise the three steps in setting objectives. Taxonomy of Measurable Variables: Bloom: Analysis. ACPHA: Reinforce.

6. Organize and emphasize why an important facet of goal achieving is keeping accurate records of the progress made toward goal accomplishment. Describe two basic methods for recording progress. Taxonomy of Measurable Variables: Bloom: Synthesis. ACPHA: Emphasize.

7. Argue as to why it is important to experience small rewards when accomplishing progress or discipline when falling short on making progress toward the goal. Taxonomy of Measurable Variables: Bloom: Evaluation. ACPHA: Emphasize.

8. Justify the purpose as to why goal aids are utilized. Taxonomy of Measurable Variables: Bloom: Evaluation. ACPHA: Emphasize.

9. Identify and measure the two issues that should both be satisfied before making the decision to change goals during goal re-evaluation. Taxonomy of Measurable Variables: Bloom: Evaluation. ACPHA: Emphasize.

10. Select and support up to 10 techniques for use in managing others through goal setting. Taxonomy of Measurable Variables: Bloom: Evaluation. ACPHA: Emphasize.

Lesson 1

Introduction to Goal Setting

Club managers are expected to perform a multitude of functions including executing their responsibilities through others. They cannot expect to manage teams and their direct reports if they cannot manage themselves. Establishing a system of goals is a valuable tool that will enable managers to manage themselves and others. Effective goal setting can provide managers with many benefits including: directing attention, encouraging high-level performance, developing innovation and persistence, and helping prevent stress. The goal-setting process includes six steps: specify the goal and how to accomplish it, create a SMART goal, identify resources and risk involved, and obtain feedback. Two effective ways to approach goal achievement are through visualization and setting objectives. Once managers have established their goals and have moved toward achieving them, they can begin to coach their employees on goal setting. Effective methods of coaching include these elements: staying in contact, praising, communicating the importance of the process, ensuring capability, allowing employees to reward and critique themselves, choosing the right time and method, publicizing goals, considering using negative feedback in a non-evaluative way, and mitigating conflict. For this section of the course I surveyed 30 hospitality industry leaders regarding their use of goal setting. Of the 22 respondents, only one said that he did not use the principles of goal setting on a daily basis.

Why Goal Setting?

When club managers do not care where they are going, goals are not important. In Carroll's, *Alice's Adventures in Wonderland*, Alice and the Cheshire Cat had the following conversation:

Alice: *Would you tell me, please, which way I ought to go from here?*

Cheshire Cat: *That depends a good deal on where you want to get to.*

Alice: *I don't much care.*

Cheshire Cat: *Then it doesn't matter which way you go.*

Goal setting is vital when managers want to know where they are going. The key to success for many senior-level managers is their ability not only to manage teams but to discipline and manage themselves. Through this skill one is able to set realistic goals and objectives and determine the most efficient and effective way to achieve them. Continual goal setting and achievement helps assure continued success.

Managers are expected to perform a multitude of functions including planning, organizing, leading, and controlling, and perhaps most important, executing their responsibilities in a way that produces desired goals. Successful managers must be able to make efficient use of time, delegate responsibility, and be aware of both the long and short term effects of their decisions. Managers cannot expect to manage other people if they cannot come to work on time, complete tasks as scheduled, and provide leadership and direction to the teams they supervise. Establishing a system of goals is a valuable tool that will enable club managers to manage themselves and others.

For the presentation of this topic, I have divided goal setting into four major sections. First I introduce the subject of goal setting by discussing some of its many benefits. The second section is devoted to the step process in establishing a goal including problem identification, strategy mapping, setting a performance goal, identifying necessary resources, recognizing risk, and the importance of obtaining constructive feedback. The third section is a discussion of a variety of methods for goal achievement once the goal is established. The fourth and final section lists techniques managers can use in managing teams through goal setting.

If managers need an incentive to read further, remember that clubs that implement goal setting deliver greater return on income to their members than clubs that do not (Terpstra & Rozell).

1.1. Mini Case: Managing Yourself

Sam is a popular manager with the members. As clubhouse manager, he works long hours, putting in the necessary high profile time during special events, and always greets everyone with a big smile. Members describe him as a great guy. The trouble is that the food & beverage department always seems to be just an inch away from a disaster. And he cannot understand why his team cannot get their act together. *After all, they are professionals*, he states emphatically. *They should know what they are supposed to be doing.*

However, an interview with Lew, the banquet captain, revealed a few of Sam's shortcomings. *He is a great five-minute man out there on the floor shaking hands and kissing babies! But he drives us crazy. We have not had a pre-meal line-up for over a year because he cannot make it to work on time. He has not posted a schedule in six months because he is too busy. Last Friday night we ran out of strip steaks at 6:00 and out of coffee by 8:00. We looked like a bunch of fools to the membership. He blamed the chef! But he is the problem and not the chef. He does not get around to approving invoices, so our vendors have not been paid in months. They will not ship to* us anymore. He just cannot manage himself at all. He certainly cannot manage us. He is a nice guy; but his lack of discipline and focus make it difficult for everyone.

Discussion Question

List some of the measures that Sam can take to gain the confidence of the food & beverage team. Now prioritize. If you were in Sam's position, what are the first three things you would do?

Manager Response 1

For Sam to gain the confidence of his food and beverage team he should come up with both a short-term and long-term plan. A long-term plan will resolve some larger issues and pave a path of future successful club management skills for Sam. However, Sam has some immediate problems to take care of and therefore he should also implement a short-term plan to take care of more time prevalent issues. Sam can start his new journey by first going back to the definition of management: planning, organizing, leading, and controlling. For any organization to be progressive and profitable, it needs to follow the basics of Management 101. Sam obviously is suffering in many of these areas and needs first to be able to manage himself before he can be asked to manage others.

In order for Sam to gain the confidence of his food and beverage team he needs to become a more effective manager. First, he needs to improve in his planning skills. He needs to be able to look forward and make decisions today for tomorrow. With new improved planning skills, Sam will be on the road to regaining his staff's confidence. Next Sam needs to organize his professional life and that of his work environment in a more proficient manner. He can make a positive start toward achieving this by first delegating some responsibilities to his department heads. When Sam's members enter the Club, they should expect everything to be ready and for the event to go off without difficulties.

Leadership ability is of extreme importance in not only a well-run organization, but also in gaining staff confidence. Sam has demonstrated admirable leadership skills when greeting his members and making them feel important. However, he also needs to express the same caring attitude toward his staff, instead of blaming them for his shortcomings.

Sam must lead by example within all parameters of the job. An effective manager must also be able to instill proper organizational controls. There should be checks and balances to provide for an efficient operation. I doubt that Sam has many of these types of controls in place.

Sam's short-term plan should deal specially with running his club more proficiently and gradually regaining the confidence of his staff. Specifically, he should first figure out what the problems are and possibly consider hiring a management consultant to detail the strengths and weaknesses of the Club and its manager's leadership skills. At the very least, Sam should hold discussions with his managerial staff and key employees to determine where improvements need to be made. Regardless of the method, he must develop a list of strengths and current problems to overcome.

Sam's next order of business is to come up with a list of objectives and goals that will help overcome his weaknesses. These objectives and goals should be very detailed with specific time schedules and built into a step-by-step program. Sam should also make an effort to involve his staff in the creation of this list of goals. Everyone needs to know that there is an agreed upon game plan in place to bring the Club to its next level of quality and expertise.

Some of Sam's goals can include: communicating with his staff on a more consistent manner; delegating more day to day duties to department heads; becoming more conscious of the clock; promoting the individual efforts of the staff to the membership rather than trying to be everything to everyone by himself; and walking the walk and talking the talk of a motivated and progressive manager.

Accountability should be Sam's third objective. Just because he has evaluated the problems at hand, set goals and objectives, he must also follow through and have some level of accountability to both himself and his team. Sam should enlist the assistance of his staff to hold him accountable for the changes he has announced, but also goals that his staff adopts in this new environment of professionalism and proficiency.

Manager Response 2

Sam needs to begin taking steps to manage his time better so that he can complete all of the tasks that he needs to accomplish on a daily basis. If Sam truly has too many responsibilities to handle by himself, he should delegate items and issues to other managers and supervisors. Once Sam displays a consistent pattern of effective management skills, he will begin to gain the respect and confidence of his staff.

If I were Sam, the first thing that I would do is make a conscious effort to arrive at work on time (early) every day. He will need to determine what time he should start his work day to achieve his goals and then stick to it without fail. This may be difficult in the beginning, but once he gets into a routine, he will realize that it actually makes his job easier.

Second, I would compose a daily list of things to do and prioritize them by number. Assigning a deadline time to each item may also prove useful. Undoubtedly, with the chaotic nature of club management, Sam will need to re-prioritize his list throughout the day. He should be careful not to focus only on the items that he enjoys doing. Instead, he may want to use a pleasurable task as a reward for completing an unpleasant task.

Third, I would schedule a specific block of time each day (at a designated time) for paperwork. During this block, there should be no interruptions from staff and or members, unless an emergency occurred. This is the time when he can ensure that invoices, scheduling, return phone calls, and the like, will be done.

Manager Response 3

Sam's measures to gain confidence of the food & beverage team:

- Look into time management: Be smart with regard to putting in face time with members, but not at cost of administrative responsibilities.

- Sam should set a schedule for himself. To rescue credibility, he should make schedule known to team members and stick to it. Sam should examine his behavior to understand why he is always late: does he go to bed too late? Is his alarm clock unreliable? Is he allowing enough time to get his children ready for school? Is he aware of the traffic patterns he might experience on the way to work? Is he lazy? Is he burned out?

- Hopefully Sam will realize that the Club's vendors are valuable customers and should be treated with the same respect that he gives to his members. If Sam makes sure the vendors are treated properly and paid in a timely fashion, he will then be in a position to hold the Chef accountable for proper ordering practices.

- Sam needs to hold himself accountable for the performance of his department. He is making a grave mistake in blaming others for his department's failings. His team will never respond positively to his leadership if he makes himself a hero, but allows his staff to appear as fools to the members.

- Sam derides his team as professionals, who should know what they are doing, but is he helping them in setting goals?
- It would be helpful if Sam were to open up communication with his team and provide them an opportunity to let him know what they need in the way of support to achieve their goals.

The first three things I would do:

1. Meet with the food & beverage team and identify the areas that are causing failures and therefore need attention. I would find out what they needed from me in the way of support to achieve their goals.
2. With the input of team members, I would set specific goals (including identifying specific areas of support needed from me).
3. Prioritize my own schedule in order to deliver promised support in a professional and timely fashion.

Manager Response 4

If Lew is any indication of the entire food and beverage department, then Sam certainly has got his work cut out for him if he wants to gain the team's confidence. Sam is close to the point of no return. The fact that his team is so easily able to see his shortcomings as their manager or coach makes you wonder if Sam has lost control of the food and beverage operation. It will not be long before the members see beyond his friendly, outwardly ways and notice that he is not performing effectively. The GM must also be aware of this problem.

In order to gain their confidence, Sam needs to do these things:

1. Acknowledge the existence of problems in his job performance.

2. Solicit the help of his boss and food and beverage team in identifying his shortcomings.

3. Admit to and apologize to his boss and team for these perceived shortcomings.

4. Rank shortcomings from most disruptive to least disruptive and try to imagine how much more efficiently the food and beverage operation would operate without these disruptions.

5. Entertain the boss' and team's input as to how to correct these problems.

6. Mull over the solutions, proactively adopt those that make the most sense, are realistic to implement, can be adhered to, and will correct the greatest number of the most disruptive shortcomings in the least amount of time.

7. He should physically involve his team in the solution through delegation He could have Lew do a weekly schedule and conduct a pre-meal line up. Perhaps the chef could assist in the authorization of invoices.

8. Set a firm date to meet with his boss and the food and beverage team to check on his progress.

9. Make sure that he does everything within his power to improve his performance.

If I were in Sam's position I would do these things:

- Unless you admit there is a problem you have no chance of solving the problem. For this reason, I would examine my conscience and come clean with myself on the shortcomings in my job performance. I would solicit the help and support of my manager and ask for his or her help in the solving of my problem.

- I would next admit my shortcomings to my team, apologize for my poor performance, solicit their help in solving the problem, and pledge my loyalty to them and the operation in solving the problem.

- Formulate a plan which establishes clear goals and measures objective effectiveness progress toward those goals.

Manager Response 5

Time Management

1. I would be encouraged (as Sam) to find ways to begin managing and leading the Food & Beverage operation instead of allowing the Food & Beverage operation to run me. Seeking out a course in time management would be high on my list in helping me to learn to plan my hours, day, week, month, year, work and life.

2. I would institute pre-shift meetings immediately. This is not only beneficial on the surface level of relating the 86 list, high-profile visitors, and soup of the day, but it will also help change negative perceptions and win back some of the confidence Sam has lost with his staff.

3. I would arrange a meeting with my prime purveyors in concert with the Club controller and arrange a payment schedule that meets the needs of the account and the Club. I would follow that up with a plan that utilizes the new skills acquired in my time management seminar. I would ensure that I maintained and updated an hourly, daily, weekly and monthly schedule.

Goals

Sam needs to begin with some basic goal setting. I recommend that he begin with goals that can be accomplished today and as he experiences achievement, then he should broaden his goal setting and achievement to longer terms.

Small victories early will give him the encouragement that he needs to develop the discipline of an integrated system of goals and objectives.

Manager Response 6

Gaining confidence with the food and beverage team could be accomplished if Sam first organizes himself, second learns to effectively manage his time, and third follows through with his newly acquired system. A team meeting discussing the problems at hand, first with the banquet captain and/or supervisors, then with the line employees is certainly in order. Making notes and ensuring the ideas come from the employees, bringing their knowledge and professionalism into the mix, and making it everyone's decision—and not just management's—would help tremendously over time. Provide the basics, such as a written schedule, a line up before shifts, organized ordering, and thoughtful follow-through on functions and responsibilities are a must in creating a successful operation. Beyond those, a service manual and job descriptions would help, too

My prioritization would first be along the lines of Sam getting himself together. He has to focus on his organizational skills and the effectiveness of his time and not to mention getting to work on time. A key to accomplishing this is the ability not to manage teams, but rather to allow teams to discipline and manage themselves. Then, bring in the staff and discuss the problems they have been encountering. Begin delegating, giving authority and responsibility with the necessary support. This will provide strong supportive leadership that can empower decision making in the absence of the leader.

Empowerment enables the staff to become better managers. Empowerment involves the process of setting mutually agreed upon goals, objectives, and tasks that have to be achieved on a daily basis toward a final outcome. A function is a series of tasks that lead to an eventual goal and a successful event.

The first three things Sam should do:

1. Establish a list of all job tasks and delegate the non-essential. Give authority and responsibility to empower the staff. Follow through on the issues delegated. For example, sign off on the schedules. Draw job descriptions that list short and long term goals.

2. Hold a team meeting to discuss the items they developed (a service manual to be written and distributed) and how these are going to be implemented, and what is then expected. Thank them for their hard work.

3. Get organized and develop a set time of work. Fluctuation is understandable. Maybe put yourself on the schedule the banquet captain completes each week, so that you know when you are expected to be on the floor. Work with a day time booklet or a list that sets up your day and week. How the members never realized what was going on should be counted as a blessing.

It sounds like the members like Sam. I doubt they never knew of the problems, though. It is imperative that he sets himself up for success by managing his time first. Once the team is on course, his essential tasks will be effortless and a part of an everyday routine.

Manager Response 7

Hold an F & B team staff meeting explaining that he recognizes that he needs to change some of his practices and more importantly how the staff can help Sam achieve this. However, also important is for Sam to show the staff what measures he has taken to change and what systems he would like to put in place to ensure his change is permanent. Sam needs to do some serious damage control if he is going to erase his past behavior and make permanent and positive change.

There are many details that Sam needs to execute and prioritize but none is bigger or more important than step one, which is personal change and understand the current state of F & B Team morale and how the operation has sunk to its present level. Sam needs to take responsibility and ownership for his lack of effective management in order for any long-term change to make a serious impact. It is obvious the change needs to be with Sam rather than the organization.

Once Sam completes step number, he needs to move to step two, which is to see what is most important to his team members and make quick, easy changes, some of which can be grouped together—as they can and should occur simultaneously.

Immediate changes that can occur the day after his revelation:

- Begin by showing up on time
- Hold enthusiastic pre-meal meetings
- Take responsibility for operational shortcomings and do not pass the blame on to other staff members or departments.

The next group of changes:

- Create daily and weekly to do schedules that will remind him that for example, every Tuesday he needs to sign invoices and that on Wednesday he needs to review inventory / forecast for the weekend.
- Communicate with staff, department heads & vendors, apologize for their recent history of un-timeliness, and work out a strategy for the future.

He should then implement these changes:

- Create a system that will help ensure timely vendor payment.
- Complete staff schedules as well as a functioning management schedule for himself, which he adheres to.

The final two steps in his short-term immediate action plan:

- Create a system of written timelines and goals for the daily and weekly operational responsibilities that are visual for the necessary staff to observe and view (not necessarily monitor, though).

- Complete a progress review and then move into phase two which will include holding a team meeting, which completes an operations analysis with larger team goals.

Lesson 2

Benefits of Goal Setting

Goals help managers translate general intentions into specific actions. Mesch defines a goal as a plan for a desired outcome. And goal-setting theory posited by Locke and Latham suggests that people who set goals perform more effectively than those who do not set goals. One GM from New England states that *Goals establish an end result, a direction of pursuit, a method of measurement, and foster team work and achievement. Goals help us perform beyond our capabilities and keep us on focused when the going gets tough.*

There are many benefits of goal setting. Some of the more notable advantages of goal setting proposed by Stallworth:

- Goals help to direct attention and actions because they give managers a target (O'Hair). People can become confused if they do not have a specific goal toward which to direct their efforts.

- Goals nurture an atmosphere that produces specific results within specific time periods.

- Goals are useful in helping people perform at peak levels. Setting goals makes managers aware of the mental, emotional, and physical energy they will need for the task and encourages them to conserve and mobilize energy carefully.

- Goals can help bolster persistence. The absence of strong goals can distract from one's mission and foster a temptation to quit when facing a challenge.

- Goals aid managers in developing innovative strategies. Club managers that set important goals will be surprised at how ingenious they can be in devising their strategies to reach their goals.

- Goal setting will provide managers with a short and long-term game plan. If set properly and realistically, managers can map out their futures with their clubs, or effect plans to achieve other aspirations.

- Goals can assist in preventing stress. A comprehensive goals program can help avoid burnout and produce positive feelings.

1.2. Mini Case: The Visionary Boss

You may know her. Susan is a visionary and big-picture person. As Vice President and creative director of one of the oldest, most prestigious advertising agencies in the Midwest, she is also President of the 900-member club where you are the chief operating officer and general manager. She has a vision for the Club, a picture of what the Club will become five years into the future. She paints with words how things will be: white-glove service, flowers at every tee, walnut paneling in the library, soft colors in the dining room, and Persian rugs in the great lounge. The Board overwhelmingly supports her plan. She turns to you and says, *make it happen*.

Gulp! You have been on the job three months and know these facts:

- The service staff is mostly part-time students that average six months at the Club before moving on.

- The tee boxes are irrigated from the roughs by large, 10-gallon-per-minute, impact sprinklers.

- Termites have been discovered in the existing roof joists above the library.

- The wall paint in the dining room contains dangerous levels of lead.

- The great lounge roof leaks. When one of the engineers was in the attic trying to repair the leak, he noticed that the sprinkler-system water pipes (fire protection) were wrapped in asbestos.

- For the past 10 years, the Club general managers have also served as assistant club treasurer. You notice that the reserve for capital replacements and projects account for the 50,000 square-foot clubhouse has not been funded for 10 years and that the account balance is $13,000, instead of the estimated $1,750,000, which should be in the account.

Discussion Question

Assuming that you do not immediately subscribe to CMAA's Managerial Openings List (MOL) and begin a job search, how can goal setting help you achieve that vision? Identify five top issues (considerations) that you will use as guiding principles to help formulate your plan.

Manager Response 1

Goal Setting will help the manager achieve this vision by laying out a plan with short and long-term goals. This will provide the Vice President and the Manager with tools to measure exactly where they are in achieving these goals, and will therefore help prevent unnecessary stress. Using short-term goals with specific results over specific time periods will help the manager to remain on target with the long-term goals.

The top five issues the manager needs to use to guide him to 2010:

1. Implement a service training program and develop long term employees.

2. The golf course irrigation system will need to be reviewed, with specific attention being given to the tee boxes.
3. The library roof needs to be inspected, as does the rest of the building.
4. Estimates should be collected for dealing with the lead paint removal and painting of the dining room.
5. Asbestos abatement and roof repair in the Great Lounge will need to be examined.

The manager should write down short-term goals for each area. He/she also needs to write down the long-term goals for the Club. Finally, the manager should institute a method for reviewing the short term goals (using objective means) to be sure that the short-term goals are progressing as planned.

The Board should be made aware of the cost of achieving these goals individually as well as the timeframes.

Manager Response 2

My first course of action would be to have contractors submit cost estimates for the necessary repairs and facility improvements using the Board's vision. With this information, I could go back to the Board with a target for funds needed to bolster the capital replacements and projects account, thus translating general intentions into specific actions.

Next, I would assemble the management staff and discuss the overall club goals set forth by the Board. Doing this would help alleviate confusion of the staff as to the direction the Club is headed. By setting goals with the staff, we would direct attention and actions which would give us a target to work toward. It would likely also foster teamwork.

With the assistance of the Food and Beverage Manager, I would review the operating budget to determine what impact hiring full time, qualified, food service personnel would have on the Club's financial situation. After submitting the findings to the Board, I would contact employment agencies, local colleges and become aware of the current labor market. These elements would help me to become prepared for the mental, emotional, and physical energy needed for the major tasks ahead.

My next course of action would be to examine why we had a high turnover and what could be done to make ourselves an attractive long term employer. I would devise strategies such as instituting a 401k program, housing assistance, and training programs that would help us reach our goals.

As a way of possibly saving money and still achieve the goals set forth, I would contact Persian rug companies and look at the possibility of using the Club as a show room for their goods. The Club would get a commission (such as 10 percent) for every rug sold and still be able to decorate the facility. Another opportunity may be to contact retail florist. We would propose that they could have an exclusive contract with the Club for private functions if they provided flowers for the Club lobby and tables at either a reduced price or free. By devising creative strategies we could reach our goals at minimum costs.

Once all the information had been compiled into short and long term goals, I would map out the future of the Club. I would also evaluate my own strengths and weaknesses in following through on these projects. I would then take classes through local colleges or through the CMAA to help me to overcome weaknesses that I identified.

Manager Response 3

First, develop a master plan for clubhouse improvements to prioritize needs, identify costs, and establish time frames of each. The plan should be directed by outside contracting professionals who would submit their findings to the Long

Range Planning Committee and/or Executive Committee (and the GM/COO).

Second, establish (if it does not already exist) a Finance Committee, to be chaired by a member Treasurer with experience in financial administration. Review the master plan goals and costs of completing, and formulate strategies of securing the necessary funding. Review the possibilities of assessing the membership to create initial funding as well as creating a long term solution of continued funding.

Third, coordinate the goals in the master plan and financial plan into a consolidated listing of prioritized goals, objectives, and strategies. Present these to member focus groups for feedback and to unify opinion. Once refined, present the final goals, master plan, and financial plan to the entire membership.

Fourth, address specific issues not included in master plan with club department heads to determine long and short term solutions to these issues.

Fifth, review with the Club President the long term vision, quantifying it wherever possible, and identifying specifics of what must occur in each of next several years for it to become reality. It is critical that the Club President enthusiastically supports the goals and strategies being formulated.

Manager Response 4

As difficult as this case seemed initially, after thinking through the issues, I find it to be a systematically simple answer.

Setting goals and objectives is the only true way to accomplish anything. Whether it is doing the laundry or shopping for holiday gifts, you must keep your ultimate goal in mind and map out the steps to achieve a satisfactory outcome.

As GM in this case, I would make a list of what the Board wants to accomplish. My goals would be in order of importance and or reality; short term to long term.

First on the list is service; this should be an ongoing quest in any club. This service issue can have immediate positive results. It will encourage members to utilize the Club more because they are being treated so well, and therefore they would recommend friends and associates to join.

Second on the list is structuring funds that go directly to the capital account. $13,000 will get this club none of what the Board anticipates. An analysis of the revenues to the Club and where they are currently earmarked is imperative. This detailed analysis will uncover probably some bad habits in spending and allocating of funds. A plan must be made as to how much per month, per year will be set to flow into this capital account. From there, projects can be structured out on time lines based on how they can be funded.

Third, a list needs to be made in order of safety, how it affects member satisfaction, etc, of all the capital projects. By doing so, a prioritized list more or less emerges—at least for discussion.

Fourth, recommendations of time lines, costs, and ultimate value should be made to the Board for their approval or restructuring.

Fifth, implementation of these projects and their time lines with costs must be communicated to the membership. A knowledgeable membership is a happy membership!

Manager Response 5

First, I would first take Susan's painted vision and create a short- and long-term game plan based on factual data including cost estimates. Any long-term plan will initially be hindered by the lack of funding for capital replacements and projects. It is important to ascertain if the Susan's long-term plan is shared by a majority of the membership, as well as the Board. Nothing of any scale can be achieved without broad support from important constituencies such as the Board, past presidents, key members, and others. After doing the proper research, the long-term plan would clearly show that there are a number of non-glamorous issues that need to be addressed before the softer side (items that members notice) can be introduced. The membership will need to be prepared for specific efforts in fundraising that might include: assessments, dues increases, bank loans, and or the sale of assets such as unused land. A long-term plan would then be formulated with the Board and promoted to the membership with specific goals and deadlines.

Second, the next important financial goal will be the immediate creation of a capital fund that will ensure that the Club's long-term needs will be properly addressed.

Third, assuming that the Club will continue to operate throughout the renovation plan, immediate attention would be paid to goals that could be reached without capital investment such as the service issue. The Food & Beverage Director would be consulted and asked to create a list of short-term goals that would quickly and positively impact the low level of service. The number one goal would be to find ways to build a core staff that would bring continuity and consistency to service within the Club. This core staff would act as a backbone, a safety net, to catch and help correct the inconsistencies offered by the short-term student staff. Specific goals would include creating incentives to retain good employees, such as paid vacations, health insurance, educational benefits, and schedules tailored to suit the needs of a working student. Another immediate goal would be the introduction of a comprehensive training program.

Fourth, the serious problems in the building would need to be addressed as short-term goals (they must be addressed!). Innovative ideas would be needed for the Club to remain an enjoyable destination while undergoing extensive repairs. The membership would be included in the restoration project using devices such as displays in the lobby illustrating and explaining the issues and letting members know the corrective plan. Also included in the display would be artist's renderings of the long-term vision of the restored club. The Club would offer a clear vision of its future for the benefit of its members, guests and, future members. This approach would be helpful in relieving members and staff from the stress resulting from a club that is perceived as deteriorating.

Fifth, all goals would include specific deadlines that would be communicated to the staff and the membership. As reached, each goal would be celebrated to emphasize the progress that is being made, producing positive feelings.

Manager Response 6

This scenario sounds like the champagne taste, draft beer budget philosophy of many clubs. Based on the capital reserves left in place, the first order of business is to come to grips with the reality of the account. From there, I would begin an assessment.

The desired outcomes require a careful review of resources. A physical review of the facility, investigating the ability of the current facility to provide the framework to accomplish this vision is an important step.

In conjunction with the Board, I would prioritize the various elements of the vision, as related to the current facility. Certain elements of the list of what is known will require short-term fixes at varying levels of immediacy.

The roof needs to be repaired immediately. This is R&M work, and bids should be secured to accomplish this project along with marshaling the necessary resources allocated to do so.

The balance of the projects requires identification of various factors:

Time. A careful consideration of the desired timetable for completion of each phase of the overall project will need to be plotted on a Pert Chart, to help facilitate agreement. Can certain projects be staged over time, or does the desired outcome require a large scale undertaking? Those questions can be answered more easily when all of the issues are delineated on a chart.

Money. Most of the issues can be addressed quickly if there is enough money. In this case, there is not much cash available. Therefore, alternatives for raising reserves to appropriate levels must be presented, reviewed, and approved. The dollars must be matched with the timetable to assure proper (and conservative) cash flow practices are observed. Alternatives would include items such as assessments, dues increases, fee increases, and or the assumption of debt.

Physical resources. Can the facility meet the needs of the members (for example, walnut paneling in the library and fine quality rugs) or is it time to look at a major renovation project to solve the environmental issues as well as the facility needs. In terms of finding the type of staff they want (experienced, full-time employees) surveys of the area, employee demographics, and projected cost of training and staffing will need to be compiled.

Ultimately these items need to be coordinated into a master plan along with goals and objectives needing to be established in order to establish an agreed upon, written plan.

Over the years, this plan will need continuous communication between management and staff, review at stages of progress of projects, and careful and studied implementation.

Manager Response 7

The first step in *making it happen* is to devise a well thought out, educated long- and short-term plan. We know that a benefit of goal setting is that goals allow us to direct attention and actions because the entire staff and membership is theoretically working towards a shared vision.

Communication is one of the most important building blocks of the foundation for success. A meeting of all department heads would be called and the President's message communicated. We would hold a brainstorming session to see how we could realize and successfully execute the President's message. Before execution though, we would have to complete the process of planning. At the first department head meeting, timelines and expectations would be set in order for all staff to complete their tasks in a focused and timely manner.

The department heads would research all that has to be done in their respective areas, as well as all associated costs. Stating these goals and timelines would allow each manger to remain focused and persistent without becoming stressed by also juggling the day-to-day operational responsibilities. With long- and short-term goals devised, department heads would be allowed to manage their own project schedule and comprehend all of the global issues and concerns. Each department head would complete a chronological plan by which their departments would be working.

All of the department head information would be collected and compiled into one unified document. Three major elements would be summarized: cost and the financial needs—plan in order for project realization, time schedules, as well as impact schedules. Once all of this information was packaged, the President's education and Board education would begin by the COO, informing them as to the ramifications of *making it happen*.

Five top considerations the Club should use in executing the plan that the Board decides upon:

1. Keep the end (outcome) in Mind
2. Cost / Quality equation

3. Timeline

4. Ethical Business Practices

5. Innovation and Creation

These five characteristics would be the foundation for all decisions. Obviously, we must always remember the main project goal, what we are to accomplish, and in this case what the Club is supposed to look and feel like; that is what is meant by keeping the end in mind. Quality and cost factors are of utmost importance and will vary what the final outcome could be. But, if everyone is aware what the end is to be, the decisions in the middle will, for the most part, tell us exactly how to get there. The timeline, sometimes the leading factor and other times, not as important as *getting it right* also makes the decision process easier by allowing us to evaluate our decisions on the impact of the schedule.

Guidelines four and five are hopefully already tenets of any well-run organization and need no explanation. As members of CMAA and effective club managers, we hope that our staffs will act in ethical and professional manners. Most of all, when planning projects of this magnitude, we hope our tasks will not only be fun but follow the saying that two heads are better than one in collaboration. We also aim to have creative and innovative teams that enjoy what they are accomplishing.

Lesson 3

Steps in Establishing a Goal

Step One: Identify the Problem

As a first step toward goal setting, specify exactly what is to be accomplished: the job, assignment, or responsibility. Club managers can use brainstorming methods to assist in identifying problems and then rank the ideas that emerge.

Brainstorming

Create a list of wants or desires as they relate to the job, assignment, or responsibility. Try to put aside inhibitions and be creative—in a dreamlike state. This is the time to catalog all options. Resist the temptation to evaluate whether or not these dreams are practical, logical, or even possible. One General Manager from Georgia shared these thoughts about the brainstorming process: *Our most successful and creative ideas come from brainstorming. We brainstorm for special projects and in general sessions to help improve overall operations.*

Ranking

Next, prioritize to determine which of these desires is most important. Select the most important option as the goal.

Step Two: Map a Strategy

Create a plan for how to accomplish the goal. Brainstorm to develop a list of possible alternatives—regardless of how impractical they appear. After recording possibilities, begin the culling process by considering the limitations of each alternative. Discard those that are unreasonable.

1.3. Mini Case: Brainstorm, Rank, and Map

Dutton Crowfield, 40-years old, is the executive assistant manager at Deep Forest Country Club. While she grew up in the private club industry, she has no formal education beyond high school. She has decided that she wants to obtain a Bachelor's degree in hospitality or business within five years.

In checking possibilities, she has discovered the following options:

- Flossmore College of Vocational Studies offers credit for life experience and hotel-motel management degrees within six months. The school is not accredited; they have a post office box address, and an 800 number. After sending for information, she received mailings from three similar schools with the same post office box in Hackensack, New Jersey.

- Eastern Louisiana Community College (5 miles away) offers an Associate's degree in hospitality management and evening classes. There are three other community colleges within 20 miles of the Club that offer 2-year business degrees.

- University of Alabama offers an external degree program (BS) in business administration entirely via the Internet.

- University of Orleans (75 miles away) offers both evening and weekend classes leading to a Bachelor's degree in hospitality management. Dutton has pretty much written off this option since it is so expensive.

- UNLV says they will accept her as a full-time undergraduate student in their hospitality program. Dutton has found that other traditional universities are interested in her, too, due to her years of experience in the industry.

Discussion Questions

1. How would you complete the brainstorming process if you were Dutton? Has she cataloged all options? Has she made any errors in the process so far?
2. How would you prioritize the list of alternatives?
3. Make a choice and begin to map a strategy for how to accomplish the goal. How would you deal with some of the limitations of the alternatives? Which limitations cause you to discard the alternative as a possibility? Which limitations can be mitigated? What would you do?

Manager Response 1

Dutton Crowfield is in a great position! There are many avenues for her to investigate in order for her to make an informed decision as to the best career move.

In the brainstorming process I would incorporate Club Managers Association of America (CMAA) and all its education offerings. She could get involved in the Assistant Manager courses. Just because Ms. Crowfield has no formal education beyond high school does not mean that her real life experiences should be discounted. She has put in many years on-the-job and probably has an enormous amount of information that those with four year college degrees could only imagine.

I would prioritize in this manner:

1. Get involved in the CMAA Assistant Managers' courses.
2. Enroll in an evening class at Eastern Louisiana Community College to get a feel for higher education. Higher education is not for everyone and does not necessarily guarantee success in life. I would hope that she would complete two or more classes and then have better clarity as to her ultimate objective. Does she want to go into a specific aspect of club management; function planning, general management, membership marketing, etc?
3. If Ms. Crowfield gets the bug from the courses at Eastern Louisiana Community College and wants to move forward toward a four year degree, then she may want to think about transferring to a school with a different degree of education in Hospitality Management like UNLV or Michigan State. She would need to have saved money or have planned out how to pay for school and how to live. Possibly she could get a part-time job at a local club.

   Dutton is in an envious spot.

Manager Response 2

I have done well in club management despite the fact that I have no formal education beyond high school. 40 years old is a great time to take a look at the direction of my professional life. If I really want to continue to grow, I must make up for my lack of formal education. Imagine how helpful a Hospitality or Business degree would be. It would certainly make it easier to find a better job, perhaps even one day, a General Manager's position.

I seem to have a lot of options available to me. I could leave Louisiana and start a new life as a student in Las Vegas. That would be awesome, I am sure that I could easily find a good restaurant job, so I could pay my way. I bet there are country clubs there that would love to hire someone with my background and would be willing to give me a work schedule that fit with my school schedule. But, I do love my job and enjoy life here in Louisiana, so perhaps a better option would be to take a correspondence course with a vocational college or an external degree program over the Internet. I really want to make sure that I am investing my time and money in something that will help me professionally successful, and I would like to find a way to move the process along as quickly as possible. I wonder if my manager could be of assistance. Maybe she knows of a suitable course or perhaps the Club could help me with my education expenses. She is always telling me how great CMAA is. Maybe she could get me involved in an education program with them. I need to take a close look at all my options.

Prioritize Alternatives. My goal is to attain a Bachelor's degree in hospitality within the next five years. I will prioritize my alternatives by eliminating options that will not help me achieve this goal. I will also keep in mind such practical issues as budget and compatibility of lifestyle.

Choice. Of my options, there are only two that meet my goal of attaining a Bachelor's degree in hospitality. I am not interested in the University of Alabama's external degree program, as it is all business with no hospitality. The University of Orleans would be an attractive opportunity if I could afford the fees, but they are out of my range. Attending UNLV would require a long-distance move and a complete change in lifestyle. However, the school offers everything I am looking for.

This would be my strategy if I were to attend UNLV:

- Complete all application forms.

- Identify any scholarship programs that might be available, especially for mature students.

- Ask my GM to contact clubs in the Las Vegas area that might be able to provide employment.

I would not receive any meaningful education by attending Flossmore College. And, as that school is not accredited, it would be of very little help to my professional development. Eastern Louisiana is very small and regional. My decision to attend UNLV is the right one to achieve my professional and personal goals.

Manager Response 3

If I were Dutton I would have reviewed what schools in the area could help me to accomplish my goal while still working at the Club. (It appears that she took this step.) She seems to have catalogued her options fairly well; however it was not clear to me if she still needed to work while getting her education, or whether she could afford to go to school full time. If colleges were interested in her, she should pursue scholarship opportunities to save money.

The priority should be to get the most powerful degree she possibly can within her constraints. If she plans to continue working full time, then perhaps the best option would be for her to go for the Bachelor of Science from the University of Alabama. This option would work with her schedule. Her goal should be to get the best degree for her future, one that could also be marketable if she ever needed or wanted to leave the Club field. If her goal is to obtain a Bachelor's degree, then this appears to be her only real alternative, unless she moves and can find work at another club.

My choice would be for the University of Alabama because it is a four-year degree which could be done around my schedule. The learning would have to be self motivated and there would be no support from the typical class room setting of peers and live interaction with professors. The choice to discard the other opportunities was mainly due to the fact that the club business is demanding from a time perspective. Long drives to school after or before work will take its toll after time.

Setting and working to achieve personal goals will not be easy for Dutton. However, the learning, satisfaction, and career opportunities that she will have after completing her goal should prove to be well worth the effort.

Manager Response 4

Dutton's goal is to obtain a Bachelor's degree in either hospitality management or business within the next five years. Her brainstorming process has led to some very interesting possibilities. Dutton made one mistake in that she prematurely eliminated the University of Orleans prior to ranking her ideas. The best brainstorming occurs when a list of ideas is developed (focus on numbers) regardless of how impractical they appear (focus on quality). Dutton has collected and cataloged a good number of options to help her obtain her goal. Dutton will have to decide whether or not she plans to continue working in her position as Executive Assistant Manager at Deep Forest Country Club while she continues her education. This decision will aid her in mapping out a plan.

In becoming Dutton in answering this question, I will assume that I have to continue in my current position as Executive Assistant Manager for both financial and practical reasons. This decision will influence the way I prioritize options and map a strategy for achieving the goal. After brainstorming possibilities, it is time to prioritize, helping me narrow focus and reach my goal.

UNLV or any other traditional university would not be practical as I am unable to devote myself full time as an undergraduate student. Therefore, I would have to eliminate this as a viable option.

The University of Orleans offers classes conducive to my schedule and offers the program I am looking for. Unfortunately, the commute is 75 miles one way and cost for the program is prohibitive. This is probably not an option which would work for me.

I have also considered pursuing my Associate's degree at a nearby community college. It may not accomplish my ultimate goal, but I can always continue my education after obtaining my Associate's degree. The college courses are affordable and will work with my current schedule. This would compromise my original plan, but may be a reasonable way to go.

Flossmore College of Vocational Studies offers a hotel-motel management degree within six months. I could consider this option as well. However, the school is not accredited, so I would not consider it a viable option.

In reviewing, the University of Alabama offers the most attractive option for me. Not only does working via the Internet offer me the flexibility I need in my current position; it is convenient and affordable as well. Upon completion of the program, I will have achieved my goal, attaining a Bachelor's degree in business.

Manager Response 5

I would complete the brainstorming process by getting more information from the University of Alabama regarding their degree program. Perhaps Dutton could do some combination of full time, on campus and Internet, external study.

I would also get more information from UNLV and other universities. These universities may have other options available that she has not explored.

I would get more information from the University of Orleans. They may have more options available to get her a degree in 5 years.

Flossmore College and Eastern Louisiana Community College do not appear to get her to her goal, so I would disregard them.

My priorities:

1. The University of Orleans

2. The University of Alabama

3. UNLV and others

My personal choice, given the information, would be The University of Orleans. Here I would be able to obtain a degree in Hospitality Management within the 5 years specified.

I would begin with my employer, Deep Forest Country Club, and sell my boss on the fact that I would be a better employee. Many companies have continuing education assistance programs. I would propose a way for DFCC to assist financially for my classes, such as having to get a B grade or better. If I did not meet that requirement, then DFCC would not be responsible for any financial obligation. I would lay out the long-term benefits to DFCC by having me obtain a degree.

I would also contact the University to see if there were any scholarships available that I might apply for.

Money is a minor issue facing Dutton. She should concentrate on how to reach her goal. The goal should not be compromised.

Manager Response 6

To complete the process, I would review all options similar to the UNLV offer, which is to matriculate as a traditional student.

In free thinking, the options should have some structure, but the imposed time limitation will limit the extent of her free thinking. Her options include Associate's (two-year) degrees at two facilities. An Associate's degree is not a Bachelor's (four-year) degree, so the free thinking is flawed in this context.

Additionally, depending on her underlying reason for achieving the degree (if it is due to her desire to increase her qualifications for a GM position) she might consider not seeking a degree, but instead enhancing her background through Business Management Institute (CMAA's BMI educational programs) or similar professional training programs.

To prioritize, first I would eliminate all Associate's degree programs since they do not meet the original criteria. Drop Flossmore since it is not accredited. She has already rejected the University of Orleans due to expense.

This leaves two options: The University of Alabama external degree program (best option), or leaving the Club and matriculating as a full-time student.

I would select the University of Alabama program since it allows me the best options. I can continue my work and go to school full time, thereby earning the degree within the desired time period.

The main challenge will be juggling school responsibilities with work. Both are full-time requirements. If she is willing to work diligently for five years, the goal can be achieved.

I applaud her willingness and drive to complete her Bachelor's degree.

Manager Response 7

I would advise Dutton to begin again and include at least one other person. When doing creative brainstorming with others, the collective ideas are infinitely more productive than individual sessions. Additionally, it appears that Dutton's brainstorming was too focused as she took into account the limitations of options such as the University of Orleans. Also, the scope of options was not necessarily as vast as it could have been.

If I were Dutton and beginning again I would start by listing categories of options:

- Remain Employed in her current job and complete the education.

- Move to the area where her school of choice is and continue working in the Club environment.

- Leave the current job in order to enter a full time schooling process.

Now that the broader areas are defined, I would brainstorm by each of those categories, which would yield seemingly limitless options. Once that was completed, I would separate ideas by those that appeal to me most versus that which might make the most sense. Next, I would research the financial aspects of all ideas, taking into account concepts of tuition assistance, scholarships, work study, etc; I would still not discard any options. At that point, I would begin to rank all of my options, even those that I do not feel like I would chose. I would keep my lists separate, desire versus practical. After ranking choices, I would closely review my top two choices on each list, carefully looking into each as if I were going to commit to that option (mapping strategies).

Strategy decisions depend on some of Dutton's life parameters and how far is she willing to go in order to accomplish what she wants. She must weigh her desires against practicality and other factors in her life that of which we are not aware. Does Dutton have an immediate family, children, or just a close network of family in her local area that she is or is not comfortable leaving? Does she have and adventurous spirit that will spur her to study far away? Is she looking at this as a life change? Does she want to remain at her present club for years to come and will taking a long leave of absence put this in jeopardy? All of those decisions play into the major decision.

As for what I would do, I am not sure of the position I will be in when I am 40. I would think I would be married with a young family, and them being my priority I do not think I would be willing to go far from home. If the Club atmosphere and my management team were right, I would probably try to complete the best program within a reasonable travel distance. The cost, although an obvious issue, would be secondary to the strength of the program and closest match to my scheduled needs. The University of Alabama would probably be my choice.

Lesson 4

Step Three: Setting SMART Goals

A SMART goal is a goal that meets all of these elements: Specific, measurable, acceptable, realistic, and timely. The following points discuss the importance of incorporating these five components into the goal-setting process.

Specific

Goals should be both explicit and unclouded, something to aim toward without misinterpretation. It is not enough simply to set positive-sounding goals (*I want to become more fit*). O'Hair found managers are more likely to succeed if their goals are specific and clear. One General Manager from Atlanta believes that focus is the key to one's success. *If I focus specifically on something long enough, I know that I probably can achieve it. If we properly plan a function and carefully focus on the details as it unfolds, we are likely to produce a huge success.*

According to Shalley, goal-setting theory asserts that specific goals improve performance by producing higher levels of effort and planning than unclear or general goals. People strive for a higher standard of success by increasing effort. Latham and Locke added that when people pursue even vague goals, they may obtain some improved sense of satisfaction over having no goals.

Club managers can channel some of this extra effort into the development of appropriate plans. Earley and his colleagues were able show that people with specific goals tend to plan and organize more than those with general goals which, in turn, create a motivational effect to follow through with the plan. Using the example about hoping to become more physically fit begins to transform from a general wish to a distinct possibility by amending the statement to the more specific statement, *I will become more physically fit by beginning a jogging program.* This idea becomes more salient and develops into a goal as the process evolves.

Measurable

It is important that goals are measurable (objective) because measurement permits objectivity which helps define goals in terms of actions that one can readily see. Measurement in terms of either or both times (such as 14 minutes) and counts (1-mile course) can be as simple as an informal check list, or it may be a complex and sophisticated evaluation form that measures performance in a variety of categories. For example, at the beginning of your jogging program, you could establish a baseline by timing yourself over a one-mile course. If your time is 14 minutes, you have established that as your baseline. It is reasonable to infer that with proper training, your time can improve, which is an indication of enhanced fitness condition. You may decide that you will jog 45 minutes, five days a week, for four weeks. And at the beginning of each week, you will time your first mile to see how you are progressing.

Acceptable

Goals should not be imposed, but rather self-desired and thereby acceptable—whether assigned or self conceived. When club managers accept their goals and make a commitment to achieving them, goals have a much better chance of being realized. However, if the goal is more imposed than desired, the goal may be perceived as more difficult to attain, thereby resulting in frustration instead of accomplishment. Is achieving an improved fitness level an acceptable, self-desired goal to you and one that you are committed to achieving?

Acceptance and commitment create determination for reaching a goal—regardless of the goal's origin. Locke summarized the determinants of goal acceptance and commitment into three categories: external influences, interactive factors, and internal factors.

External influences and legitimate authority. Managers have both personal and club related goals. Boards have goals that are often times pushed on managers. In order for managers to be as effective as possible in goal achievement, they must deal with this dilemma of sorting out which goals are most important. In effect, managers must try to reconcile conflicting goals and attempt to make them congruent for themselves as well as for the teams they supervise. According to Gatewood, Taylor, and Ferrell this merging of individual and organizational needs is seen as the biggest challenge in goal attainment.

Managers should take responsibility for and assume ownership of their goals—all goals. Those that are sent down from the Board should be carefully incorporated as guiding principles into operational goals where they become more salient. It may not be easy. The culture of the Club will regulate the amount of influence club managers have on influencing top-down goals. A Club Manager in Annapolis, Maryland offered insight regarding his past experience in a restaurant company: *The corporate office set goals, the general managers were enforcers. Department heads had very little say. Now that I am a club manager, I try to involve everyone in the process, so goals become more meaningful.*

Ideally, club managers should go about the process of developing and implementing work-related goals with the same structure and zeal they would utilize with their personal goals, instead of accepting them as habitual responses, respect for authority, or due to the power of the person assigning the goal. With long work weeks the norm for managers, the process of buying off on and personalizing club goals is a key issue with which to make peace.

Earley summarized that assigned goals affect individuals in these positive ways:

1. Provide a sense of purpose, direction, and clarity concerning expectations.
2. Stretch individuals' beliefs as to what they think they can achieve.
3. Lead individuals toward developing high quality plans to achieve their goals.

Interactive factors. Although assigned goals increase commitment, Mathis and Jackson suggest that participatory goal setting produces even greater commitment. Participation was a subject of primary concern to management during the mid century. Maier's research asserts that employees tend to set higher goals in a participatory setting than supervisors alone would dare to impose, since employees seem to be more acutely aware of the factors within their control.

Studies have not yet definitively proven how competition affects commitment. However, Locke found that individuals set significantly higher goals and performed significantly better in competitive situations than those who were not competing.

Internal factors. Personal goals and self efficacy judgments have direct effects on performance. Zander suggested that individuals are equally committed to self-set and goals set and agreed to through participation.

Individuals will set more difficult personal goals for themselves than for others because they see themselves as more able to perform. In other words, individuals have lower expectations for others than for themselves.

During the goal-setting process, Gellatly asserts that individuals experience a normative shift that shapes their self efficacy—the belief in their capabilities. When an individual believes that they can accomplish a task, they will push themselves. By contrast, not even incentives will motivate an individual with low self-efficacy. In other words, self-efficacy is more a more fundamental internal value than reward. People will not strive for rewards they believe are unattainable, but they will commit to goals they believe they can reach.

1.4. Mini Case: Setting a Specific Goal

Sally Butterfield, dock master and manager at The Harborside Club, made an appointment to discuss budget problems with her boss, Paul Lewis, the GM. Sally planned to ask Paul for an increase in operating funds because the yachting department was having a tough time making ends meet. Sally and Paul occasionally played tennis at the same park and their children attended the same school, so Sally felt comfortable about the meeting. She did not plan out what she was going to say because she felt sure that Paul would see the situation her way.

When Sally arrived at Paul's office, she was kept waiting for over 20 minutes. When Paul finally saw her, he told Sally that he had to leave for BMI V in 10 minutes. He looked at Sally and said, *This is a tough year for budgets. All departments seem to need more money. I can help only those that can really demonstrate specific needs.*

Sally had come into the meeting unprepared—no data, hard facts, or specific goals. She did not even have a specific amount in mind. She had planned to use the meeting to get additional funding from Paul on the basis of their friendship. She left the meeting with Paul encouraging her to keep up the hard work, but no increase.

Sally's experience shows the importance of specific goals. They are valuable because they take set conditions into account and identify targets. Specific goals allow a person to plan her or his actions and behaviors. Sally should have set specific goals such as:

- *I will present four points each with supporting material.*
- *I will prioritize my points so that if we run out of time, the most important ones will be covered.*
- *I will show how our department is in greatest need of extra funds.*
- *I will ask for a 20 percent budget increase, in hopes that Paul will actually give me 15 percent.*

By setting specific and high goals, Sally would have been in a better position for handling such a difficult situation.

Discussion Question

Have you faced a similar situation with your boss? Recall the specifics of that encounter. Using hindsight, what steps could you have taken to have made the session work to your advantage?

Manager Response 1

The situation Sally faced with Paul is similar to one I faced with my boss this past year. I am GM of a golf club, which is now in its second year of operation. Cart paths were not completed on six of the 18 holes of the golf course. We lost substantial revenue and member goodwill during periods when the course was closed to carts due to inclement weather. The President ordered completion of two paths on holes on the back nine, making this half of the course complete and available every day. He did not direct any improvements for the front nine.

This spring I asked to meet with him, and had the Superintendent and Director of Golf attend the meeting as well.

We three had agreed that the paths on the front nine had to be completed this year, and were sure he would concur and order the work—that he would come up with the money. What actually happened was that he listened, asked us to quantify the precise costs, and approved the project with the understanding that we would find the dollars to pay for it. We had no answers, and only then learned that the original construction budget had been closed out. Had we known specifics of cost and a plan to fund the project, we would have saved weeks of wasted time, and our reputations.

We did return to meet with the President finding $25,000 that we had received from a Workers Comp refund. This was just a fortunate coincidence. If I had to approach the same situation again, I would have first researched the project thoroughly to help ensure that I could answer quantitative questions. Tough lesson.

Manager Response 2

My club has a policy that performance evaluations are done twice during the Club's fiscal year. It gives me, the General Manager, the opportunity to get direct feedback from department heads and evaluate their performance on a regular basis. It is during the October evaluations this year that my Executive Chef requested a 20 percent salary increase for himself for the upcoming budget. This request, if I agreed, would require me to seek the approval of the Board.

I began to prepare information that would help me determine if his request was justified. I knew that it was important for me to be specific when I made my presentation to the Board. I also felt that it was necessary for me to feel confident and supportive of his request before any presentation was made. I also had to prepare myself for obvious questions from the Board—if I supported his request—as to how senior management could have let the Chef's salary get into an uncompetitive range. I knew that the outcome of the meeting was dependent on how well I presented my case.

I began by completing an evaluation of the Executive Chef's contributions over his last 15 years of employment. I looked at his years of loyal service, his direct impact on club dining, member satisfaction, and private party volume. I measured on a scale of 1 to 5 how well he managed his staff, his ability to grow both personally and professionally and how well he handled member complaints and concerns. I also completed a survey of other clubs in the area to find out what Executive Chefs were being paid. I was careful to compare only those that matched us closely in food sales volume, number of months and days open for business, and the responsibilities of the Executive Chef. Once I completed my evaluation, I realized that I supported the Chef's proposal for a 20 percent salary increase. I was now in a position to present to the Board at our next meeting.

I presented the Board with my request for a 20 percent increase in salary for the Executive Chef for the upcoming year. I also presented the results of my survey and performance evaluation. Being specific helped ensure that my requested increase for that department was clear and objective. Producing evaluations and survey results gave the Board the opportunity to measure his performance and current salary against the industry. I made sure that I communicated my results of the survey clearly and concisely. I realized from the results of the survey that the Executive Chef was in fact under paid by about 20-25 percent according to the industry standard. I explained that his loyalty and service to the Club over the years, had allowed management to become disconnected from the market (since we had not gone through the process of hiring an Executive Chef for over 15 years). I presented his most recent performance evaluation, which supported my case for the increase. I also had to make the Board aware that his loyalty and dedication to one club for 15 years was rare and that he is considered a leader in his industry. Another club would be happy to have him and would pay the going rate. After careful consideration the Board approved my request.

Manager Response 3

Last spring I asked the President about hiring a student intern for the summer without doing my homework and mapping a strategy. Naturally, the President said no, since I did not set specific or measurable goals related to what it was that I was trying to accomplish for the Club.

If I had to do it again, I would go into the meeting with a more formal and fully-developed presentation that would include these elements:

Specific goals for the position.

A method for objectively measuring these goals.

A job description listing what the intern would accomplish and where he or she would work during the summer.

Cost and where the money would come from.

How this position would contribute to the Club's mission and vision statement.

Before going into this meeting, in addition to developing a fully-developed presentation, I should have developed SMART goals, specific, measurable, attainable, realistic, and timely. Being turned down by the President was an embarrassing incident that I should have never let happen.

This spring, I met with the President to make a similar request. This time, however, I was prepared. My request for a summer-season student intern was approved.

Manager Response 4

I faced a similar situation with a previous General Manager. We were and still are close friends with the relationship we forged during his tenure at the Club.

We had recently reopened our clubhouse after a complete rebuild of one year. We were exceeding budgeted revenue for a la Carte dining. As a result, labor was also high when compared to budget—as well as everything else expense related. I was feeling pressure from him to reduce labor, *because we had a budget to meet*. The basis for my defense was that we were making the same return percentage as budgeted.

The problem escalated when I decided to talk to him about labor percentage while driving to a CMAA meeting about two hours away. I thought that a casual conversation mixed in-between everything else would be a great way to discuss labor. I was apprehensive about speaking about it formally, because I was close to the issue and saw it as a *no brainier*. As we were driving, I brought the issue up. I was unprepared other than knowing the general numbers in my head. I had computed them several times while stewing over our previous conversation on the subject.

As we got involved in the conversation, and it had taken several wrong turns, I realized I had made a huge mistake. On both of our parts, we were guilty of having communication problems with too many remodeling concerns and too little time spent making sure that we were aligned in our thinking. This, compounded by the business onrush of the first six months of the reopening, had left us with too much to discuss and catch up on. We had a seemingly unfocused conversation that led everywhere from labor cost, to maintenance picking up trash in the parking lot, to birds making a mess on top of the new building. The original conversation I wanted to have never really even happened, other than on a surface level.

As a result of my missing the opportunity to discuss the specific labor issue, a couple of days later, I asked for a specific meeting. I came prepared with a financial sheet, copies of the budget, and a couple of carefully-prepared points that I wanted to address. The end result was a better understanding between us both. I now understood his point of view and he realized that we were on the money with labor cost.

In retrospect, I would never try to use an informal setting again to explain a business point or rely on a personal relationship to achieve a goal.

Manager Response 5

When I prepared my first departmental operations budget, the General Manager met with me to discuss the various line items. He asked me for the conceptual picture of what I was trying to achieve. Of course, I had no idea what he was talking about. He explained that it boiled down to *the big picture*. I went on to explain the ideas I had for my department and the future. When I took a breath, he asked if I had thought strategically, if I had done any projections or written any assumptions, or if I had collaborated with my staff and fellow managers to come up with this vision. I had not.

I simply was flying by the seat of my pants and I became embarrassed that I had not thought things through. He began to take me apart as he shot holes in my ideas or asked questions for which I should have had answers. While he was patient and helpful, I soon realized that I had been humiliated—and I knew that I would never let something similar happen again. He told me that he had made the same mistakes and proceeded to assist me in developing my vision for where I wanted the department to be. Slowly, I began to see the light and envision a system whereby I could back up the assumptions that I was making instead of pulling numbers out of the air.

This is what I should have done:

- Developed a big picture vision of my department—as an SBU (strategic business unit), ensuring that it complemented the overall vision of the Club.

- Gotten input from all constituencies—my staff, fellow department managers, members, and the General Manager—regarding forecasts, goals, and objectives.

- Formulated a game plan to achieve my financial goals for the year utilizing past performance statistics as a guide, current trends, pre-booked business forecasts, cover counts, check averages, etc. In short, I should have written assumptions for every line item, which were then supported by objective measures (to assist with periodic review). Objective measures are anything that you can either count or time—such as covers, key ratios, dollar volume, and even how long it takes (in terms of seconds) to greet a member at the Maitre d' stand.
- Created a written rationale showing that my goals are in keeping with the needs, wants, and standards of the Club's membership and paid staff.
- Been specific with regard to timing of goal completion. I should have done seasonal projections, which would help smooth the budgeting process—especially the variance process at the end of each period.

Since then, I have approached most tasks in the same manner, resulting in more successful completion of my goals. The business plan for my department is involved, but it presents a rational plan of listing goals and tying it back to budget by period. All of my detailed assumptions are backed up by objective measures. The organization of the process has made me a much more effective manager.

Manager Response 6

In facing a situation where a manager has to map out goals and objectives to produce a specific result, nothing comes more to mind more than negotiating contracts. And who has not been through that ordeal? It was my first one-on-one review with the GM. I knew I was worth more money than I was getting paid, but I lacked the confidence and support material to substantiate my claim. The final outcome was both favorable and a learning process. Also, in this case I learned the importance of being patient in a conversation—and not to be defensive.

In hindsight, I would have made a specific plan of what I wanted to achieve coming out of the meeting. Salary, future, and responsibilities were the topics to be discussed. Then, I would have investigated the material to support my desired results. I should have done a comparative survey of what other clubs were paying people in my position and to what kind of benefits they were entitled. Then, I would analyze the financial statement that I was responsible for and draw a conclusion from the numbers. Hard facts supported by my blood and sweat.

In the end, I was rewarded generously, but it could have gone all wrong in a hurry. And to boot, I had just bought a house, and my wife was pregnant with our first child. I am grateful to that GM. He listened, was willing to work with me, and we have all—the Club, the GM, and I—enjoyed a prosperous relationship.

Manager Response 7

I have been fortunate to learn, early on, from some very wise club managers whom reinforced the idea of having one's homework completed before addressing any situation that you are about to enter. Whether it is completing a club wide budget for your general manager or finance committee or as simple as going to speak with an unhappy member, you need to have the necessary information. If not, you will almost always be defeated.

A server tells you that Mr. Jones wants to see you. My first thought is to ask myself the reason behind Mr. Jones (known as a member that is difficult to satisfy) wanting to speak with me? I will always ask the server about the quality of the dining experience, so far. Has everything been accurate and timely? Were any mistakes made or has Mr. Jones grumbled about any particular detail? Once you have a foundation, you can assimilate a game plan and be that much more on the offensive side than the defensive side, you might have a small inside look to what motivated Mr. Jones. This preparation might be what allows you to soothe over and help solve any issues Mr. Jones might have. And of course there is always the opportunity that Mr. Jones just wants to say, *hello*.

A more serious example is one that I just recently completed. Being at my current club for less than one year and never being in the lead position—always an assistant—completing a club's food and beverage budget was a bit of a daunting task. However, I took all of the necessary steps to make the budget presentation a smooth process and without many changes.

My first step was to compile all of the necessary base forms and paperwork that I could, as well as corresponding information on the last three years of budget numbers for every line item. Once I had an understanding of the historical data, I was able to compare it to current and short-term, future trends. Armed with those hard numbers and theoretical future information, I was able to make limited educated predictions on the upcoming budget numbers. Once a very rough first draft was in place, my game plan was to speak to everyone involved in the budget process on an individual basis and ask for their comments and criticisms. That information produced draft two. Knowing the power in numbers we held two group budget review sessions, each followed by new editions of the budget. As I made the final edits, after doing all of my homework, I was able to present the aggressive budget to our general manager and controller in a very confident manner. All questions could be answered with logical, well thought out answers and explanations. After few minor revisions we were completed.

If I had not completed a thorough analysis following all the steps and tools that I knew existed, the presentation aspect of the budget process would not have gone well. Numbers and prediction might not have been as accurate and I might not have had the necessary rationale for what was put into print.

Lesson 5

Step Three: Setting SMART Goals

(Continued)

Realistic

Goals should be challenging, but within an individual's capabilities and limitations. Goals should not represent whatever levels of achievement a manager decides would be *nice* to attain. Wishful thinking has no place in effective goal setting. For goals to serve as a tool for stretching an individual to reach their full potential, they must be challenging but achievable. Therefore, before beginning goal setting, club managers should consider their stretch capabilities and honestly examine whether they have the knowledge, skills, resources, and abilities needed to successfully accomplish their goals. Satisfying this criterion means setting goals in light of several important considerations that have been proposed by Thompson and Strickland:

- What performance levels will conditions realistically allow?
- What results will it take to be a successful performer?
- What is an individual capable of accomplishing when pushed?

Managers should emphasize that their goals extend their abilities. Though it may take extra determination and hard work to achieve difficult goals, it will be far more rewarding than those goals that can be achieved with little effort. Research by

O'Hair has found that when challenging goals are set instead of easy goals, performance is usually better. This is true because achieving only easy goals may keep one from realizing their full potential. One GM in Chicago stated, *The process of lofty goal setting keeps everyone striving for improvement, rather than allowing the easier alternative. We want our managers continually stretching their limits.* On the other hand, managers should not set goals that will be impossible to achieve, thereby setting themselves up for failure. Experiencing failure makes people less apt to set goals in the future.

For example, most of us probably will never be able to run a four-minute mile, so stating that as a goal for one's personal fitness program is not productive. But it is a good idea to push beyond what you honestly feel would be your best performance. You know from your baseline measurement that you can jog a 14-minute mile in your present fitness condition. Furthermore, you may remember three years ago, after one month of easy-to-moderate training, you were able to run a 12-minute mile. To set that as a goal would not allow you to reach your full potential. On the other hand, you may feel that if you really train hard, you may be able to jog a 10-minute mile two minutes faster than ever before. The 10-minute mile goal, one that broadens your previous capability, will be a far more rewarding goal.

Timely

Managers should not constrain themselves with procedures and deadlines. While goals should be specific, they must be allowed to change over time. *As the world evolves, circumstances change,* says one Club Manager in Ocean City, Maryland. *We cannot just set and achieve goals in a vacuum as there are too many exterior variables such as weather, regulations, or economics affecting our business. We must be able to change too, even if it means abandoning a goal altogether and creating a new one.* Setting highly specific, inflexible goals may give a manager an unfavorable reputation as being too rigid, or unresponsive to the real world. For example, if you have set achievement of your 10-minute mile goal over a four-week timeline and sprain your ankle at the end of the third week, you will likely need to adjust your deadline.

1.5. Mini Case: Realistic and Timely Goals

Doug Hogan is the rooms division manager at the Llenroc Club, a private hotel and club on the upper east-side of Manhattan. He has challenged the reservations team to improve hotel occupancy dramatically. His incentive bonus is based on increased occupancy and he sees an opportunity to make enough bonus money to buy a new car if they do well enough. He says that he has not challenged them with increasing occupancy to a specific percentage, because, *I do not want to leave money on the table.* He wants them to do everything they can do to raise occupancy as much as possible. He knows the following facts:

- The club hotel currently runs an annualized 80 percent occupancy rate.

- Similar properties average a 79-82 percent occupancy rate. Current market conditions are pushing occupancy rates down slightly.

- If they can increase occupancy by 20 percent, thereby achieving a 96 percent occupancy rate, his year-end bonus will be $19,000—enough to pay cash for a new small car.

- The Llenroc's advertising budget has been cut 50 percent for the upcoming year.

- The City of New York has discovered a natural-gas leak under a building three doors down from the Club hotel. The City estimates heavy construction in front of the entrance to the Llenroc for 90 days beginning next month—prime season.

- The hotel commission has recently discovered that Chorlofueron 67 (a plastic polymer used to waterproof commercial bedding) causes cancer in lab rats. They are pushing for a law that will prevent use of commercial bedding containing Chorlofueron 67. They have the solid backing of New York State Legislature and the law will likely pass next quarter.

- The Llenroc has had an exclusive contract for commercial bedding with Sleeptime Beddy-Bye Mattress Company of Tenafly, New Jersey for over 25 years. Sleeptime pioneered the use of Chorlofueron 67 over 20 years ago. It is used in all of their bedding.

Doug has decided to push forward with his goal since; *I could really use a new car.*

Discussion Questions

1. What is your reaction to the way Doug challenged the reservations staff? Why do you feel that way?
2. Is the goal realistic, within the Club hotel's capabilities, with regard to the following points:
   - What performance levels will conditions realistically allow?
   - What results will it take to be a successful performer?
   - What a team is capable of accomplishing when pushed?
3. Is the goal timely? Explain why or why not.

Manager Response 1

Doug's method of challenging the staff was ineffective management that is doomed to fail. The goal is not specific or measurable, and there is no incentive for the staff to reach it or even to try. The only real goal is for Doug to earn a bonus to buy a car, and it is likely that the staff is not aware of this motivation.

The goal is not realistic under the best of circumstances, and certainly not under those present in the scenario. There is no reason to expect occupancy to increase dramatically without a plan to allocate time and resources. In this case, the advertising budget is decreasing, and no plan has been initiated to improve performance, so there is no way levels will exceed averages.

- Conditions will likely result in a modest reduction, rather than an increase, because construction will make access to the property more difficult and the lack of advertising funds will reduce the recognition of the hotel's name.

- The result to be a successful performer in this case is reaching 96 percent occupancy. Since only Doug knows this strike number, the staff cannot achieve the goal because they do not understand the goal. If they try to achieve it for Doug (for the boss), they will still not succeed, and the resulting demoralization will likely damage the organization further.

- The team is certainly capable of accomplishing more than any one individual believes is possible under favorable circumstances. In the case of Llenroc, they are not capable of achieving Doug's goal because of the issues listed above.

Whether the goal is timely remains to be seen, as the date of the bonus period is not clear. Even if it were, however, given the fact that the City estimates 90 days of construction, and the mattress crisis to follow shortly afterward, there is probably no way that short term occupancy percentage can be expected to rise.

Manager Response 2

Doug has not effectively challenged his reservations staff. His goal was not specific, realistic or timely. Goals need to be clearly stated. For Doug to avoid confusion among his reservations staff the goal he is looking to achieve must be specific. Doug's expectations are unrealistic and untimely. The obstacles outlined were clearly not taken into consideration when determining the goal. The only consideration Doug made to determine the desired percentage increase or the timely manner in which it should be achieved was how much bonus money it would generate and how quickly he needed to purchase a new car.

Doug's expectations for achieving a 20 percent increase in occupancy in the Llenroc hotel over the next year are unrealistic. Given the conditions in the market he will be facing over the next several months, Doug may be hard pressed to achieve the 80 percent of the occupancy he has been running.

Here are some of the specific issues that will contribute to a downward trend in business over the next several months:

Marketing budget cuts of 50 percent. Increased marketing would have a direct effect on increased volume. Doug would have to beef up his marketing strategies to get better turn out. With such severe budget cuts, he will have less of an opportunity to reach out to his consumers.

Heavy construction scheduled for three months. Since the front of the hotel entrance is going to be affected by construction for at least 90 days, consumers may decide to avoid the inconveniences of the Llenroc hotel.

Law being passed within next three months preventing use of Chorlofueron 67. Once the law has been passed the Llenroc hotel will have to start to replace all the bedding in the hotel as the company they have used for the last 25 years to supply bedding for the hotel uses Chorlofueron 67. This will cause some of the rooms to be unavailable as the bedding is replaced to conform to the new regulations.

The goal is not timely. Doug is pushing his team into trying to achieve a goal, which is going to be negatively affected by external variables. Doug is not only setting up his team to fail he is not taking these variables into consideration when stating a time frame in which he would like to see this goal achieved. It would be wise for Doug, given the circumstances, to abandon this goal and create a new one. Changing the goal to maintain the 80 percent occupancy rate during an upcoming transitional period would be more realistic and timely for now.

Manager Response 3

Doug has set his team up for failure by not helping facilitate specific, mutually agreed upon goals along with realistic time lines. This is clear in the way that he assigned the goal in view of the realities of the marketplace.

Similar properties are running an 82 percent occupancy rate. With conditions pushing rates down, upcoming construction, gas leaks, advertising budget cuts, and the bed issue, the goal should be more along the lines of maintaining current occupancy in the near term.

When challenging goals are agreed to instead of just easy goals, performance usually improves. An easy goal will keep one from realizing their full potential. Doug's goal is too challenging, unrealistic, and seemingly impossible to achieve. The organization does not have the resources to accomplish the goal. Doug is setting his team up for failure.

The goal is not timely. The conditions described above suggest that the team will be lucky just to maintain its present position. In all likelihood, occupancy will go down due to budget cuts and construction.

Manager Response 4

Doug has set his goals way too high. He has not been realistic in what he can accomplish. Unfortunately his real goal is to get a new car for himself. This is not a goal that his staff will feel committed to and support. Also, he made no attempt to get his staff involved in the goal setting process.

The goal is not realistic even in an upward trending market. However, given the realities of the local area and market conditions, his goal is undoubtedly headed for failure. To review, he is facing known, historical occupancy rates, which do not suggest that the goal is attainable. He also knows that the Llenroc is running about average when compared to similar properties—so there is no reason to believe that the Llenroc could dramatically increase its occupancy. Worse, he is facing problems of the advertising budget being slashed by 50 percent, construction equipment related to the gas leak will be blocking access to the hotel property during prime season, and chemical problems in the Sleeptime mattresses may necessitate an expensive and disruptive replacement of all bedding.

The goal is unrealistic. While setting high goals may help employees increase productivity, setting unrealistic goals will lead to poor performance, because the staff will not feel they can be attained.

This goal is also not timely. It needs to be adjusted based on the adverse conditions that the property will be facing. Perhaps Doug needs to put his bonus in the bank each year and set a goal that he will be able to buy a new car a few years down the road.

Manager Response 5

Doug's challenge to the staff is out of proportion to the abilities of anyone in their situation. Considering he is already meeting current standard within his market, a 20 percent increase in occupancy is not going to happen. Never mind the fact that Doug expects such a large increase in occupancy before his next compensation meeting. It is all too much, too fast, too greedy, and too unrealistic.

If that was not enough to set him back, heavy construction, lab rats getting cancer, a 50 percent decrease in the marketing budget, and not allowing for the unknown which undoubtedly will rear its head. Surely, Doug must realize he has a problem. With the obstacles in front of him, he should be thinking of a plan to merely keep the Club performing at its current occupancy level. Maintaining current levels of operations will be tough given the conditions he is facing. This would translate into a successful season for the Club.

For Doug to be an effective manager, he will need to address the problem issues and brainstorm ideas to overcome and or work around them. With the advertising budget being cut, they will need to become better self-promoters, or use their dollars which will produce the highest return. With no way of getting around construction, temporary valet servicing, alternative entrancing, giving a complimentary hard hat with every room, or *Excuse the Mess, New York City, is at it again*, signs and creative ideas will need to be formulated and put into action.

With 25 years of history with one company, it might be time to push the Sleeptime Beddy-Bye Mattress Company to become the leader they were 20 years ago. Negotiating with the company to make changes to their product and providing a reasonable exchange program or some similar plan is in order.

The staff certainly is capable of increasing their productivity and guest satisfaction, which will result in a return to higher occupancy over time. I also suggest that groups of staff can achieve far more than thought possible given even a small chance to work as a team. Doug should invest time with the staff, to get their input and their buy-in into the goal.

Manager Response 6

Doug challenged his staff for his own personal gain. With the new situations brought out in the case, he should abandon or drastically change his goal. In either case, he should de-focus his want for personal gain and be concerned about the Club. He will not make the eventual goal as it stands and therefore will defeat his staff by giving them an unattainable goal.

The goal is not realistic given the current conditions. The performance of the operations will be drastically reduced as soon as the construction starts, which will likely send the Club into a downward spiral of occupancy. And, those who are in residence will not want to be there. Most likely they will lose a significant percentage of their guests to other hotels. To be a successful performer under these conditions, the goal has got to be adjusted. Even if the team could mitigate the construction and the Chorlofueron 67 issues, the lofty goal of 96 percent occupancy is unrealistic to achieve. Added to this is the advertising budget being cut. To run 80 percent occupancy is good, when taking into consideration the entire year. The time factor has not been set. The goal is measurable but not timely. Timing would allow him to alter the goal now and push the timetable to a realistic period after the hotel's issues are addressed. Taking this time to brainstorm and come up with a plan to gain occupancy after the issues have been settled with the help of the staff will help. Make the team a part of the planning of the solution and let them see what they will receive if they succeed is a positive way to manage the challenge. Doug will find that having his staff come up with many solutions to the project will benefit him in the long run.

Manager Response 7

This is a self-motivated want, not necessarily a great business practice goal; created more out of personal greed than the desire to raise the occupancy rate to its highest possible rate. Goals of this nature are usually more destructive and negative than a positive team building success for any company or club.

Goals, most definitely, need to be tangible and measurable. This goal, selfish it may be is not measurable. Doug told his staff they need to attain a 96 percent occupancy rate regardless of the outside environmental factors. This is an unfair challenge that is not only unfair but also difficult or impossible to achieve.

What Doug is unaware of is he could develop a measurable standard at 96 percent and if it was a realistic goal, his staff would probably have an end result that was better than what he expected. Another key step in team goal setting is to get the group involved in defining the parameters and expectations of the goal. When the latter is done, there is a greater buy in factor and usually better results.

Is the goal realistic, within the Club hotel's capabilities, with regard to the following points?

- What performance levels will conditions realistically allow?
- What results will it take to be a successful performer?
- What is a team capable of accomplishing when pushed?
- Is the goal timely? Explain why or why not.

Considering myself a realist, I do not believe that this goal is within the hotel's capabilities. Similar properties average 79-82 percent and Doug's property registers an 80 percent occupancy rate. Regardless of the bedding issue, three months of prime season with heavy construction on your doorstep, along with the already down turning market, the hotel should be pleased if they could at least maintain the 80 percent—much less increase it several percentage points. Taking into account the bedding issue, rooms will have to be closed, which means fewer rooms to sell, an inconvenience to the guests, as well as an increase in expenses. All that combined with less money to advertise and market does not translate to an improved business climate.

To be a successful performer, Doug's property will need time, an established time chart with measurable, flexible standards, and expectations. All results must be measurable and truly achievable. The gas leak and construction will deny ease of access and make location, a key factor, a negative aspect of staying at the Club.

A team is capable of accomplishing incredibly high standards—well above and beyond the goals that have been set for them. However, when nothing is given as a tangible target, and there exist all of the negative environmental factors, the group has the potential to feel dejected and psychologically beaten even before they begin. Group dynamics falter and nothing positive will be achieved.

With regard to the appropriateness for the timeline, there is no timeline, but rather just an undefined deadline that the employees are unaware of. Nothing states they have 10 months to accomplish their highest occupancy rate. Doug has a timeline, but Doug is not completing the goal, his staff is and hence, his staff needs to be informed of both the deadline and then create a corresponding timeline of success.

Lesson 6

Step Four: Identify Resources

Time, equipment, money, favors, encouragement, and moral support are just a few of the resources managers may need to achieve their goals. Anticipating resource needs will strengthen plans and actions, and planning how to utilize resources can make goals more real and concrete. Using our 10-minute mile example, you should consider issues such as how you will work your run into your daily schedule, where you will keep your workout clothes, how you will freshen-up afterward, and if your staff will support your quest. After all, the staff is bound to enjoy the stress-relieving benefits that come from your fitness program!

Step Five: Recognize Risk, Contingencies, and Conflict

Risk

To increase the probability of success, consider the risks connected with accomplishing the goal. Risks refer to what might be lost by pursuing the goal by one method over other alternatives identified in the brainstorming process. In your 10-minute mile quest, how much higher is your risk of injury (and perhaps goal failure) if you use your old Nikes instead of spending $95 for a new pair?

Contingencies

Prepare for contingencies. Do you have an alternate location to run if you live in an area where severe weather is a possibility? Can you use the clubhouse locker room, or should you consider the possibility of a fitness club membership for showering and changing? What happens if a last-minute meeting comes up as you are walking out the door to go run? Devise goals so that a large number of potential obstacles can be removed or mitigated in order to have a better shot at achieving the desired end results.

Conflict

When pursuing multiple goals managers will likely devote more time and effort to one goal than another, often trading off between quantity and quality goals. Task difficulty and interest will determine the goal selection and performance. If managers choose difficult *quality* and *quantity* goals or if they are not confident of their abilities, they can often feel overloaded and unable to improve. As a result, they will begin to tradeoff performance quality for performance quantity (Gilliland and Lamis).

One Food & Beverage Director in Seattle expressed this concept succinctly: *We name proprietary brands in our specifications to make sure our members are getting the highest quality. Last week we could not buy Ore Ida or Lamb's shoestring fries, just the distributor's private label. Instead of our normal five-ounce portion, we served eight-ounce portions to try to head off any possible complaints.*

1.6. Mini Case: Risk, Contingencies, and Conflict

Mary Berman, GM of Babbling Brook Country Club in Starstruck, Colorado had finally received the go-ahead from the Board to add a $250,000 dining terrace to the clubhouse. It was a beauty! Seating for 300 under a covered arbor, flagstone, paddle fans, weather curtains, and overhead patio heaters. The way she figured it (and sold it to the Board), she could virtually double food & beverage revenues with outside events. There were just a few small glitches in her plan. We had the following conversation regarding the expansion:

- The $250,000 does not include money for patio tables and chairs estimated at $30,000—*I forgot to put that into the package. And after a two-year battle for Board approval, I cannot go back to them now.*

- We did not go over exactly all of the details with the building department during the permitting process. *I was afraid they would make us add on to the parking lot or add more toilet facilities. That would have killed the project. I think we can finesse the inspector as we go along.*

- The patio is on the view side of the clubhouse. The kitchen is upstairs and on the back side of the building about 300 feet away. *Yeah, but we did not have the money to build a new kitchen, too. We can roll everything from the kitchen to the top of the stairs in hot boxes. I will just bring in a few extra bussers to service the buffet lines. It should all work well.*

- Approval was a two-year process that barely passed. The incoming President led the opposition. *That is true, but I think I can win him over.*

- You decided to stage the overhead timbers on the site using a helicopter. *I know we are taking a risk with the overhead power lines being within 50 feet of the site, but the crane to reach from the parking lot to the site was an extra $250 I could not justify spending.*

- Digging the foundation footings will require the water to be shut off for eight days. *I arranged for a water truck to pump through an over-ground pipe during that period.*

Are you concerned that occurs during the member-guest golf tournament? *I got the dates confused. The concrete contractor says he will try to have it finished early. Besides, we have a short window of opportunity. We have to get the footings dug before the frost heaves the ground. The golfers will just have to bear with us. It will be worth it.*

- What about on-going operations while construction is underway? *I can handle them both. The members know that I am going to be busy with construction. I think they will let me slide on operations. I am prepared to comp. a few dinners, if necessary.*

Discussion Questions

What could Mary have done to better anticipate the questions of resources, contingencies, and conflict. Identify some the major problems that could occur either during construction or afterward. Given the scenario, how would you have managed the project differently?

Manager Response 1

Mary would have benefited by setting up a planning committee to meet with monthly to discuss all stages of the project.

Resources. The individuals on the committee would be asking questions that a single person (Mary) undertaking such a large project would not have the time or energy to explore in order for successful completion. For example, the $30,000 needed for furniture could be reduced by changing vendors and/or adjusting the design. Additionally people from the committee could have assisted with product research.

Contingencies. With committee input and backing, the go-ahead from the Board may not have taken two years, thus allowing the project to proceed in a more timely fashion. To resolve funding conflicts and the possibility of creating problems with scheduled member events, delaying the project until early spring or next fall may be Mary's only alternative.

Conflict. The ideal purpose and goal of the planning committee would be to serve in the best overall interest of the members. With Board approval, this would help ensure support during the construction process and with answering members' concerns and questions.

Budget. In any construction project there are usually unforeseen and/or hidden costs. Issues of this sort might occur because of wiring problems, structural deficiencies, etc., and could quickly break the budget—depending on the severity of discovery.

Members. On-going operations should not be discontinued any more than absolutely necessary, as doing so would cause inconvenience and discord among the membership. This could be detrimental and end up causing a long-term problem due to a drop in utilization of the Club, bad reputation, and possible resignations.

The steps that I would have taken in managing the project:

- Set up a planning committee consisting of at least one member representative from each of the existing committees.
- Establish project goals.
- Create a basic, middle, and worst case budget with assumptions and a completion scenario for each.
- Allow for incidentals and other hidden costs in the budget.
- Possibly develop a member survey to get a broader view of membership desires and expectations.

Manager Response 2

Here is what Mary could have done better to anticipate the questions of resources, contingencies, and conflict.

With more thorough planning, Mary could be more successful personally and with this project. She should think things through and create a number of lists to keep the issues straight. By reducing her thoughts to lists, this would help her to anticipate most of the foreseeable problems. She should recognize all of the known risks and make plans for workarounds for each of those risks. She should have utilized the brainstorming process with her colleagues and key committees. This would help her be prepared for unknowns. Mary will be overloaded during this period and will need to be very careful to ensure that quality and membership are not compromised during the construction process.

Here are some of the major problems that could occur either during construction or afterward:

Mary's major problem is her lack of thoroughness. She will have many problems because of this failing. How will her Board feel when they find out that she missed the financial planning on this project by a huge amount? She was too concerned with getting the project approved and purposely failed to report possible expenses, because she was afraid her project would get killed.

By not being thorough, Mary can expect both trouble and non-budgeted additional expenses. Her major problems are these:

1. She forgot about the furnishings. Where will the money come from?
2. She cannot rely on finessing the inspector. If the code states that they must have so many restrooms for so much seating then they must. Same with the parking. She cannot expect the inspector to violate state code and to compromise his

position just to help her out. Again, where will the money come from when she needs to correct this oversight?

3. Not budgeting for a crane.
4. The kitchen location is also a problem, though maybe not major.
5. The scheduling of the project. Bad timing. It is not a good idea to alienate members during the busiest tournament of the year.

Her lack of proper planning may cause her to lose the respect of her members, staff, and Board. Any one of these constituencies losing respect for her ability could jeopardize Mary's employment at the Club.

This is how I would have managed the project:

I would have contacted my CMAA chapter to see if they had knowledge of any other manager who had gone through this type of project, contacted him or her and solicited advice. I would have brainstormed and tried to list everything it would have taken to have made this project happen successfully. Then, I would have listed all the associated risks and devised a plan of action. Most importantly, I would have been thorough in my planning and given all the facts and figures to my Board and then would have tried to press the project forward from that point. If they shot it down, then I would have done additional work and resubmitted my proposal.

Manager Response 3

Mary needs to address the outstanding issues prior to the start of construction. She needs to open up the line of communication with the Board and with the new President. Mary should disclose all of the facts; the additional money needed for patio tables and chairs, any changes as a result of the inspector, the difficulty regarding service from the kitchen, the use of a helicopter to save $250 on a $250,000 project, and the problem with the water, possibly, during the Member-Guest weekend. Once these issues have been addressed, then the construction process should begin to move forward.

Whenever construction is underway, timetables are difficult to adhere to. There are many variables that are beyond anyone's control. The weather can affect everything from the start of construction to how long each segment of construction takes. Demolition always opens up new questions. What is behind a wall may not show up on any drawings. You surely would not want to construct anything that the building inspector has not approved or you may have to tear it down and rebuild it after drawings have been approved.

Given the scenario, I would go the Board and let them know that we cannot start construction until all these issues have been addressed. I feel we should also have some sort of back-up plan. Maybe we spread the project out over 2 fiscal years.

The way that the mini case is stated, Mary is setting herself up for an impossible goal. It may (will likely) affect her career negatively. It would be better to delay the project than for her to find herself unemployed.

Manager Response 4

Mary seems to be way out on a limb. Mary has done a poor job in planning her goal. There are times when you must lead a project that you feel is necessary for the Club as a whole, even when you do not agree with it entirely. However, her lack of planning, foresight, and listing contingencies has not only jeopardized her job performance, but it may have put the Club's wellbeing and service to the members at risk, as well. This is not a positive career move!

In making any large capital improvement, I always include a range of 10 to 15 percent extra for cost overrides, delays, and other uncontrollable factors. Plans have to be made, so that they will not interfere with the normal member flow any more than necessary. Members should look forward to the new project instead of being so inconvenienced they are praying for it all to end.

I refer back to Mary's goal. She seems to have pushed for the project instead of motivating the Board and winning them over so that the goal became a part of everyone's agenda. This is an early indicator that a goal will fail. There does not appear to be any communication with the membership as to the plan she proposes. Therefore, the members are clueless as to the facts. This usually leads to unexpected inconvenience, discontent, and perhaps revolt in some manner. Effective and thoughtful communication with the membership is an intricate part of successfully achieving large projects such as this.

Mary's *small* glitches can be partially overcome by some tactful utilization of member connections. In many private clubs, contacting the appropriate member who may have connections at city hall may help ease and facilitate the permit situation. The extra money that should have been built into the project for contingencies could have covered the crane issue. The other glitches are a bit more difficult. One solution is to put the project on hold until a more favorable time frame can be established. As for the kitchen being 300 feet away, Mary should plan to hire food runners to help mitigate the distance issue.

Mary is prepared to comp a few dinners. Perhaps she should be prepared to comp the Member-Guest. The ill will she is creating cannot be overcome with a few free dinners. Her lack of planning, anticipating, and attention to normal operations would not be tolerated in many clubs. Remodeling and reconstruction contribute highly to GM turnover. Mary, by continuing on this road to disaster is likely to be looking for a job sooner rather than later.

If I were Mary, I would make it my top priority to re-think member inconvenience, anticipate member needs, and get realistic with the budget, timing, and staging. Once done, I would enlist the support of and ownership by the entire Board. Their input and support are vital in dealing with the member issues that will arise. I would also brush up on my planning and organization skills. In its present state, Mary's project will turn into a train wreck.

Manager Response 5

Mary is in deep trouble. She has not evaluated her resources and is in no position to begin the project she is excited about taking on. Financially, she has admittedly left out the cost of furnishings, has failed to consider the cost of adding parking and toilet facilities, as well as costs of other items needed in securing permission from building inspectors. She also likely has not allowed contingency funds for those extra issues that always seem to need to be addressed.

But, perhaps even more important than the financial shortcomings, she failed to rally support for the project. The project barely passed and does not have the support of the incoming President. Once things begin to go wrong, which is likely to happen, Mary will need to have built a base of member support and alliances to help in convincing the splinter groups of negative members that the project is good for the Club. She does not have this power base, and is jeopardizing her influence and future with the Club as a result. A manager should never take a political stand for or against a project when there is opposition. Mary did not follow this rule and now stands to serve as the scapegoat for those opposed to the renovation.

Other considerations of resources that Mary should have planned for include the helicopter use for the timbers and the water truck use during the member-guest event. With more thought given to alternatives, these situations could have been avoided. Mary has accepted a sizeable risk by implementing these options, without a real need to do so.

Mary should have involved the Board in brainstorming contingency plans regarding the water shutdown, the helicopter, and the operational problems that the kitchen distance will create. She thinks she can handle it all on her own, and that is a risk no manager should take.

Finally, an overriding motivation of Mary's has been the increasing food and beverage sales—quantity over quality—during construction. This is the wrong reason to move forward with the project.

If I were in Mary's position, I would have tried to not go forward with the project until the entire Board was in agreement. If there were reasons some Board members were opposed, those reasons could be worked out in advance. I would also have convinced the Board of the necessity of hiring a professional club planner to study the project, evaluate the options, and recommend the best way to proceed. If the project were to proceed at that point, it would be as part of an overall long range plan for the clubhouse, which would include future changes to kitchen facilities, restrooms, and parking. After buyoff occurred, the project would be owned by the Board and its master planner. The manager would then be implementing a project as agreed upon and directed by the Board.

Manager Response 6

Mary is headed down a painful path that will end in a disaster. She created a bad situation for herself by not following her plan and mapping all aspects of the goal. Mary did not anticipate the risks that may and likely will occur. If she had done so, the Board, or the new President, playing the role of the devil's advocate, could have helped flesh-out the fine tuning of the proposal. She could have discovered flaws in her plan and made an ally or two at the same time.

Mary needed to write action plans to account for every aspect of the plan. Anticipation of the potential risks was critical.

Mary risked losing the plan, but then won the vote. However, she will undoubtedly lose her job as the project proceeds. Factors and plans change during construction. While the overall goal is maintained, individual steps are constantly being re-evaluated and altered to accommodate the realities of construction unknowns and severe weather. Considering that there was no room for fault in her plan, contingency plans (funds) were never thought out and planned. If x happens then y has to happen; but since no scenarios were mapped, Murphy's Law of *anything that can go wrong will go wrong* takes over and Mary will very likely crash and burn.

Mary needs to answer the great question, *What if?* Looking at the phases to be completed, I foresee problematic areas. Conflicts abound. She believes that if she is busy managing the project, her daily responsibilities will be allowed to fail—and that the membership will understand. She should build teamwork and bring in the staff to engender their involvement and commitment. As currently set, the goal is unreachable and the reason for the goal is not feasible.

The problems foreseen for the construction phase are many. The case did not say how the Board felt about outside events being held in prime space of the Club. So, the general membership would be on her like a pack of wolves if they have the negative feeling towards outside events.

The chairs and tables will break the budget for sure, but worse, did she think about staff, china, glass, flow and silver? The building inspector may not approve the building. Relying on smoothing the inspector is not a plan that makes good business sense. She should have focused on due diligence.

The matter of the proximity of the kitchen to the new structure is poor planning and will impede the flow of service dramatically. The new President will remember his fight and revisit the vigor he once fought with, and she will pay the price by taking the blame.

The power lines will be problematic. There should be many contingency plans in place for this step. If the lines are down, then you lose the entire club and not just the new building progress. The $250 will be well spent.

Having anything go through or on the course on a member-guest event will not be tolerated by the membership. At any club with golf, the member-guest is the most important event of the year.

The time frame of the plan is important. And, if she is relying on a contractor to finish on time, never mind early, she surely is suffering from reality problems (and delusions). The members will ultimately pay for the dinners that she is prepared to comp. Who is she helping? Here is where the team concept comes into play.

I would immediately scrap the plan and start over. I would work to get the new Board behind the scrapping of the plan and do my homework. I would listen to what the members want. I would then help to establish the overall goal in terms of interim goals, which could be measured for evaluation. I would then plan the course of action involving the staff. If I hit a snag, I would deal with the problem and reassess the steps necessary to achieve the goal.

Manager Response 7

Mary could have executed many protective measures in order to guard against her current situation. Not only could she have consulted with outside professionals, Mary should have been open, honest, and detail oriented in all of her dealings. Mary should have looked at the bigger picture and not been so focused on reaching her own desired outcome. Not having enough money, not being honest with the building inspector, taking shortcuts, and not sacrificing the operational outcome are all aspects of ineffective decision-making. Additionally, one should never take shortcuts on daily operations or negatively affect major club events, such as the Member-Guest.

Mary should have sought the assistance of a consulting company, professional project manager, or even taken a secondary role in this project management process. Mary should have been more thorough and complete in the planning process and should have exhausted all possible outcomes and results in hope of planning against any surprises. As well, Mary should have completed a timeline and matched it with the Club's calendar.

Major problems that could occur either during construction or afterward.

Budget, timelines, accidents, negative member perception, as well as negative member and staff morale are all detrimental effects of project management. When the planning process is short changed, the project will never have the best possible outcome. The least amount of surprises mean the closer to both budget and timeline guarantees and the only method to achieve this is through complete, detailed oriented, proper planning.

In this case, extra money likely will not surface and there might really not be any money to purchase tables and chairs. The building inspector might not approve the process without major modifications or they might find code violations, which will need to be reworked and thereby increasing both the timeline and expense line. Loss of business could occur by disrupting the member guest tournament. The members will complain which will create a public relations nightmare. But the guests, potential members, and users of this club will be turned off so they will not want to apply for membership. Additionally, they spread the word about the negative experience that they encountered. Many other potential disasters could occur.

How I would have managed the project.

One of the most important parts of project management is to complete and execute a thorough fact-finding and research mission that will result in complete preparation. The more preparation involved, the more all possible options and worst case scenarios are explored, the less surprises that will be encountered. A project budget with a reasonable percentage for contingencies and an overage budget need to be completed to as much of an exact science as possible. Additionally, a chronological timeline and variance report must not only be initially completed but also updated on a period basis.

Additionally, pending the size and scope of the project, if I were to direct the project, someone would need to be appointed to manage daily operations. During times of renovation, everyone is a bit more sensitive and stressed out, members and staff alike. If normal operations are not heightened and improved the morale of everyone will decrease and the optimism for the project will decrease.

Most of all, all *glitches* no matter how large or small need to be anticipated, or at least dealt with in an immediate, open and honest manner. The other aspect of this situation is that if I were to be the project manager, I would hire at least one consulting company to review the plans in entirety before beginning the project.

Miscellaneous points to help ensure success:

- The project would not begin until we had a sufficient budget that included a percentage for overage.
- All details would be discussed with the building department to cover details and decrease the chance for glitches.
- There would be no operational assumptions, it either works well or we redesign and change our plans to make the new plans work and be received positively. And if additional renovations had to be completed in order for the whole plan to come together, then the entire renovation plan would be put off or at least phased.

- In any renovation, we would need to plan for minimal impact and inconvenience to the operation and membership. The member guest, typically the most important club event is not one to compromise. If daily operations are going to be impacted, an alternative must be provided. And, the alternative must be better than the normal service and experience.

Lesson 7

Step Six: Get Feedback

Feedback clarifies messages and verifies shared meaning. Feedback makes goal setting more effective because it indicates when and where club managers may need to adjust their direction or methods so that they are achieving their best.

Feedback can also provide encouragement. Locke, Chah, Harrison, and Lustgarten found that if managers receive messages that support their goals and their progress toward them, they are more likely to reach those goals and set higher ones in the future.

Goal-setting theory proposed by Mitchell and Silver states that feedback results in higher effort and performance than lack of feedback. People use feedback to compare the difference between their performance and established goals and make necessary adjustments. When an individual receives negative feedback, he or she feels dissatisfied because his or her performance does not meet established standards. Individuals respond to negative feedback by setting higher goals than those that receive positive feedback. Mesch found that the dissatisfaction from negative feedback prompts them to develop more task strategies than those that received positive feedback.

Mesch went on to conclude that in the short term, negative feedback positively affects goal setting. However, at a certain point the dissatisfaction created by negative feedback can outweigh the benefits. High levels of dissatisfaction can lead to negative behavior and an increase in absenteeism and employee turnover. Even in the short term, negative feedback can be detrimental if the individual does not believe his effort ever will result in positive feedback. Negative feedback might not be appropriate when there is a lack of organizational support, low trust, a poor relationship with the feedback source, and low self efficacy. Conversely, a positive relationship with the feedback source, a high-trust environment, support for goal accomplishment, high self efficacy, and rigorous criteria for acceptable performance may enhance the feedback relationship.

Furthermore, the more difficult and more specific goals become, the more feedback managers need. In essence, the process reinforces itself according to O'Hair: Setting higher goals leads to better effort and elevated performance; learning of success through feedback encourages still higher goals in the future. Talk about your 10-minute mile goal with other runners, read running magazines, try an organized fun run event such as the one held during the CMAA World Conference. Develop an informal support group that can provide constructive feedback regarding your goal.

Goal selection and establishment using the preceding steps are perhaps the most important stages in establishing what people want to do. By this time in the process:

- The goal should be identified.
- A strategy for how the goal will be accomplished should be mapped out.
- The performance goal should be challenging, flexible, and measurable.
- Issues such as time, money, and other necessary resources for goal achievement should have been considered.
- Risk and rewards relative to the alternative selected should be understood. Similarly, a well-devised strategy for contingencies that may arise should be in place.

- Finally, a support group for receiving constructive feedback from others should be assembled.

1.7. Mini Case: Feedback

Larry Case, manager of Winged Griffin Polo Club in Gatorland, Florida knows what he wants out of life. *I want to run the Boston Marathon in 3:25. It has been a personal goal for five years. In fact, I am training hard, hoping to be accepted this year.* Larry works 80-hour weeks managing the equestrian activities for a young, active membership and trains on Monday (his long weekly run) and during late-afternoon breaks (between lunch and dinner split shifts).

The track coach for distance running at University of Florida is a club member and has noticed Larry's running clothes hanging in the locker room. He has offered to take a look at Larry's running style an offer a few pointers. *Maybe I can sharpen your skills a bit, Larry. No big deal. We keep lots of stats and pre-written training programs at the University. I will be happy to give you some pointers. Maybe you would like to come to practice on Monday afternoon and meet some of the others who are training for Boston. In fact, we have a group of five that are peaking-up for New York City. You could take a training run with them if you would like to find out what they are going through right now.*

Thanks coach. What a generous offer. I just don't want to take advantage, especially since you are a member and all.

That is not a problem in any way. Larry, I will see you on Monday.

Discussion Question

We have discussed the importance of feedback. However, this case puts a twist on that subject by involving a member.

Are Larry's concerns valid? If certain circumstances are not clear from the case, state under what circumstances something may or may not be okay. What does Larry stand to gain? What does Larry stand to lose? What would you do if you were in his situation?

Manager Response 1

There is no set rule as to under what circumstances a manager should or should not accept a favor from a member. It is a judgment call, and should be based upon what the manager believes would cost the member in personal time, money, or resources. It also has to do with the cost to the manager of owing the member in the future in terms of club favors. Going in to the equation should also be the relationship between the manager and the member. If the manager does not know the member, then there is no relationship. If this were to be the case, then the manager might decline. If, on the other hand, the member was a frequent club user, had events at the Club, and participated on committees of the Club, then the manager would be in a position to accept an offer of assistance. The manager should not ask for assistance unless there was a personal friendship already in place.

Larry stands to gain the feedback he has needed for some time, which could make the difference in progressing toward his goal or not. It may also help him define the direction he should take toward his goal in training techniques and time allocated. If I were in Larry's position, I would gratefully accept the coaches offer, and show up at the track the following Monday. I would then have the coach evaluate my technique and provide advice, thank him, and leave him alone. Once introduced to other runners, they could provide further feedback, allowing the coach to feel as though he had fulfilled his obligation to help and is now off the hook.

Manager Response 2

Larry is fortunate to have a member show interest in his personal life. This means that the member sees Larry as more than a faceless employee or from a servant level.

Feedback is essential in obtaining one's goal. A harmonious blend of both negative and positive feedback must be processed and acted upon in order to reach the goals that have been set.

Larry has established his goal, but that seems to be an arbitrary end-result state. He trains when he has time without objective critique. He should be able to measure his improvement toward the achievement. This will help ensure that he continues to progress toward the goal.

There are risks involved in forming a non-club relationship with a member. One of the biggest problems is other members feeling that favoritism is being shown to the member involved. This is never a good situation in a private club. Larry has a valid concern. What Larry has to gain is a better chance to achieve his goal. Being monitored by a professional in a professional setting with others, who also have athletic goals, greatly increases his chances of success. Larry may lose some credibility within the Club if he works closely with one particular member. Larry has the ability to gain achieving a lifelong dream. It depends on the nuance of the situation, which cannot be conveyed in this scenario. In any case, if Larry is considering accepting help from the member, he must be very careful.

I would discuss the situation with the Board President and make him or her aware of my goals outside the Club and what has been offered by the coach. If we were both in agreement with me accepting the offer, I would return to the coach and undergo a professional appraisal. With the Board being aware of the circumstances, and with their support, this should help alleviate any problems. Those members who object could be satisfied in knowing that the Board is aware of the relationship and approved it. The Board is more likely to look upon Larry as an individual with dreams and aspirations instead of an employee who is trying to take advantage of a situation. If the President did not approve my proposal, I would politely thank and diplomatically advise the coach and move toward my goal on my own.

Manager Response 3

Larry's concerns are valid. In this instance it would appear to be beneficial for Larry to receive feedback on his running style. However, Larry could establish a relationship with the member that he might not enjoy. This would be the case if the member started to give Larry *helpful suggestions* as to how to manage things at the Club. If the member sees Larry as the student, he might try to treat him like that all the time.

What if Larry's running style stinks and the member hates it? Could Larry lose face with the member? What if the member decides Larry does not train hard enough to attain his goals? Again, could the member bring this feeling to the Club and evaluate Larry as being inept? If Larry sets the ground rules for the training relationship, this could theoretically be averted and develop into a great personal gain. Larry needs to make sure that he details the guidelines of the relationship with the member to the best of his ability.

Larry could gain or lose in this relationship; it depends upon how the member envisions Larry. If I were in this situation, I would thank the member and keep my personal goals and ambitions to myself. At times, when a member helps a club manager, he or she eventually wants the favor returned. This can come back to haunt a manager. Keep your personal life your own.

Manager Response 4

Larry's concerns are valid. He has set a personal goal in which the Club is not involved. The coach has approached Larry on his own—without prompting—offering professional advice. Larry has the opportunity to decline this involvement in his personal goal. He may, however, accept the coach's generosity and seek suggestions or ideas and insight that he might explore on his own. This could be using the Internet, reading articles, or possibly viewing training videos that the coach could provide. Accepting anything more may involve the member too much. Additionally, it could hurt Larry's self confidence in accomplishing his goals on his own terms.

If I were Larry, I would graciously decline the coach's offer. However, I would ask for suggestions to research on my own time, and thank him for his interest.

Manager Response 5

My club has a strict policy that would not allow Larry to become involved with a member in this manner. We have found that employee relationships with members outside of the Club rarely provide long term benefit to anyone. However, for the purpose of answering this question, I will assume that this policy does not exist.

Larry has set a goal to run the Boston Marathon in 3:25. Although he has been training hard he has been unable to reach his goal over the last five years. Larry's goal puts him in an intermediate group of athletes. The realities of an 80 hour per week work schedule and limited training time have not allowed him the flexibility to concentrate on what needs to be done. I am assuming that the time that Larry spends training for the most part is time spent alone with very little feedback on his performance by others.

By taking up the track coach on his offer, Larry will be able to have someone provide him with the feedback he needs on his running style, goal, and training techniques. Having the ability to run with the other people who are training for Boston could be both inspirational and helpful to Larry. Through feedback,

Larry could make comparisons between different running styles and make some adjustments, where necessary, to his own style. The encouragement Larry receives from the coach or the group could produce a higher performance effort and make his goal achievement more likely. However, Larry would need to be aware that he would be associating with elite class runners, who do not typically work and train. Training is their most important focus.

However, the severity of the drawback to Larry becoming involved with the coach and other runners depends more on his level of involvement with them. Consulting with them for a session or two may provide him with the feedback he would need to assess his own situation. On balance, Larry would be better off training regularly with an individual or group of people who are more closely matched with his lifestyle.

If Larry does not get positive feedback, the negativity may discourage him from actually continuing to pursue his goal. Larry's personal responsibilities may differ greatly from the responsibilities of the other runners making it impossible to compare training times, schedules, and goals. This is where becoming involved with a member may become sensitive. Larry may become so influenced by the feedback he receives that it may affect his work performance. Larry may even start to rethink his long hours and begin to devote more time to his running schedule. His performance on the job may begin to suffer creating an awkward situation between himself and the member. The other possibility is that the feedback may be so negative that Larry finds it uncomfortable to be around the coach in his work environment.

If I were Larry I would find a group to associate with that could provide me with the feedback necessary to make my goals more attainable.

Manager Response 6

Larry is not doing any harm to his career or crossing the line as long as he is very careful. He should accept the invitation once. If he has been training for the marathon for over a year and is serious about running, he probably will gain a great deal of knowledge from the coach and the rest of the runners at the University.

The member issue should be addressed only if it gets weird or Larry senses a problem with it. The way the other runners treat him may be a factor. Circumstances that will dictate uneasiness would be an ongoing relationship to which the coach feels like he is obligated to help Larry. And, another would be if Larry takes what the coach is doing for him for granted. Also, if the coach finds that Larry is good and pushes him to do better and gives him either positive or negative feedback strongly, the relationship will probably go downhill fast. The line would be crossed.

Larry stands to gain valuable information from a professional trainer that has extended an offer to asses and provide his opinion. He could gain much from the coach. He stands to lose the trust of a member, and possibly his job (worst case scenario).

If I were Larry, I would take the coach up on the offer and see how it goes. The first time that we met, I would explain my concerns of not wanting to take advantage. I would definitely not continue training with the coach. The one-time feedback would be great.

Manager Response 7

Larry's concerns are valid. Any time a manager crosses the professional realm into a member's personal realm, the manager has to be very careful. In this case, because the situation is informal, I might participate. However, I would be careful about the manner in which I approached the situation. This type of situation does not open anyone up to any sensitive issues. The only two issues that might be important would be Larry's ability to receive negative feedback and criticism from the member without reacting to it personally (carryover hard feelings from the track to the Club.) The other factor would be for Larry not to take up too much of the member's time.

Regarding other circumstances, it depends on the topics. If the member was a financial advisor and was offering to help the manager with financial planning, I might suggest that the manager seek financial assistance elsewhere as financial matters are more private and sensitive in nature. The member could argue to other members that the manager was compensated too much or might comment on other parts of the manager's life that need not be known by the membership.

In this more informal scenario, Larry seeks to gain knowledge, abilities and outcomes that he might not have achieved otherwise. This is a special opportunity that does not pertain to sensitive issues; it is not as if Larry can just look in the phone book and receive the same type of training opportunity from many other sources. Additionally, Larry can gain the opportunity to build a good relationship with a club member while extending his talents outside of the Club. Additionally, and at the heart of the situation, is the possibility of getting closer to his personal goal than ever before, running the Boston Marathon in 3:28.

Larry, in this case, does not have much to lose. Whenever you enter into a relationship with a member outside of work, there is always the chance that you may lose respect and professional integrity. In this case I do not think Larry is entering into anything that is too sensitive.

I would probably enter into the situation. I would ask if the coach would want compensation or see if there was some other, non-club related manner, whereby I contribute to express my gratitude. I would also be sure not over extend my stay , even if I really did want more knowledge, I would ask the coach to maybe recommend another facility or running coach.

Lesson 8

The Goal Statement

When the decisions in the steps for establishing a goal have been successfully made, commit them to writing. Review and adjust or clarify the steps as necessary. Be specific. Using the information produced in the step process, create a written goal statement that includes answers to the seven following points:

- Who? Sam Jones.

- What? Adopt the goal to run a 10-minute mile.

- Where? On the track at Canyon College.

- When? Within four weeks of beginning my jogging program January 1. Without a deadline, there is less urgency, resulting in laxness and the risk of losing interest.

- Why? I have selected this goal to help me begin a jogging program.

- How? I will schedule my 45-minute jogging routine five days per week—just like any other appointment.

- Who cares? A regular jogging program will enable me to become physically fit, reduce stress, and allow me uninterrupted time to think about the strategic direction of my club.

Once written, the goal will have more meaning and importance to the creator. One GM in Roanoke, Virginia adds, *I first became familiar with the importance of this process in school. Our journalism teacher pounded it into our heads at every opportunity. To this day I still ask those questions, not only when I write, but when I plan. This format is a major key to our success.* Once the goal is established, move forward to the physical and cognitive steps of goal setting.

1.8. Mini Case: The Goal Statement

Chris Johnson, GM of the City Club of Anorak, Maine worked hard and long to develop an important personal goal. At five feet eight inches tall and 377 pounds, Chris had resolved to lose 200 pounds. Here is what Chris wrote in the written goal statement:

- Who? Chris Johnson
- What? I will try to lose 200 pounds.
- When? Soon.
- Where? Wherever.
- Why? I am tired of being fat.
- How? I will join one of those diet programs advertised on TV.
- Who cares? Lots of people.

Discussion Question

What is your reaction to the way Chris has written the goal statement? Could you help Chris strengthen any answers to the seven points?

Manager Response 1

Chris did an excellent job outlining the *Who* part of his written goal statement. Past that, not much else would help him to achieve his goal. His goal statement is vague and will be easily cast aside; as it does not appear that he really wants to lose the weight.

This would be a better way for Chris to write his goal statement.

Who: Chris Johnson.

What: I will lose 200 pounds.

When: Within the next 18 months.

Where: Any time that I eat or times that I workout.

Why: I am unhappy with my physical appearance, am concerned about my future good health, and am dissatisfied with my level of physical shape.

How: I will consult my physician to help determine the best way to lose this weight. I will abide by his or her recommendation no matter how difficult it will be.

Who Cares: I care and the people who care about me want for me to live a long and healthy life. I will feel better physically and mentally.

Manager Response 2

Chris Johnson's written goal statement is not only too aggressive but is not specific. Although Chris has expressed his desired goal and put it in writing, he has been unable to identify the physical and cognitive steps he plans to use to achieve his goal. Chris would be more successful if he set his goal to lose less weight over a shorter period of time. With the successful completion of shorter goals, Chris would receive the encouragement and feedback from small successes to go on to continue with new goals and continued weight loss.

To provide strength to Chris' seven points I would have done the following:

Who? Chris Johnson

What? Adopt an interim goal to lose 50 pounds.

Where? I will only eat at work and home, where I can be in control of the ingredients used in the preparation of my meals and portions.

When? Within 6 months beginning on the 1st of January. This takes into consideration that during the winter months and holiday season, I find it more difficult to control my eating. The spring and summer months will be a great time period for weight loss.

Why? I have selected this goal to help me begin a long-range diet program, which will result in a total weight loss of 200 lbs.

How? I will schedule my eating, prepare my own meals, and control my portions and calorie intake in consultation with a nutritionist who I will see once every two weeks. She will provide me with the feedback and encouragement necessary for me to stay focused and on schedule to achieving my goal. I will also keep a food journal of everything I eat including what time of the day I eat it and the exercise that I do.

Who cares? A regular diet program will enable me to be a happier, healthier more productive person. I will live a longer and healthier life if I lose this weight.

Manager Response 3

My first suggestion to Chris is that his goals need to be more realistic. He needs to add more details in mapping his strategy. He also needs to be more specific in his time factors. The way he has written his goals, he will get frustrated early and probably end up failing. He should set 25 pound increments with specific times to help avoid this from happening.

He needs to thoroughly analyze the resources available to him and brainstorm his options to be more realistic, specific, and objective. The list of who cares should have his name on it!

In short, Chris has not set goals that will allow him to succeed.

Who? Chris Johnson

What? Adopt an overall goal to lose 200 pounds in 25 pound increments (which will serve as my mini goals).

Where? I will count calories and only eat in places where I can stay on my plan. For example, I will not eat in fast-food establishments.

When? I will begin January 1. Each month, I will drop a minimum of five pounds. When I have dropped 25 pounds, I will celebrate by buying three new pairs of slacks, shirts, and sport jackets and throw out my old ones. I will continue my plan until I achieve a weight loss of 50 pounds. When I have lost 50 pounds, I will buy new clothes again to help ensure that I do not fall back into my bigger sizes. The process will continue until I reach my overall goal of 200 pounds

Why? I have established these steps to help me begin a program, which will result in a total weight loss of 200 lbs.

How? I will adopt an overall goal of losing 200 pounds in conjunction with a lifestyle change, which will include exercise, diet, and consultation with my physician. I will adopt mini goals in 25 pound increments to help provide positive reinforcement.

Who cares? This diet program will help me to dramatically increase the quality of my life. First, I care. Second, my family and friends care.

Manager Response 4

Chris is not specific in his written goal statement. I would strengthen the seven points by answering this way:

What? The goal Chris has set is not adequate. Trying implies failure. I would instead write: Adopt a goal to lose 200 pounds.

When? Chris answers by saying soon. What is soon? This is too vague. My goal would be: I will lose 200 pounds over eight months, losing 25 pounds per month. I would space the goal over a period of time whereby I could see improvement over time. Accomplishing a loss of 25 pounds each month would give me a reason to get excited and help carry me onward toward my overall goal.

Where? Wherever is once again too vague. Chris needs to be more specific. Where should read something like this: Wherever and whenever I decide to put food into my mouth.

Why? It is not because he is tired of being fat. He has set this goal because he wants to lose weight.

How? His *how* response needs a good deal of work. One of those diet programs is too general. He should pick one program and focus on it. My how would read this way: I will embrace a protein-based diet eliminating most carbohydrates in my diet. I would also adopt a regular exercise program to help ensure success.

Who cares should read as follows: By losing 200 pounds, I will improve my appearance. As my appearance improves, so will my personal self image. People will relate to me in a more positive manner. My health will also improve. I will have more energy and stamina and become a happier person overall.

Manager Response 5

Chris' goal statement is too big to undertake without the help of interim goals. He has set his sights on losing 200 pounds and is understandably overwhelmed. His answers to the six questions lack definitive interim actions and accomplishment and motivation.

He can help himself create a more attainable goal by constructing a basic outline. He should state his goal of losing 200 pounds as his overarching goal.

From this list he can visualize a process that he must follow. This process should consist of interim goal statements with his ultimate goal being the focus of end result. For instance, if he set his time frame at one year he could incorporate interim goal statements at one month periods. After that year he can continue the same path or re-evaluate and develop an adjusted plan. At this point, his overarching goal will change and become more attainable, since he may only have 100 pounds left to lose.

Chris' first part of the plan might look like this:

Who? Chris Johnson

What? Establish a diet and exercise program with monthly interim goals to lose weight, with the ultimate goal of losing 200 pounds.

Where? Brisk, morning walks through the park and utilizing the gym and exercise machines at the YMCA.

When? Make an appointment with my doctor by the end of this week and begin a program based on his recommendation immediately after the appointment.

Why? First, health concerns and low energy level. Second, I want to make the quality of my life more enjoyable.

How? Change my eating habits by cutting back on fats, calories, and portions and eating more healthy and nutritious foods. Start a morning walk routine and an exercise program at least five days per week (possibly alternating between the two to keep my interest).

Who Cares? I do. I must do this for myself and the people who care about me. We will all reap the benefits of my improved health and self esteem.

Chris' next step in the plan may be even more detailed. He might challenge himself with more specific tasks or take on new athletic interests such as biking, sailing, running, etc.

Manager Response 6

Chris has set a lofty goal, but one that is necessary for him to be healthy. Being five feet eight inches and weighing 377 pounds is not healthy. His goal needs to be more precisely defined, made concrete, and measurable. Adopting the goal of losing 200 pounds would leave him at 177 pounds. Good, but time matters. If he loses the weight too quickly he runs a risk of being hospitalized. The when needs to be revised and re thought. Do not try, do. I will lose 200 pounds. When needs to be defined. A doctor's consultation will need to come into play. This will set up the when and how. Where needs to be everywhere—the goal should consume him. Why could be expanded upon. Being unhealthy and fatigued with inhibiting work performance along with personal confidence, are some of the whys that could be added. His answer as to *how*, needs professional direction. A doctor needs to be involved. TV diet programs are not safe for a person of that size. Who cares? Hopefully, he cares. He must care or he would not be concerned about losing this weight.

Setting the goal is one thing. Defining and pinpointing an ultimate outcome with mini celebrations is another. Measurable, attainable goals that can be altered according to varying conditions are paramount. Once the goal is in writing and it is perceived as a reachable goal with a clear vision, the steamrolling effect can happen. If the goal is too outlandish, then negative reinforcement could backfire and kill the goal. Short, sweet, and concise goals with a plan of attack are what make winners.

Manager Response 7

Chris's goal is not only ambitious, but it is also a serious challenge. The increasing importance and difficulty of the goal create an increasing need for effective planning and reducing the planning to a written goal. My first reaction to the written goal statement is that there has not been enough emphasis placed on the seriousness of the first step. The goal statement is not specific or detailed enough to be effective. The progressive checkpoints are not measurable. And the goal is not personal enough to stir the motivation that will be needed to achieve such a large goal.

The question of *who* is sufficient. However, the question of *what* should be stated in the following manner: *I will permanently lose my body fat. My end goal is to lose 200 pounds.*

When, should be stated, *I will successfully have lost all 200 pounds over a one year time period beginning on some stated starting date and ending 365 days later.*

Where, would read, *on regular outside workouts on the trail by the river, the State Park, and the Fitness First Gym in downtown Anorak.*

Why? Not only am I tired of being fat, decreasing my unhealthful weight will increase my life expectancy, quality of life, all health details (blood pressure, heart rate, cholesterol, etc). *Not only is this important to me, it is also important to my wife and children.*

How? I will begin by getting a physical exam by my Doctor. Pending his comments I will solicit a personal trainer from Fitness First as well as seek assistance and guidance from a local nutritionist referred from my doctor. I will create exercise plans and workouts that will change over time. The workouts will be balanced between cardio and weightlifting.

Who Cares? I care, my wife cares, my children care, and even the people at work care. They want to see me become a better, healthier and happier person who lives the life he has potential to live.

Lesson 9

Achieving the Goal

Before beginning the achievement phase of the goal there should now be an established, written goal in place. The written goal statement is a declaration of the outcome one plans to accomplish. Now consider how and when to accomplish the goal. Two effective ways to approach the achievement of one's goals are the cognitive approach and the physical approach.

The Cognitive Approach: Visualization

The cognitive approach takes place within the mind and involves visualizing an outcome. The fundamental premise behind visualization assumes that the subconscious cannot distinguish between an actual experience and one vividly imagined. By concentrating on the goal and believing that it is attainable, it is likely that the subconscious mind will begin to play a role in helping with goal achievement.

There are four steps involved with visualization, which will prove beneficial toward the final outcome:

1. Develop an enthusiastic and positive attitude. Have confidence that the goal is attainable. If not, no amount of work will be able to overcome that fault.

2. Relax. Sit back in a comfortable chair and allow your body to unwind. Close your eyes and breathe easily, slowly, and deeply.

3. Imagine accomplishment. Envision success in detail. Fill your mind with thoughts of achievement. Dwell on these positive thoughts and enjoy the pleasant feeling. Now, imagine a single situation where you achieve your goal. Visualize this success time and time again. Convince yourself that the scenario exists. Repetition is important in helping convince the subconscious that the success is real.

4. Reorientation. After an intense session, clear your mind. Allow time to reorient with your surroundings and resume your daily activities. This may be helpful in avoiding any possible obsession or loss of touch with reality regarding the goal.

Physical Approach: Setting Objectives

The physical approach is the *doing* as opposed to the *thinking* orientation of the cognitive approach. The physical approach includes the setting of objectives. Objectives are short-term milestones that enable managers to map out the conditions that must be met for goals to be reached. Just as there are steps to establishing a goal and visualizing it, Locke proposed three steps in setting objectives.

- Establish the time frame. Set a time frame for accomplishing the goal. Evaluate how time is spent, eliminating or spending less time on minor activities to allow more time for goal-achieving activities.

- Set interim goals. Break goals into a series of small stepping-stones that will lead to accomplishment of the main goal. Interim successes will help reinforce these steps and inspire you to press onward. The goal becomes more manageable and less overwhelming when goals are broken down into objectives.

- Set a deadline. Regular deadlines act as powerful motivators in helping managers reach their goals. Deadlines help determine what must be accomplished and how it must be accomplished. Be as specific as possible. Set periodic checks to determine closeness to achieving the goal and reassess progress. Determine where expectations have been met, exceeded, or fallen short of the goal. If deficient, take appropriate action to get back on schedule.

Recording Progress

An important facet of goal achieving is keeping accurate records of the progress made toward goal accomplishment. Progress will likely come as slow transformation that is not readily recognized without accurate recording of daily activities. It is important, therefore, to maintain precise records. There are two basic methods for recording progress:

Frequency Count

A frequency count involves calculating the number of times a particular event occurs. This is the easiest and most common method of assessment. For example, if you have committed to jogging five times per week in your 10-minute mile goal, a frequency count will help assess progress being made.

Time Duration

This method involves timing the length of the activity. If you have committed to jogging for 45 minutes each session in your 10-minute mile goal, you can keep track of your progress by using the chronograph feature of a sports watch.

Reinforcing

Knowing how to measure the progress of goal accomplishment, one should also establish appropriate methods for reward and discipline when accomplishing or falling short on making progress toward the goal.

In choosing to use positive (reward) and negative (discipline) reinforcement, ensure that the criteria are realistic and attainable. By establishing criteria, managers have measurable control as to what degree a reward or discipline will be administered.

It is important to experience small rewards such as positive self acknowledgment early and frequently to help increase the likelihood of maintaining the goal quest. Similarly, discipline for non achievement should not be so severe as to cause one to give up.

Small lapses and regressions may occur during the process. Do not permit them to cause discouragement. Rather, let the lapse become the impetus for renewed and redoubled effort toward the goal.

Goal Aids

Aids are utilized to help managers keep their goals before them at all times—ever-present but not intrusive. They are most effective when practiced on a daily basis.

One club manager uses time spent in driving to work as quiet time for reviewing and emphasizing goal aspiration. Another does daily step exercises to the accompaniment of *I wish to get my Master Club Manager (MCM) credential, I want to get my MCM, and I will get my MCM.* The progression moves from fantasy, to desire, to determination.

Goal Re-evaluation

Goals are likely to change with time. There is nothing wrong with that. However, the decision to change goals should be both rational and conscious. Where accomplishment was underestimated, consider setting higher goals. Similarly, where accomplishment was overestimated, this is the time to adjust to more realistic goals (just be sure to keep them challenging). Re-evaluate. Have efforts been maximized? Was the goal attainable and realistic within the established time period? Re-evaluation means re-thinking and making necessary adjustments. It does not mean quitting.

Re-evaluation may indicate the desirability of changing an interim goal. Do so, if necessary. The aim is to achieve the goal, not to let it beat you.

1.9. Mini Case: Visualization

Tuesday evening after the last member had left the Club, Pat Brown, manager of the Women's Social Club of Bellview, Virginia sat back in one of the overstuffed leather wing-back chairs in the South Parlor deciding it was time to begin imagining that her goal could be achieved using the cognitive approach she had heard about recently. This is what she did:

- She was not sure if this new-age method would work. But, she was willing to try it once to see if it would.

- Since there was no one in the Club, she tuned-in her favorite oldies radio station and cranked-up the volume to the Tuesday night Dinner with the Beatles program.

- She began to imagine accomplishment, while singing along with Yesterday. She continued to imagine accomplishment to the accompaniment of Yellow Submarine and I Am The Walrus. She continued to relax and imagine and fell asleep after about 10 minutes.

- She awoke approximately an hour later feeling refreshed. *Hey, maybe this stuff really works!*

Discussion Question

What is the likelihood that Pat's method of visualization will work? What, if anything, would you advise her to do differently?

Manager Response 1

Although the Club may be empty and quiet, I would not try relaxing and visualizing there. Sitting in one of the public rooms at the Club would distract me from the intended goal of visualizing. I would hear or see something that would get me thinking managerial thoughts like, *has this room been dusted according to standards; a light bulb is burned out; the speakers are crackling, the doorways need to be touched*-up, etc.

Playing music loudly or maybe even at all would seem to be a distraction from relaxing and concentrating for the visualization process. Certainly catchy vocals would detract from the intended purpose.

Pat is probably quite tired and getting an hour of naptime seems to have done her some good; but she did not accomplish what she set out to do. She took a refreshing nap, but did not go through the process of visualization.

There is no mention of the goal she was to visualize, nor is there mention of what happened as a result. Sounds like she just got a good nap!

The likelihood of her achieving her intended results are poor. I would encourage her to relax in a quiet spot, away from work, and if she feels strongly about music, I would listen to light, Classical or New Age music.

Manager Response 2

Pat got started on her road to visualization by loosening up and relaxing her mind and body. However, by actually falling asleep she violated a key principle to visualization. While this type of behavior is beneficial to the mind and body, she just relaxed too much. To start the visualizing process, she must begin with her goal in mind (after relaxing) and actually envision herself achieving the goal. Additionally, she is probably enjoying the music too much by putting it into the foreground; she is not focusing on her goal.

Perhaps she could start her routine of visualization by relaxing to the music. However, at some point, she must turn it off or down to a background volume, so that her mind can focus on the goals she wants to achieve. When the daily stresses of life and job have left her body, she can make her subconscious mind believe that she has already achieved the goal. Then, her actions are guided by the visualization of accomplishment. Her subconscious mind needs to believe the goal has already happened and then the necessary subconscious actions will make her goal and visualization become a reality.

Manager Response 3

Pat did not effectively use the elements of visualization to help her achieve her goal.

Develop an Enthusiastic and Positive Attitude. To begin, Pat seemed to be skeptical about achieving her goal through visualization. The exercise may have been more successful if Pat had been more open-minded. She referred to this approach as a *new age* method and expressed some concerns about its effectiveness. Before beginning the exercise Pat should have been more accepting and positive toward the visualization process. Pat, give it a chance.

Relax and Imagine Accomplishment. Pat had the right idea initially in that she tuned into her favorite radio station and began to relax and unwind. Although Pat began to imagine the success of achieving her goal, she fell asleep within only ten minutes and slept for approximately one hour. Pat should have allowed herself enough time to envision her success over and over in great detail. She should have filled her mind with thoughts of achievement reliving the satisfied feeling of goal achievement.

Reorientation. Pat awoke after one-hour feeling refreshed by her extended nap, not from a successful visualization exercise. Pat should have awakened, cleared her mind, and reoriented herself to her surroundings by gradually resuming daily activities. Pat's not reorienting herself with her surroundings may result in a detachment from the present. This could result in employees feeling that she is a space cadet at worst and detached from operations at least. In either case, skipping this step, if the process is used during operating hours, would probably result in a negative reaction to Pat's behavior from employees and members.

Manager Response 4

Pat's method of visualization will not work. She made several fundamental errors in her methodology. First, she needs to develop an enthusiastic and positive attitude. She starts off being unsure of this process. She should focus on the goal and have confidence that the goal is attainable. Without this, she is doomed for failure.

Her relaxation technique is not effective. Listening to the Beatles with the volume turned up full blast is not relaxing. Where are the slow, deep breaths?

She also does a poor job of imagining accomplishment. She is not envisioning every detail. She is filling her mind with thoughts about the Beatles, instead of achievement of her goal. Where is the reinforcement?

About the only positive thing she did was wake up after she fell asleep. Her reorientation process appears to be working just fine.

In summary, Pat needs to develop a positive attitude, relax, focus on her goal, imagine accomplishment in detail, and then reorient.

Manager Response 5

Pat has made a great choice in music, so I think everything will work out for her. Pat was not sure this new-age method would work, but she gave it a shot. So she is on the right track in that she is going to give it a shot. You could read into this both ways. I tend to believe she is honestly trying, even if she mess it up past that point.

She should probably go home to be more effective. The music will only create a distraction and no one could think while *Yellow Submarine* is playing. While she is imagining her accomplishments, she is not committing to remembering complete detail. Therefore, she is losing the sense of what she is doing and goes off to sleep. After an hour nap, she has to get up, drive home, and try to fall asleep again, and she is probably no closure to her goal then she were to go home and watch Leno.

I would advise her to go home and leave the music off. She should relax in her own comfortable chair and imagine accomplishment by visualizing completion of her new goal.

After a period of time spent visualizing, she should reorient and then, perhaps, go to bed. More than likely she will have a big day of accomplishment tomorrow.

Manager Response 6

When I close the Club, all I want to do is go home to my wife and child. I do not want to sit and try a new visualization technique. Nor do I think that is the proper time to try visualizing. Pat was tired after a long day and it was probably late by the time she awakened. The likelihood that Pat's method of visualization worked is slim. Her goal was never stated and not clear-cut. The pre requisite for visualization is to have a written, established goal. There are four steps to cognitive visualization: a positive attitude, relaxation, imagination, and reorientation. She fell asleep in a wing-backed chair.

I would establish my goal and focus. Focus is the key to attaining clarity on something that I want to accomplish. Relax, take a breath, and think without distraction. I would not recommend singing. Get the goal in your head and think of the many ways of accomplishment. Then prioritize your thinking by picking the most efficient and logical way to get there. Now, convincing yourself should not be hard fought—it should come simply and clearly. Next, imagine the goal happening repeatedly and in great detail. As in the movie *Caddy Shack*, I would try to become the ball. After your mind has been set to the chosen path and your vision has cleared, then work the plan.

Drop back and evaluate from time to time interim goals, the overarching goal, and the master plan. This is where being a Monday morning quarterback helps and is insightful rather than regretful. If Pat had gone home to get a good night's sleep and practiced visualization in the morning—over breakfast—she would have been far more successful.

Manager Response 7

I would advise Pat to change several aspects of her visualization session. Visualization is not nap time; it is a serious tool that when used appropriately can be a major asset.

In this case Pat's goal is never mentioned, so we do not know the specifics and therefore, cannot give specific criticism to her process.

However, we can tell that unless the music is part of the goal, music should not be played. The act of visualization is so intense that even if the music were playing, it would not be heard. The focus on the act of the goal is so real that after completing visualization, it feels as if one has physically gone through the process. Yes, the body is energized by the process and most often wound up, but it is not negatively stressed.

The process should be done in a private area without distraction and time limits. You should also not have to be concerned that a colleague or a member is going to walk in on the process. Visualization should be executed when your body is ready and awake, not necessarily after a long day at work. Last, visualization is not just imagination and dreaming, it is a combination of focus, mental execution and specific thoughts that will trigger a connection between the mental and physical process.

Lesson 10

Managing Goal Achievement

Once managers have established their goals, and have moved toward achieving them successfully, they can begin to coach the employees and teams they manage on goal setting. One GM in the California desert had this to say: *Goal setting cannot be implemented without effective, regular coaching. I ensure that goals:*

- Are created by those that will achieve them
- Have measurable mileposts along the way
- Include incentive
- Build in steps from simple to difficult
- Are split between objective and subjective measures.

Employees and teams should choose and set goals for using the same methods that have been described above. Managers should encourage employees to set both personal goals and those that relate to their team performance at the Club. A General Manager in Palm Beach Gardens, Florida describes his process: *I spend a good deal of time with each member of my senior management team—about 15 total—asking them to come up with seven to ten major goals they want to accomplish. I also have my own list, again seven to ten in number. We discuss all of the goals, eliminate those that are unrealistic or un-measurable, modify others, and adopt some as they are. We eventually agree on the specific goals.*

Managers may want to share one of their job goals as an example to help their team members understand the concept. If managers can institute a program whereby all employees set and achieve goals, their clubs will run more efficiently and more productively as the staff will understand where they are going and why they are going there. One GM in Dallas had this to say: *I meet with my direct reports every week in order to give each individual an hour of my undivided attention without interruption. We use forms as guides to ensure we cover all areas—accomplishments, work in progress, questions, opportunities, work ahead, and comments on the support managers need from me. We even set daily objectives to help achieve goals. I believe that for goals to be achieved successfully, they should be set democratically but implemented dictatorially by the team leader.*

Stay in close contact. After employees and teams have begun to establish work goals, managers should review their plans to ensure they are consistent with the larger-perspective club goals. Managers should encourage and support their teams' goal-setting efforts. Meet with them on a regular basis to discuss progress, problems, and goal refinement.

Praise often. Words of praise go a long way with many people. If teams are not making progress, discuss reasons why, and if necessary change the goal.

Communicate the importance of the process. If certain team members are not interested in the goal-setting process, managers should explain that it is important to the Club and to those employees' growth within the company. Make sure that employees understand the importance and benefits of goal setting in all aspects of their life. One General Manager in Scottsdale offers his thoughts, *I try to have goals set at the lowest levels of the organization—almost everyone is involved. Once goals are adopted, I meet with my staff on a regular basis to assess how we are progressing and use them as a basis for rating supervisors' performance. Everyone understands the importance of the process.*

Make sure teams are capable. Pay close attention to changes in employees' feelings of self-efficacy, recognizing that they are more likely to experience low self confidence in stressful situations, where anxiety replaces motivation. Locke found that participatory goal setting can channel anxiety into motivation and increase self-efficacy, leading to greater goal commitment than possible through assigned goals. Gellatly added that managers can raise team confidence and reduce anxiety by providing information, training and supportive behavior.

Allow teams to reward and critique themselves during the coaching process. Managers can increase organizational commitment and performance by encouraging employees to engage in self-generated rewards and feedback during review sessions. People are more likely to accept and derive meaning from self-generated feedback than from supervisor-generated feedback.

Choose the right time. Goals may be presented at the beginning of a week, a new project, or when quarterly reports or performance appraisals are given. If there is a time lag between the assignment of a goal and performance, additional information input that intervenes in the process may cause changes in the originally set goals and distract attention necessary to reach the desired performance level.

Select the right method. During the early stages of skill acquisition, performance goals may be distracting and, therefore, counterproductive. According to Matthews, different types of goals (e.g., learning vs. performance) may be helpful during different phases of skill acquisition. For example, if you wish to increase productivity in the engineering department, then you should charge the engineering team with a difficult performance goal rather than a do-your-best job, or no productivity goal.

Publicize goals. Managers can increase goal commitment to goals by making goals public to other departments rather than keeping them private. The public spotlight and pressure will help motivate commitment.

Consider using negative feedback. Managers who expect more from teams often achieve better performance than those who demand less. If trust and a good relationship are present, negative feedback can help increase and motivate team performance. But, this word of caution: If managers plan to give negative feedback, they should be sure to give it in a specific, non-evaluative way so that teams are challenged to work harder to achieve.

Avoid goal conflict. Managers should ensure that team goals facilitate the attainment of organizational goals. If managers reward teams for a *quantity* goal while being asked to make a *quality* goal a top priority, they will commit less to both the quantity and quality goals (Mitchell).

1.10. Mini Case: Managing Goal Achievement

Ralph Springer, manager of the Country Club of Jefferson Springs, Arkansas, jumped to his feet, *Enough already! I want to get going with helping my team begin the implementation process of goal setting.* Ralph began a comprehensive program vowing to eventually involve every employee at the Club. To get things going, he decided to share one of his job goals as an example to help team members understand the concept. Over a period of time, the Club began to run more smoothly.

- By staying in close contact, everyone understood where they were headed and how they would get there.
- Ralph began a praise program. Here is how he described it: *I requisition $200 worth of $20 bills from petty cash each month. At least twice a week I make sure that I catch someone doing something right and lay a twenty on them! It is most effective when there are plenty of staffers around.*
- *We all get together—everyone is invited (and on the clock)—to talk about what we are about and to reinforce the importance of achieving our goals. New employees catch*

fire quickly after hearing others share their successes. We flesh out our challenges, too. I try to share at least one miserable failure to let them know that it is okay to goof up along the way. This is not rocket science so much as it is determination.

- I try to help teams have everything they need to succeed. I figure by leveraging myself through our club teams, I am about three times as effective as I used to be. Department heads cans commit up to $1,000 without my approval, line employees can commit up to $200. The rule is they put a note on my desk telling me what it was for. I know it sounds crazy, but I will support them even if they spend the money to buy chocolate milkshakes for our day campers—as long as it seemed like the right thing to do at the time. If I disagree, we will discuss it later in private and work out a scenario for the future. It works for me.

- My role has become that of a facilitator. Each department polices itself among its team members. They figure their goals and objectives and their bonus plans. They are also responsible for reviewing themselves. Oh, I have plenty of input into the system—especially from the big-picture perspective. But the direction for how goals will be achieved—the objectives—are set by our teams. They are much harder on themselves than I ever was. Occasionally, they will blow-up at each other to motivate the other. I think it works now because of the trust that exists. Before we got into this new-wave management stuff, we were often at each others' throats.

- We make our goals public. The entire staff knows what we have committed to achieving. It can be a bit daunting to air our stretch goals, but I have found that if everyone knows what we are trying to accomplish, we work as a more cohesive unit.

Discussion Question

Ralph's management method of participative goal setting and achievement sounds strange to some people. Take a position and either defend his style or point out its weaknesses.

Manager Response 1

I support Ralph's ability to take the 10 techniques for use in managing others and applying them in a real situation with his staff. From the report he gave, it seems clear he has implemented each step in the process, and has maintained a hands-on approach by staying involved in the big picture without micromanaging the daily objectives.

While I support Ralph overall, I do have these reservations:

Ralph's empowerment strategy has worked well for him, but I am reminded of John Jordan's (Past President of Club Managers Association of America) statement, for goals to be achieved successfully, they should be set democratically but implemented dictatorially by the team leader. Most employees would not be as self motivated as Ralph's. In many club situations, if given this degree of freedom, chaos would ensue.

In the real world of clubs, the manager has the responsibility for (and his career riding on) the success of goal achievement. He or she alone must identify the course of action to be followed. It is therefore the manager's call as to what accomplishments should be valued, what objectives should to be selected, and what shortcomings should be highlighted. Giving over control of the processes to the staff may work in instances in which a high degree of trust exists; but this is likely not the case in many clubs.

Ralph's decision to provide access to funds and decision making ability as to how they are spent is risky. Again, if he has a high degree of trust in each of his staff members, then he can succeed. If, on the other hand, there are staff members interested in serving only their own needs, then the open book management policies could come back to hurt the manager.

Ralph is a highly motivated and enthusiastic coach/cheerleader for his team. Other managers who do not possess this level of enthusiasm would make a mistake in thinking that it would work just as well for them. Unless the manager can commit himself to continually providing the amount of praise, support, and empathy toward staff members that the process requires, then he will only alienate staff members and defeat the entire purpose. The 10 techniques can work in some situations, but not as a cookie cutter solution for every club yet. This is highly-evolved management and is where we should all be aiming.

Manager Response 2

Ralph's management style is aggressive. It is almost so aggressive that it could get out of control if he does not monitor it closely. The plan in place seems surrounded by the expenditure of money to make things better and the monetary reward for doing things right. Maybe he should praise the employees who are doing things well and bring money into the picture on special occasions or for exceeding expectations. The employees could get used to the constant monetary reward and come to expect it simply for meeting baseline expectations. We should hire people and expect them to do the *right thing* as part of their base pay. Ralph should institute an incentive program for all employees, which is based on going above and beyond baseline expectations.

He has a wonderful foundation to get ideas from everyone in the golf shop. I did not see mentioned that he brings in a dictatorial attitude from time to time. When it comes down to it is he is the one running the golf shop. Ideas from everyone are great. However, Ralph should manage and lead the staff. A balanced approach will allow for input, but as the leader, Ralph should decide what ultimately goes.

The ideas shared throughout the department and communication of common goals is excellent. Everyone knows why they are doing something and understands the established goal. That is the best thing he can do with his department and staff. Overall, I agree with his management style. However, I would compliment more and pay rewards for exceptional performance.

Manager Response 3

Ralph uses many concepts which are important in building a team and being a respected leader of a department. For instance, he uses empowerment, delegation, encouragement, instant reward/recognition, goal setting, and resourcefulness. Additionally, he does not micro-manage his staff.

While I like his approach, he needs to be more involved in the goal setting for his direct reports. Especially, Ralph should make sure that he facilitates goals that stretch his staff to perform more effectively than they believe that they are capable of doing. He needs to communicate his goals clearly, so his department heads can set their goals at the department level with overall club goals in mind. He should sit down with his managers on a regular basis to give them direct feedback on their goal achievements and measure their successes and failures.

Ralph may be too hands off and should make sure he is aware of their goals with regard to employee development. He uses praise and recognition quite well, but he must be there to encourage more objectively defined goals for everyone.

Manager Response 4

Ralph's method sounds somewhat different than that of conventional management. However, he is heading in the right direction. I would modify some of his actions and add others.

Stay in close contact. Ralph appears to be right on the money with this element of leadership.

Praise often. Here Ralph took the expensive approach. Words of praise can go a long way. While it is always good practice to catch someone doing something right, it does not have to cost $20. Money is not the sole or the most important motivator. This money could have been spent more effectively elsewhere.

Communicate the importance of the process. Ralph got his team together to go over achieving the goals, but many of them are likely only pretending to listen in order to get another $20. The money has become the goal, not the real goals.

Make sure teams are capable. Ralph needs to help his employees know that they can achieve their goals, not just get $20 bills. He should provide support, information, and training.

Allow teams to reward and critique themselves during the coaching process. He has allowed his team to reward and critique themselves, but occasionally, they will blow-up at each other to motivate the other. This needs to be brought under control. More direction should be given to help them interact. While some amount of conflict is helpful, too much is destructive to the organization.

Ralph has set out to eventually involve every employee. He needs to first set his goals, write them down, and commit to them. His initial goal is too vague. How can his staff begin to set goals if the leader has not set his? Ralph has jumped into the program without doing enough of the foundational work on the front end. He should take his time, plan his goals, and only then help set goals for his staff. Once everyone is on the same page, they can move forward toward goal achievement.

Manager Response 5

Ralph's management method of participative goal setting was extremely effective. Ralph's method incorporated a number of elements which lead to effective goal setting and achievement.

To begin, Ralph was brilliant in sharing one of his own job goals as an example to make sure all employees were of similar understanding. Ralph was sure to include every employee in the golf department, so that all employees were involved in the goal process. Having everyone involved ensured that the Club would run more efficiently and productively. It meant that the staff understood as a team where they were going and what they were doing.

Ralph stayed in close contact with the employees supporting and encouraging their goal setting efforts. He also met with them on a regular basis to discuss the problems and the progress. Ralph created a praise program which created a vehicle for his team to be complemented and communicatively effectively in front of other team members. This technique was not only effective for the person receiving the reward, but for the other employees to observe the recognition and therefore work harder to one day be recognized and rewarded as well.

Ralph maintained an open line of communication with his employees. He made sure they understood the importance and benefits of the goal. Ralph not only invited each employee to be present at his meetings to discuss the goals, he paid them for their time as well. The message he sent to his employees by doing this was that he recognized that their time was valuable and that their input was essential. His team's self efficacy likely increased due to Ralph's belief in them.

Ralph always made sure that his team was capable. He knew that raising team confidence and reducing anxiety was obtained by providing information on training and supporting behavior. Ralph's decision to allow his team to make commitments without first asking for permission was extremely effective. This must have boosted the employees' self-confidence as well as promoted a trusting relationship between Ralph and his employees. Ralph later provided them with feedback based on their decisions. Given the open and honest relationship Ralph established with his staff, even if the feedback were to be negative it would have still proved to be effective.

Ralph made sure that the team had lots of opportunity for interaction with each other. The employees set their own goals, objectives, and bonus plans leading them to reward and critique each other. This feedback from team members would be effective for goal achievement. Ralph also made sure his goals were public. Publicity not only puts the pressure on the team to perform; it also motivates them to succeed in a more visible position.

Nice going, Ralph!

Manager Response 6

In a time when it is hard to get and hold good employees, I have to agree with Mr. Springer. His adopted management style is rewarding for service and quality, not cash flow. But, that can be budgeted.

Employing his methods, he will gain new employees more easily and keep the ones that are key tools, thereby thwarting off high turnover rates and poor employee morale. He is a monetary motivator. This does work well and quickly in a workforce during low unemployment or where qualified employees for clubs are otherwise scarce. The involvement is a right side up triangle with everything trickling downward. That is not the good end of the trickledown theory. The productivity of his work force in the golf department had to increase with the expense. But if considering the cost of hiring and firing and training into the mix, one would undoubtedly come out ahead, even with the increased expenses incurred. So, yes, I believe in this type of environment.

Do I think I can implement this exactly, *no*. And, it would not fit my management style. However, taking bits and pieces out and plugging in my style will work to make the employees I work with more productive and motivated to move onward and upward in their careers. The almighty dollar sure is an effective temporary motivator. The motivation was there. And, as long as the guiding force was leading—and not sitting back—it would be an effective implementation.

Manager Response 7

As different, non-traditional, or seemingly new wave as it might be, the program has tremendous merit. Not only is this incentive program very successful, efficient, and contributing to a much stronger culture and organizational environment, it also is built upon the foundation of the ten-step guideline that define the strategy of managing others through goal setting.

One of the first principles Ralph mentions is that he remains in close contact with all of his staff in order to communicate the goal and keep focused. The $20.00 gimmick is just that, but it is both successful and positive in nature. The reward is a sense of immediate feedback in a public environment. This point not only covers timing and method, but is a way to praise often and reinforce positive behaviors.

As long as the pre-agreed boundaries are not violated, we are concerned with the end result of the goal. By doing so, we allow each person to reach that point by their own method. Each team has the right to develop their own method, as long as the results are goal oriented and produce the desired outcome. At a club, that goal usually gets down to some measure of improved member perception of service or some increase in bottom line cash flow—maybe both.

Ralph has become the facilitator. In that role, he is no longer the doer and thinker on a focused situation. When you reach the level of Ralph is as the global facilitator, he is truly able to manage the operation and guide his teams strategically He provides his team with the tools and resources which allow them to set their own objectives and conduct their own evaluations.

As long as the teams have been properly trained and educated in the process, the same result that is shared by Ralph will be experienced by all. The teams will succeed at higher levels and will review themselves on a much tougher scale. The goals are created by the team, are measurable, include incentives, and are monitored along the way for proper feedback, creating a near perfect situation. Negative feedback is provided and accepted. Since the foundation layer of trust has been created, the individual team members act as strict self-monitors.

This is the essence of excellence in strategic thinking and management.

Summary

Club managers are expected to perform a multitude of functions including planning, organizing, leading, and controlling, and perhaps most important, executing their responsibilities through others—leading teams. Managers cannot expect to manage others if they cannot manage themselves. Establishing a system of goals is a valuable tool that will enable managers to do both—manage themselves and others.

Club managers should recognize some of the many benefits of goal setting including:

- Directing attention and actions.

- Mobilizing peak-level performance.

- Bolstering persistence.

- Developing innovative strategies.
- Providing a short and long-term game plan.
- Preventing stress and burnout.

As a first step toward goal setting, identify the problem. Specify what is to be accomplished: the job, assignment, or responsibility to be completed. Managers can use brainstorming methods to assist in identifying problems and then rank the ideas that emerge.

The second step includes creating a plan for how to accomplish the goal. Develop a list of all possible alternatives and then discard those that are unreasonable.

Step three lists elements to include when creating a SMART performance goal. SMART goals are those that are: specific, measurable, attainable, realistic, and timely.

Step four identifies resources such as time, equipment, money, favors, encouragement, and moral support managers may need to achieve their goals. Anticipating resource needs will strengthen plans and actions, and planning how to utilize resources can make goals more real and concrete.

Step five refers to the risk involved by pursuing the goal using one method over another, planning for potential obstacles that develop, and the eventual tradeoffs among conflicting goals. Trading off between quantity and quality goals is one of the most common conflicts.

Step six discusses the need for constructive feedback. Feedback makes goal setting effective because it indicates when and where managers may need to adjust their direction or methods so that they are achieving their best.

When the decisions in the steps for establishing a goal have been successfully made, commit them to writing. The goal statement is a declaration of the outcome one plans to accomplish. Review and adjust or clarify the steps as necessary.

Be specific. Using the information produced in the step process, create a written goal statement that provides the answers to who, what, when, where, why, how, and who cares?

Once an established, written goal exists, managers can then move toward achievement of the goal. Two of the effective ways to approach goal achievement are the cognitive approach and the physical approach. The cognitive approach is a mental procedure, a visualization that assumes that by concentrating on the goal and believing that it is attainable, it is likely that the subconscious mind will begin to play a valuable role in helping with goal achievement.

The physical approach includes the setting of objectives that enable managers to reach their goals. Just as there are steps to establishing a goal, and visualizing it, there are steps in setting objectives:

- State the requirements and methods.
- Establish the time frame.
- Set interim goals.
- Set a deadline.

An important facet of goal achieving is keeping accurate records of the progress made toward goal accomplishment. The fact that progress will likely come as slow transformation makes it important to keep precise records by frequency count or time duration.

Managers should also establish appropriate methods for reward and discipline when accomplishing or falling short on making progress toward the goal. Positive (reward) and negative (discipline) reinforcement ensure that the criteria are realistic and attainable. It is important to experience small rewards early and frequently to help increase the likelihood of maintaining the goal quest. Similarly, small lapses and regressions may occur during the process. Discipline for non achievement should not be so severe as to cause one to give up.

Goal aids are utilized to help managers keep their goals before them at all times, becoming ever-present but not intrusive. They are most effective when practiced on a daily basis such as during the morning commute or during exercise periods.

Goals are likely to change with time and therefore should be re-evaluated. However, the decision to change goals should be both rational and conscious. Where accomplishment was underestimated, consider setting higher goals. Similarly, where accomplishment was overestimated, this is the time to adjust to more realistic goals.

Once club managers have established their goals, and have moved toward achieving them successfully, they can begin to coach their employee teams on goal setting. These are some effective methods managers can use in coaching their teams:

- Stay in close contact. Find out what support employees need from you to be successful.

- Praise often. Compliments help teams feel appreciated and valuable to the goal achievement process.

- Communicate the importance of the process to everyone involved.

- Make sure team members are capable of achieving the goal.

- Allow teams to reward and critique themselves. People are more likely to accept and derive meaning from self-generated feedback than from supervisor-generated feedback.

- Choose the right time. A time lag between the assignment and actual achieving of the goal may cause changes in the originally set goals and thereby distract attention away from the goal.

- Select the right method. Different types of goals such as learning goals may be helpful and more appropriate to set than performance goals when people are acquiring information and skills.

- Publicize goals. The public spotlight and pressure will help motivate commitment.

- Consider using negative feedback. But, this word of caution: If managers plan to give negative feedback, they should be sure to give it in a specific, non-evaluative way so that teams are challenged to work harder to achieve.

- Avoid goal conflict. Managers must ensure that team goals facilitate (rather than conflict with) the attainment of organizational goals.

Chapter 2

Why Teams Are Important

This is the second of four major topics in the course Organizational Behavior: Team Processes in Private Clubs. So far, we have covered:

Goal setting: Managing yourself to manage others.

In this second topic we will discuss the importance of teams to one's success as a club manager. A complete listing of the four topics covered in this book:

1. Goal setting: managing yourself to manage others,
2. Why teams are important,
3. Phases in team development, and
4. Decision making.

About This Topic

The Why Teams Are Important Topic is divided into 5 lessons. Each lesson will take approximately 30-45 minutes to read and understand. Furthermore, each lesson will take another 30-45 minutes to envision ways in which one can apply the ideas presented in the text.

Note: I want to gratefully acknowledge the valuable contributions of Professor Florence Berger and Jeffrey Catrett to this section.

Organization

The unifying and recurring stream used throughout this text is in providing readers with information that will allow them to become better and more effective managers in their positions. Each chapter topic begins with the introduction and discussion of theories, concepts, ideas, and best practices relative to the subject topic.

Following the presentation of theories and ideas, I have designed mini cases, which propose scenarios that can be solved, managed, and or mitigated using this new knowledge. The application exercises (the mini cases) are best solved using a combination of both new knowledge and past knowledge that has come from training, education, logic, and experience.

Finally, for each mini case, I have re-printed seven example answers from managers with whom I have worked in the past. I have found that readers benefit tremendously from having a variety of answer examples drawn from managers from all corners of the globe and each with different perspectives, educations, and backgrounds.

Competencies

1. Given a scenario of *because they are there*, the student will, in his or her own words, be able to argue with at least two reasons as to why failing to deal with groups and teams can cause managerial problems within clubs. Taxonomy of Measurable Variables: Bloom: Evaluation. ACPHA: Emphasize.

2. Using the concept of *affiliation*, the student will be able to justify in his or her own words the following terms:

    - Belonging

    - The implication or promise

- Recognition
- Identity

Taxonomy of Measurable Variables: Bloom: Evaluation. ACPHA: Emphasize.

3. Given the roots of group and team process, the student will be able to interpret America's role in development of groups and teams in other countries. Taxonomy of Measurable Variables: Bloom: Application. ACPHA: Reinforce.

4. Referring to the Zander research, the student will be able identify and discuss 15 reasons why people join groups or teams. Taxonomy of Measurable Variables: Bloom: Comprehension. ACPHA: Introduce.

5. Referring to the Zander research, the student will be able to construct the 3 conditions under which teams form. Taxonomy of Measurable Variables: Bloom: Application. ACPHA: Reinforce.

6. Referring to the Hare research, the student will be able to organize and emphasize four reasons why teams are often found to be more successful than individuals. Taxonomy of Measurable Variables: Bloom: Synthesis. ACPHA: Emphasize.

7. Given the results of the Employee Involvement (EI) and Total Quality Management (TQM) study of Fortune 1000 companies described in the text, the student will be able to interpret the main ideas of what the authors (Morhman, Lawler, and Ledford) explain regarding EI and TQM programs and financial performance of the companies surveyed. Taxonomy of Measurable Variables: Bloom: Evaluation. ACPHA: Emphasize.

Lesson 1

Why Teams are Important

When asked why they take on Everest's heights or risk frostbite on Antarctica's Erebus, mountaineers customarily respond, *Because they are there.* The same answer can, in a sense, be applied to the question, *Why are teams important; why should we seek to study them and to manage them within organizations*? Regardless of whether one likes it, teams are there. The club itself, including operations departments, committees, informal groups, subgroups, and formal teams within it represent team activity which must be acknowledged and dealt with if we wish to maximize performance and productivity. Not dealing with groups or ignoring teams is simply failing to recognize and manage the fact that they exist and will certainly affect club outcomes. Failing to incorporate them into the structure of work activity is equivalent to refusing to manage any other vital element in the overall work environment within the Club.

Affiliation

Ahrne searches for a fundamental reason for team existence and individual involvement in teams. Ahrne uses the term *affiliation* to describe one of the principal reasons why groups and teams exist and why individuals choose to join them.

In the beginning there is organization. The basic human experience is belonging and dependence. Affiliation is a prerequisite for most human action. To belong means to have a place to go, to have certain rights as well as commitments. Affiliation implies a promise or an obligation to come back. To be able or allowed to come back, the affiliates of an organization must be recognized. As an affiliate of an organization, other affiliates give you an identity, they begin to recognize you, and they care what you do. Ahrne conceptualized that individuality is mainly a combination and construct of previous and present organizational affiliations.

Ahrne's conception of the organized nature of human activity suggests an important, if basic, reason why groups and teams should be studied and managed within organizations. Groups and teams clearly exist within clubs and other organizations. We are drawn to participate in organizations in order to survive in modern society, and we are automatically enrolled in formal and informal groups and teams.

The Urge to be an Individual

While Ahrne asserts the importance of affiliation, he does not underestimate individualistic urges by group and team members. People depend on organizations and spend much of their time in the realms of organizations. Many actions are motivated by organizational affiliation and commitment. Yet, people resist being organized and often refuse compliance. People do not become easily fused with their positions within an organizational structure.

Ahrne has pointed to the dichotomy which exists within us to varying degrees. Individuals seek group participation and at the same time tend to reject it. Depending upon their backgrounds, managers will tend to feel more strongly about team relationships or more strongly about individualism and will, accordingly, either accept or reject the importance of teams within the overall work environment. The very mention of team work and team process triggers surprisingly passionate responses in managers ranging from a warm expression of pro-team sentiment to a hot denial of the group structure and institutionalization, which threaten the status of the individual. Some managers embrace team-based decision-making as perfectly natural given the existence of groups all around us; others reject it outright as an unnatural way of doing business which undermines leadership.

Before we can begin to consider how teams can be managed effectively in clubs, we must first get an understanding of what triggers these emotional responses. We must take on squarely the skeptic who thinks that teams are a temporary fad which undermines the efficiency and dignity inherent in individual work.

We will begin by placing group or individual preference within its historical and social context. We will then turn to the question of why people form or join teams, in order to determine when teams are more effective than individuals. We will consider the learning effects achieved through cooperative rather than competitive means. We will look at whether or not management of teams really results in increased profitably. And finally we will consider teams within the context of the club industry.

2.1. Mini Case: I Want to be a Star

Many managers have worked with staff members who have a star attitude similar to that of Frankie Breyer. Let's look in on her as she prepares for a Friday night dinner shift in the Elm Room, Canandaigua Country Club's formal dining room.

Work as a team. Take care of the side work. Sort the linen. Re-set the tables. Cover for others when they are on break. I am tired of hearing Jamie, the food and beverage director, telling us that over and over at lineup. She should realize that I can wait more tables than any two of the other wait staff combined. I should not have to do all that side work junk. I should be working the floor. What she should do is assign a bus person and a bread and butter attendant to me alone. I could really make some good money in gratuities if people would just get out of my way and let me do what I am capable of doing. In fact, that is a great idea. I am going to see Jamie and tell her just how I feel. The club is holding me back by making me work as part of a team. All I need is a bus person and a bread and butter attendant and I could double my sales. This group stuff is a bunch of bunk. I am not waiting around for this teamwork fad to blow over.

Discussion Question

Assume for a moment that you are Jamie Fogg, the food and beverage director, the Club distributes gratuities based on individual sales, and Frankie Breyer has come to see you with the agenda described in the mini case above. Using the text points of affiliation and the urge to be an individual as guides, and assuming you will support the team concept, how would you counsel Frankie?

Manager Response 1

I would sit down with Frankie and listen to her suggestions. I would then politely, but firmly, roll out what it is that we are trying to achieve as a club (overall) and as a dining staff (more specifically). The answer is teamwork. I would outline to her the pros and cons of working her style of *me first* versus as a team. The pros would outweigh the cons for a team concept. In the concept of T.E.A.M., which means, together everyone accomplishes more.

I have had similar experiences with wait staff in my career. For instance, at our club we share the tips in a pool (tip shares are based on hours worked) for all dining. Some of the veterans feel they will only work and do the side work they feel is appropriate and let the newer staff do the dirty duties. This leads to resentment and a wall built between new and old. We have addressed this issue by conducting training for all staff on teamwork accomplishment. Everyone is assigned duties and held accountable.

The results are that everyone working together accomplishes the work in a shorter period of time, which allows everyone to go home earlier. It also allows us to cross train staff on all duties, as we rotate them daily. We have measured these results by member satisfaction and scores have increased 12 percent since we implemented the team concept. Morale has improved because people tend to be more satisfied with work when they work together. Managers support this concept by leading by example.

With Frankie, her ideas may achieve personal success in increasing her tips. But, this form of goal accomplishment suggests everyone working as individuals and adds disincentive to working as one team to share the work load. I would inform Frankie that she will need to try our team concept with an open mind and a positive attitude. We would evaluate her ability to meet our team goals and review them with her after 30 days.

Manager Response 2

Frankie needs to review the concept of the team and understand why it is in place. It may be true that Frankie is the *best* wait person at the Club. If she really is she probably makes more money than the other severs since tips are based on sales (I am assuming that tips are not pooled at this club). But the question should be presented to Frankie is this: How long could she continue to be the best wait person if she is not prepared to serve tables? With no side work, how will she make it through her shift without running out of table top items such as sugar, blue packets, pink packets, and yellow packets (and other condiments, too)? She will not have enough napkins or silverware to reset her tables. Is it right that she gets to wait on tables and not do side work, while everyone else is expected to so?

The fundamental elements of teams need to be reviewed with Frankie so that she understands why they (team elements) are in the best interest of the Club, as a whole, in this situation. Frankie relies on the team, whether she acknowledges it or not. While a basic human experience is belonging and dependence, people resist being organized and often refuse to comply. People are not easily fused with their positions within an organizational structure. Some people support a team concept when they get to equally share the burden. However, they also believe that they each deserve their perception of their proportionate share of the good.

The whole is greater than the sum. Frankie needs to understand that teams do not need any particular individuals (stars). Successful teams are made up of individuals with a common goal and who understand their function in achieving that goal. Jamie should get Frankie to back away and focus on the big picture. If Frankie cannot do this, then the team would be better off without her.

I take a hard line opinion on this issue. I have managed a number of *stars* in food & beverage departments and have learned that if they cannot *get and implement* the team concept, then they need to go elsewhere. The baggage that comes with this type of employee is usually too much to overcome their favorable sales ability.

Manager Response 3

I would respond to Frankie along these lines:

Frankie, you are one of my best servers. You handle the members professionally and efficiently. You also are capable of handling more tables than any other server. I recognize your capabilities and empathize with your frustration.

However, let us look at the big picture. Can you, by yourself, handle the entire dining room? Can you, by yourself, wait on every member? Of course, the answer is that you cannot. Sure, you are more efficient than the rest of the staff, but you need their support to help with the load.

If there are problems with work distribution, I will look into those. Side work should be shared equally by all. If that is not what is happening, it is my job to get it straight.

Covering for each other when people are on break is a situation that works both ways. How would you feel if nobody covered during your breaks? You probably would be upset.

In closing, everybody must share certain duties. You should be grateful that you are able to do twice as much and therefore make twice as much in gratuities as the rest of the team. (This club does not pool gratuities.) You should view it as a case of the rest of the team helping you make your income, because they are assisting you with side work.

I will monitor things to assure that everybody shares equally in group work.

Manager Response 4

If I were Jaime Fogg and Frankie Breyer came to see me complaining about being a part of our team and expressing a need to work alone and independent from the others, I would make these key points.

I would tell her how valuable she is as an employee with so much experience and dedication. I would let her know how much I appreciate her efforts and admire her for her loyalty. I would sympathize somewhat with her desire to be more of an individual. However, I would not sympathize too much, since I would want her to begin to see the value in working as part of the team. I would point out and explain the concept of *affiliation* and why groups and teams exist. It would be helpful for me to get Frankie to understand the need to belong to a group. Having her realize that being a part of a team gives her identity and that her relationships with the other affiliates would be more rewarding than working alone. I would discourage her from working independently, as it would promote a lack of participation and less team involvement.

If I could I would like to convince Frankie to become more of a team leader that participates in all of the side work, resetting tables, and sorting linen, thereby serving as a positive example to those employees that are new or in training. Having Frankie act as a mentor to the new hires would serve both to include her in the group but help satisfy her need to be more independently perceived.

If Frankie does not resist this idea, she will begin to realize the benefits to belonging to a group. She will be rewarded for her efforts and recognized for her hard work. Until people allow themselves the opportunity to experience the benefits of group participation, they do not know what they are missing. Frankie will realize over time that it is better to make good money and be in a healthier, more productive and interactive environment, than to work alone and isolated from the group—regardless of how much more money she can make.

Manager Response 5

Frankie, you have asked why you have to participate in our team concept in serving our membership. You believe that you could increase your own income if you were freed from operating as a part of the team. I can see that you have a strong interest in being an individual, and you obviously have skills that make you a valuable part of our staff. Let me see if I can convince you of the value of the team concept with a bit of background.

First, we all have a need to be a part of a group, or to have an affiliation. This need to affiliate is what drives us to be a part of groups and is part of why teams exist. People affiliate so they have a place to belong. It also provides us with recognition for the work we do, and gives us an identity. While I know your individuality is important to you, even this individuality comes from your past and current affiliations. Think back to when you first joined the Club staff and desperately needed help and training from your peers (the other members of the team). If they had thought of only themselves and the financial gain they could earn if they did not have to take time in helping you, you would never have obtained the skills that you now possess.

You are experiencing a loss of identity because you have an incomplete participation in the team. If you would let others help you and be there to help them, you would see the Club as a whole service system and each of us individually would benefit.

I think you would agree that every member of our staff can learn more about what our members want by working cooperatively than by working competitively. As a result, we would all be better at what we do, and member use of the Club would increase. Everyone in the team would make more money and be happier. The club would be more financially successful, and could afford to make improvements to the facilities and pay the staff higher wages.

Give the team concept a chance for one month. Now, by giving it a chance, I mean give it 100 percent of your support and maintain a positive attitude. We will meet again at the end of the month and discuss your observations.

Manager Response 6

I agree with some of Frankie's points. Instead of butting heads, I would take a different approach and get her involved as a team leader and as a standard setter. I would make her a part of the solution and have her join in on a team building standard. She sounds like a great server that knows her potential both for income and workload.

I would make it worth her while. Involve her. Frankie would not have joined the team without prior knowledge of the business performance levels, or else she would not be there. A candid discussion of reality may also be in order. Has she read her job description? Or, if there are no such descriptions, I would make her a part on the team to create job descriptions and duties.

Whatever path that I chose, I would not let her leave my office before we had agreed on a resolution. The best way to break Frankie of her individual status is to make her a benchmark example. She will be included and bolster a team of which she is a part, which will make her earnings more lucrative and productivity more dynamic. Frankie will be a good influence on others' production if I can just get her on the team.

She asked for a bus person and a bread person, so this *is* a work team! And, while they must work together, they each have their own distinctive roles to perform in the overall process and eventual outcome. In doubling her sales, she, along with her team would find that they are making more money the more that they cooperate and work together. If they are a test group that maps out the makeup of future teams, then she would have even more of an understanding of the necessity for reliance and cooperation to attain the goal.

Manager Response 7

I would first make sure that Frankie and I were not just sitting down before or after a shift when emotion might be high. The conversation would take place at an off time and in a relaxed but controlled setting. I would be an active listener, attentive to everything Frankie wanted to say. Once Frankie had made her pitch, I would summarize everything just said to make her feel good about the trust factor and to help her know that I heard and understood her points. Next, I would summarize all of her strong points and the beneficial factors she brings to the team, staff, and membership.

Now that trust and understanding had been stated in the conversation, I would see how we could transform Frankie's desire to take on more responsibility, while possibly coaching the staff to become as productive as Frankie is, in her eyes. Together, we could devise training situations, a possible head server position, and even involve Frankie in the orientation of new servers. We would put Frankie to the test and have her put action behind her words. We would give Frankie a chance to affiliate better with the team in more of a leadership capacity, making her feel better. She, in this enhanced role, would have an impact on future staff and co-workers, which would be putting the responsibility back on her. This new role could lead to greater financial rewards through higher gratuities paid if Frankie were able to produce measurable, improved staff results.

If Jaime were to elevate this potential long term morale and employee issue into a positive light, the situation would be a win for everyone involved. The negative is that if Frankie walked out and was not satisfied, she would still feel hassled while making other employees believe that they were being mistreated. By focusing on the team atmosphere, Jaime can make a stronger, more loyal, and team focused employee out of Frankie. Ideally, she would become someone who is willing to help develop others, thereby creating even more of a team culture. For Frankie, who craves the team environment but still desires the independence, the plan seems to have all of the aspects for success. In the spotlight and responsible for creating change, Frankie is independent, yet working with others to improve the overall program.

Lesson 2

Team or Individual?

If you have taken an academic business course lately or attended a CMAA-sponsored program on team dynamics and thereby have experienced the emphasis on team effort and group projects, you have probably learned first-hand how beneficial team effort can be. Certainly in your club you have experienced the satisfaction of orchestrating a successful social event through a concerted team effort. However, utilizing teams is not always the most efficient way to manage. Read on for some further insights into the history of team versus individual accomplishment.

Group Process Versus Individualism

Man is a social animal. Aristotle's starting point for the study of human interaction in *The Politics* simply accepted that to talk of the human species as individuals outside of societal groups would be akin to speaking of ants outside of their communities. Western thought has been characterized since the time of the ancients by a tension between individuality and collectivism. Over time, Western thought began to split into two major camps. One tradition emphasized the importance of the individual, the other the importance of the group or society.

Swiss philosopher, Rousseau, in his major seventeenth century work, *The Social Contract*, describes an historical metamorphosis of the individual prior to society, the noble savage, into the domesticated civil servant of civilized life in society.

The idea that humans only agreed to begin joining groups in order to make life easier and more productive developed into what has come to be known as *natural rights theory*. Natural rights theory reached its zenith at the time of the American Revolution and is clearly reflected in the American Declaration of Independence. *We hold these truths to be self-evident: That all men are created equal and that they are endowed by their Creator with certain inalienable rights, that among these are life, liberty and the pursuit of happiness. To secure these rights, governments are formed among men....* To this day, some people believe that groups exist as a kind of unnatural entity to secure rights for individuals. This fundamental belief in the importance of the individual is reflected in the competitiveness of American business and society.

Roots of Team Process

American business has begun to consider the usefulness of team process within firms in achieving quality and ensuring efficiency. At first glance, it would appear that group and team process is an idea borrowed from Toyota, Honda, and Nissan. An argument could be made that Americans simply are not brought up to accept this way of thinking or working and that the effort to impose group methods will prove to be a temporary artificial business construct that will go away once the experiment fails. What works in Asia will not work in America, and sooner or later we will figure this out and get back to business as usual (and team work will likely vanish out of business schools).

A closer look at the study of the productive power of teams, however, reveals a very different story. More than any other country, it is America, ironically, which has produced the team models business is recognizing and incorporating into modern practice.

Some Western managers view today's emphasis on group process as a theme, perhaps temporary, emerging from research into the success of the Japanese style of management popular during the 1970s and 1980s. While much of the research into *team management* or *management teams* is rooted in much earlier and mainly American inquiry.

Scientific analysis of team and individual motivations and behaviors can be traced to the development of the social sciences during the nineteenth century, when natural science methodologies began to merge with theoretical approaches to social science. From its inception, psychology has concerned itself with the relationship between the purely individual elements of a person's character and the intrinsically social or group elements. The use of groups as a vehicle for psychological therapy and organizational adjustment testifies to the importance of group interaction to the overall well-being of the individual.

The applied management sciences of organizational behavior and organizational psychology draw from the social sciences in terms of methodology and tradition. In the Hawthorne Studies, conducted at Western Electric's Hawthorne Works in Cicero, Illinois, researcher Roethlisberger began to recognize the existence of informal organizations or groups within the formal organization of the work environment. The power of peer groups and the importance of team influence on individual behavior and productivity were confirmed during the Hawthorne experiments. The entire field of organizational behavior is, by its very definition, the study of the interaction of individuals within group contexts.

Specific study of small group processes was begun in America during the Second World War by Rickman and Bion in studies of military effectiveness and military rehabilitation. Their findings established early guidelines for group analysis and posited the importance of the group or team to the individual. According to Bion, *the group is as fundamental a part of the individual as the unconscious. The team is the sum of its parts and has very little to do with the individuals in it.*

The mid century produced a volume of material concerning small group process. In *Interaction Process Analysis*, Bales set categories for analyzing team interactions at the verbal level. Bales discovered the so-called J-curve of verbal commitment within teams, whereby groups, regardless of size or purpose, tend to demonstrate the same patterns of verbal activity by members. This echoes Blon's suggestion that teams have their own identities separate from the individuals involved in them.

Evidence of the importance of team impact on the individual was reported during the mid century by Solomon Asch and William Foote Whyte. In experiments with groups of varying sizes and purposes, Asch demonstrated that individuals are increasingly willing to accept inaccurate information if team consensus counters their individual judgments. Using amateur sporting events as a research arena, Whyte found that individual performance is determined more by social status than by pure talent.

Throughout the 1950s and 1960s, researchers in related disciplines conducted experiments designed to increase knowledge about team behavior and its effects on the individual. The concept of teams developed primarily during the 1970s and 1980s through the work of Patten, Dyer and others.

Deming took his team-based Total Quality Management ideas from America to Japan because he had been unable to convince U.S. managers to try his approach. The ideas and approaches made so famous by Toyota, Honda, and Nissan management actually have their roots in American inquiry.

Having now examined groups in the broader contexts of historical beliefs and academic evolution, we will now consider situations in which teams are more effective than individuals.

Lesson 3

Why People Join Teams

Zander spent more than 30 years analyzing team process and the interplay of individuals with teams. Purposes for team formation that are particularly useful within a club context are presented in the following list:

- To protect themselves from harm
- To solve a problem
- To reduce costs
- To make resources available
- To accomplish complex tasks
- To make routine tasks more tolerable
- To set rules or standards
- To change the opinions of outsiders
- To teach skills
- To make improvements to systems
- To integrate and operationalize information
- To create leisure time
- To provide advice
- To evaluate other teammates

- To administer a function within a club

Teams form when:

- Existing conditions are unsatisfactory or offer an opportunity for improvement.
- Members believe that their team action can succeed.
- Conditions in the Club encourage persons to establish and participate on a team.

On the other hand, managers can detect reasons why some individuals dislike group and or team work.

- When conditions are inappropriate for team development.
- No clear purpose or outcome is definable.
- Doubt exists as to the effectiveness of group effort over individual effort.
- The overall environment does not encourage or reward team participation.

Teams can be More Effective Than Individuals

Hare compares individual effort and team effort in terms of advantages and disadvantages. Hare begins his comparison by establishing that some tasks simply cannot be performed by an individual because of the volume of activity required. For those tasks which could be performed either by an individual or a team, Hare quotes research by Hill which indicates:

> . . . groups generally are found to be better than the average individuals, but seldom better than the best. The productivity of a group tends to be less than that of the same number of individuals if no division of labor is required, if there are problems of control, or if the group develops a norm against high productivity. In terms of

the number of individual hours required for a task, an individual is usually more productive than a group.

Why teams are often found to be more successful than individuals:

- There are more people to remember facts, identify objects, or produce ideas
- There are more people to evaluate decisions and actions
- Teams do better than individuals on tasks requiring high levels of creativity (Hare).

In summary, the fact that groups and teams exist is reason enough to study their behavior, their influence on the individual, and how they can be managed for the benefit of the Club.

Characteristics of Effective Teams

Effective teams utilize members' abilities in the attainment of group goals. And teams have better chances to continue to be effective as long as they elicit contributions from their members. One way to think about the relationship between a member and the team is as a type of exchange. Team members give time, energy, knowledge, and abilities. The team, on the other hand, provides its members with need satisfaction. Team membership has the potential to satisfy several basic human needs. Individual member needs that are met through group and team involvement include the need for achievement, need for affiliation, and need for power (McClelland).

Ten characteristics of effective teams (Likert):

1. Roles and expectations are understood by all members.
2. Members have developed a good working relationship.
3. Members are attracted to the team and are loyal to the leader.

4. Members have a high degree of trust and confidence in one another.

5. Activities such as decision making and problem solving occur within a supportive atmosphere.

6. The leader's role is to create a supportive atmosphere in which group work occurs. The leader seeks information from members about decisions that will affect them and provides information that they need to do their jobs better.

7. The team attempts to develop each member's full potential.

8. An atmosphere that encourages members to influence each other is maintained.

9. Communication among members and the leader is encouraged.

10. If problems exist, free and open communication brings problems to the surface.

Lesson 4

Learning Styles

Much credence is given to the term *learning organization* by managers even if they do not recognize the importance of team process to successful club management. Endless Board presentations are given in which managers claim that their clubs are indeed learning organizations and that they are structured for change and prepared to meet the challenges of an evolving business climate.

As part of the general topic concerning teams and individual orientation, it is useful to consider the differences in learning achievement when team or individual learning approaches are incorporated. Can any club or other organization truly call itself a learning organization if team learning approaches are ignored?

A manager caught in the crush of studying for the CMAA certification examination may believe that individual learning is preferable to group learning. However, that manager may be confusing the accomplishment of assigned tasks and the achievement of grades (the smaller picture) with the actual pursuit of learning outcomes (the larger picture). While certain tasks (such as studying for the Club manager certification examination) may be accomplished more efficiently and with a higher degree of success by individuals, but this alone does not answer the question of whether individuals tend to learn more effectively in cooperative team formats or in competitive individual formats.

Until the early part of this century, education in the U.S. assumed that the classroom was best managed as a competitive arena designed to bring out the talents and strengths of individuals as compared to their classmates. To this day, many American classrooms are organized on competitive models.

More recently, however, studies have begun to show that academic achievement for all students was positively affected by team or team learning models. Slavin reviewed 45 studies from a variety of nations and reported that 37 of these studies suggested that academic achievement is facilitated by group and team approaches, that learning is improved when group and team approaches are utilized, and that none of the studies showed greater success of competitive approaches over cooperative approaches. Based on this and other evidence, it seems that any self-styled learning organization which truly intends to promote the maximum productivity effects involved with learning should incorporate cooperative group and team structures.

Although cooperative team-learning structures can be frustrating for certain individual adult learners, organizational learning is positively affected by cooperative approaches. A club manager who has grown up in the competitive tradition and is seeking to achieve maximum competitive success is likely to feel frustrated by this style of learning. In the final analysis, it is the overall productivity outcome of the learning organization which should interest managers and not the individual performance of competitive players. The educational literature suggests that group-based cooperative learning works.

2.4. Mini Case: The Wedding Cake Team

We now look in on Jorge Hurrera, a prep cook at The Country Club of Salton Sea. He is part of a training session being conducted by chef Louis Richards.

I cannot believe it. The chef put Ricky on our team to develop in-house wedding cakes. That is baloney. I just cannot understand why he would make all of us put up with having to bring Ricky along—all he does is hold us back. When we get into production, he is just not what we need on our team. We need the best people available. If he cannot keep up, he should be off of the team. The chef keeps talking about cooperative versus competitive learning—what a crock! The strong eagles should push the weak eagles out of the nest.

Discussion Question

Using the findings discussed in the text, if you were the chef and overheard these remarks, how would you counsel Jorge in the direction of cooperative learning versus competitive learning?

Manager Response 1

As the chef of The Country Club of Salton Sea, I would begin by explaining to Jorge that to develop in-house wedding cakes, a team or cooperative approach is essential. I would sympathize with Jorge's frustration to a degree and ask him to help Ricky develop—as once he catches on he will be a valuable piece in the whole team puzzle. I would explain the importance of overall productivity outcome of the learning organization over the individual performance of competitive players.

Jorge needs to realize that clubs are learning organizations structured for change and must be prepared to meet the challenges of an evolving business climate. Jorge needs to be open-minded and allow Ricky to contribute his ideas and methods of cake decorating to the group. The team may benefit from some of Ricky's fresh ideas.

I would stress that academic achievement for all students is positively affected by team or team learning models and that Ricky deserves an opportunity to learn and grow as part of the team. Ricky's talents may take some time and patience to develop. However, eventually it will only add to the success of the entire wedding cake team.

Manager Response 2

As Jorge's attitude regarding education is competitive, his reaction to anything associated with being weak, is negative. My counseling session would begin by removing the competitive nature from the team in Jorge's eyes. The big picture for Jorge is the production of wedding cakes. It should not focus personally on who else knows how to prepare wedding cakes. Because Jorge's learning curve is shorter than that of Ricky's, his (Ricky's) association with Jorge has dealt Jorge a blow within his narrow and competitive focus.

I would begin by explaining to Jorge that putting together wedding cakes requires a variety of skills. To be sure, Ricky will not be ready to fashion marzipan tulips in a variety of muted spring colors at the outset of production. However there will be many things whereby Ricky can make a positive contribution. For instance, he will be able to produce the thousands of royal icing teardrops that some cakes require. There are dozens of eggs to break, cake pans to butter, cases of butter to unwrap, etc. The more Ricky understands about the process, the stronger the team can become. As important, Ricky will have the background to continually improve his skill, thereby making his contribution to the team increasingly more important over time.

I would ask Jorge to consider this big picture view. The end result is skills development to produce a better product by more people. To that end, the learning curve of the group has to be considered. I may agree with Jorge that in other educational situations, Rickey may not win. However, the big picture, at The Country Club of Salton Sea is the production of its own, customized wedding cakes. Bringing Ricky along is an important step toward realizing that goal. Further, I would counsel Jorge that helping Ricky with his learning curve will strengthen Jorge's own development. Ricky may be able to help cover for Jorge when he is on vacation.

I would recognize Jorge's desire for achievement. His contribution to the organization is important. In appealing to Jorge's nobler sense and focusing his attention away from himself to that of the group, Jorge, Ricky, and The Country Club of Salton Sea will benefit.

Manager Response 3

Jorge appears to have the desire and commitment to get the job done. He also seems to want to service the members' needs. This positive energy can be transferred into good team energy by explaining to him how the team concept will enable Jorge to improve his productivity. If Jorge can understand that by working with the potential that Ricky has shown, instead of fighting against Ricky, then Ricky, the team, and even Jorge can learn from the experience.

I would also explain that the team cooperative concept must have been working in the past, because the current team is doing a great job. They are pushing each other to perform as part of the group, which produces some of the positive elements of the competitive approach in the process.

The competitive approach will weed out the weak links of the team. However, it is the strong cooperative team working together and helping each other that will outperform any individual working alone.

Manager Response 4

Jorge seems to be competitive when it comes to learning. This is natural, as many American classrooms are organized around competitive models. Much of business life is geared around achieving the best results in your given category. If you are able to achieve this level, then you are considered a success. If we are not the best, then often we are a failure.

Jorge needs to be counseled regarding his comments about Ricky. They are not in line with teamwork or a group oriented environment. While I am sure that the Chef wants some level of competition going on during the training exercise, he needs for it to be done in a cooperative way. In essence, the more cooks who are trained to do wedding cakes, the better the kitchen will function, especially when emergency situations happen. The ultimate payoff is exceptional service to the members. Perhaps if the Chef reviews these details with Jorge and explains to him that Ricky needs to learn it as well, maybe Jorge will be more responsive. Does Jorge want to do 100 percent of the wedding cake business at the Club? Jorge needs to back away to see the bigger picture. Jorge cannot take the time off if he is the only one trained to properly produce wedding cakes.

Jorge needs to come on line as a team member. The Chef should insist on it. If not, maybe the Chef should get an employee who works in the best interest of the Chef and the Club.

Manager Response 5

If I were Chef Richards and overheard Jorge's remarks, I would sit him down and try to show him the big picture along these lines:

Jorge, I understand your frustration. However, put yourself in my place. My goal is to have the entire team proficient in the production of wedding cakes. It does the organization no good if only a few members of the team can master the skills. By working in groups, all members benefit and learn by working with each other. You should try to be more open minded. You may actually be surprised in that you come to regard Ricky as a valuable contributor to the team. Please, promise me that you will give it a try.

Using cooperative learning makes the entire team more knowledgeable. This is an important lesson. As you continue to advance and progress through management positions, you will have to learn how to work with people of varying abilities. Not all people will be as talented as you. However, it is important that you learn to help your people develop and perform at maximum levels.

In summary, I must be concerned with the development and advancement of all of my staff and not just a few people. I need your support. Please commit yourself to giving this wedding cake team concept a chance to work.

Manager Response 6

If I were the Chef, I would talk to Jorge about the reasons why I paired the group. It could be that Ricky could pick up the pace from the motivation in the team environment and learn ways to increase his productivity. If he is with a group that is more talented, he will hopefully tend to excel further and faster than he thinks is possible.

In this instance, the team approach is sounder than the individual approach. There may be some functions that Ricky can perform that the others cannot. There are many facets involved in achieving the eventual goal. The actual production and brainstorming could be more individualistic, while the final outcome could be made by a group decision. Pushing each other to excel and cooperating, because you are members of the same team, usually yields positive results. The variables are direction, leadership, and clear objectives. These variables need to be defined and controlled in order to set up for success.

Jorge may not be able to lead in a team environment. Pastry work is an individual and creative art that many people do not take lightly.

Manager Response 7

If I were the Chef, I would take Jorge to a private spot, such as my office, and have a frank discussion with him. I would first let him know that we only accept team players at The Country Club of Salton Sea and that his comments were certainly not conducive to team play.

I would then explain some about the different styles of learning. I would let him know that the chosen model of learning for the Club is a team learning style, and that nothing else would be acceptable. I would share Slavin's results in that any self-styled learning organization that truly intends to promote the maximum productivity must incorporate cooperative group and team structures.

I would also let Jorge know that although he is very good and a valued team member, it is imperative for him to find contributions and appreciate what Ricky does add to the team, and that by making comments like I overheard is a real morale buster, not booster. Jorge will have to know that I mean business, and that he is expected, along with everyone else on the team, to help develop Ricky. Jorge also needs to understand that we have made the decision to take wedding cakes in-house, and that Ricky is the person best suited to this task.

I would then let Jorge know that if he has other thoughts on this newly-formed team, I would be happy to discuss them with him in the privacy of my office. Otherwise, I would assume that, being the professional he is, he will recognize the value of the team and the value of Ricky on the team, and will move forward with only the best of intentions.

Lesson 5

Team Success

Despite research indicating that teams are often more successful than individuals in solving problems, and that teams facilitate better overall achievement of learning outcomes, many managers will be hesitant to adopt group and team approaches in their clubs. The status quo is safer than experimentation, and theory is, at times, misaligned with day-to-day reality.

Have team solutions to some problems really worked in organizations in which they have been tried? Many managers and boards want an answer which shows clear bottom-line evidence for the advantages of teamwork approaches.

Morhman, Lawler, and Ledford reported the results of a study of Fortune 1000 companies conducted to determine the effectiveness of team-based Total Quality Management (TQM) programs and especially TQM programs with significant Employee Involvement (EI) in structured team formats. The authors established that the two approaches are interrelated and, in fact, devote a significant part of the article to measuring the effectiveness of the programs as complementary elements in an integrated scheme of organizational change.

The research findings reported indicate that both EI and TQM are increasingly practiced among the Fortune 1000 companies surveyed. A strong correlation is established between the adoption of employee involvement approaches and the use of TQM practice. Using a rating system monitored by the companies polled involving three performance measures—direct performance outcomes, profitability and competitiveness, and employee satisfaction and quality of work life (QWL)—the authors not only infer that companies perform more successfully using EI and TQM, but further indicate that the success of EI and TQM are interrelated in that each is more successful if the other is incorporated as an integral part of the process (Morhman).

These researchers did not limit their research to subjective self-rating systems. At the conclusion of their article, they compared the extent of use of EI and TQM with the financial performance of the companies surveyed. Their findings suggest that the more organizations use EI and TQM practices, the better their financial performance using virtually every major performance ratio analysis tool (Morhman).

This research leaves little doubt that team and group approaches emphasizing affiliate involvement do result in improvements in financial performance. While inadequate specific study has been devoted to the success of teamwork efforts in the hospitality industry, and more specifically to the private club industry, a brief review of the hospitality industry suggests that teamwork approaches are and always have been an integral part of the industry. While most private clubs are established as not for-profit organizations in the traditional sense, managers and boards are clearly quality oriented and price sensitive. If the results of these programs can improve service and help reduce the frequency of price hikes or dues increases, it seems that the findings within Fortune 1000 companies can apply to private clubs as well.

Club Groups and Teams

Few industries are as people-intensive as the private club industry. The services provided by the industry emphasize human contact and caring. Many club managers who have conducted employment interviews have been exposed to the answer, *because I love working with people*. Whatever we may think regarding the day-to-day stresses involved in working closely with people, the private club industry is an occupation for persons highly attracted to the sort of affiliation inherent in working among groups of people.

The private club industry has been organized into subgroups and teams since its early days. Any manager who has witnessed interdepartmental warfare can attest to the existence and influence of informal groups within the Club. A new receptionist is automatically enrolled in a *team* whether or not that team has been organized and empowered. Acceptance by the existing team and the support and guidance provided by existing team members will be a key to the success of that receptionist.

A glance into the history of private clubs, as evidenced through artifacts and systems still employed by older clubs, suggests that even greater teamwork existed within the industry at an earlier date. Old training manuals list detailed procedures for interactions among classical American four-person wait teams involving a bus person, a front server, a back server, and a captain. Similarly, teams existed within the kitchen and in golf maintenance.

Two considerations tended to disrupt traditional teams. First, improvements in efficiency reduced hierarchy and division of labor. Job combination, made increasingly feasible through the use of advanced technology, changed the face of traditional teams. Simultaneously, accounting and performance tracking concepts gained acceptance whereby steps were taken to increase the accountability of the individual, sometimes at the cost of team participation. Similar disruptions occurred among front office and engineering personnel, as individual accountability became the primary concern of managers seeking to curb losses and ensure productivity. This concern for accountability was strengthened by the emergence of legislation allowing for increased litigation on the part of employees.

Yet fear of losing control and losing accountability has prevented some managers from embracing participative concepts involving management of groups and teams. Many managers would answer, *we have always done it this way and it* works. In fact, *we* have not always done it this way, and some of our earlier changes may have disregarded important elements in overall property productivity. In an industry so people-intensive, hesitancy to utilize the advantages of potential for formal and informal groups is short sighted at best.

Teams Differ From Groups

We have discussed teams and groups in somewhat synonymous terms up to this point. There are, however, fundamental differences between the two. A group consists of two or more people who regularly interact with and influence one another over periods of time, perceive themselves as distinct entities (distinguishable from others), sharing common values, and striving for common objectives. Group members may share information, make decisions, and help each other, but they produce individual outputs within areas of accountability. A work group's performance is the sum of what its members accomplish as individuals. They pursue no collective outcomes requiring joint effort (Katzenback and Smith). For example, club committees composed of individuals who work together are not necessarily teams.

A team *can be defined as a small number of people with complementary skills, who are committed to a common purpose, set of performance goals, and approach for which they hold themselves mutually accountable* (Katzenback and Smith). By choosing the team path instead of the group path, people commit to take the risks of conflict, joint work-outcomes, and collective action necessary to build a common purpose, set of goals, approach, and mutual accountability. Teams strive for magnified impacts that are incremental to what their members could achieve in their individual roles.

Katzenback and Smith proposed a team performance curve to help build a framework for their concepts of group versus team:

1. Working group. This is a group for which there is no significant incremental performance need or opportunity that would require it to become a team. Members interact to share information, best practices or perspectives, and to make decisions to help individuals perform within their areas of responsibilities.

2. Pseudo-team. This is a group for which there could be a significant, incremental performance need or opportunity, but it has not focused on collective performance and is not really trying to achieve it. It has no interest in shaping a common purpose or set of performance goals, even though it may call itself a team.

3. Potential team. This is a group for which there is a significant, incremental performance need, and that really is trying to improve its performance impact. Typically, however, it requires more clarity about purpose, goals, or outcomes, and more discipline in hammering out a common working approach. It has not yet established collective accountability.

4. Real team. This is a small number of people with complementary skills who are equally committed to a common purpose, goals, and working approach for which they hold themselves mutually accountable.

5. High-performance team. This is a group that meets all of the conditions of real teams and has members who are deeply committed to one another's personal growth and success. That commitment usually transcends the team. A high performance team significantly outperforms all reasonable expectations given its membership.

Developing Groups Into Teams

Effective teamwork has been found to be a key characteristic of America's 100 best companies (French and Bell). However, teamwork does not automatically happen. If elements such as proper preparation are not in place, then quality circles, autonomous work groups, cross-functional teams, and other types of teams may not live up to expectations. If members do not trust in and support one another, meetings can degenerate into arguing that produces little more than hurt feelings and resentment.

Newly formed groups desiring to become teams, whether they are basketball players or dining room workers, wrestle with many of the same considerations: Team values, organizational conditions, skills, and the match of team roles with work preferences.

Team Values

Team members need to possess certain core values that reinforce collective accountability for cooperative outputs. Such key values encourage listening and responding constructively to others.

Organizational Conditions

Overall, teams have a better chance of functioning effectively if the following four conditions are met: Organizational support of teams, team support of organizational goals, team leaders are skilled at running meetings, and organizational tolerance for time lost while team members learn to work together.

Skills

Successful teams are usually composed of members who possess complementary skills required to do the team's task. Such skills may include technical skills necessary to meet functional requirements, problem solving and decision making skills to identify problems and decide how to proceed, and interpersonal skills like openness, active listening, feedback, support, and trust to establish and work toward common goals.

Team Roles

Team roles are sets of behaviors that contribute to goal achievement. The following nine roles need to be present if a team is to optimize its performance (Margerison and McCann):

- Advising. Advising concerns gathering and disseminating information about things like new products, services, or competitors' activities.

- Innovating. Innovating involves thinking up new ideas or ways of tackling old problems.

- Promoting. Promoting centers on selling ideas to those with the resources to implement them. In a club, an example of promoting may be the tennis professional trying to get people to sign up for the Fourth of July mixed doubles tournament.

- Developing. Developing involves assessing and developing ideas for implementation. An example of developing may be a joint effort among the general manager, an assistant manager, and the chef to roll out a new menu.

- Organizing. Organizing means setting up a structure so that the service can be provided. It involves deciding who will do what and when. Organizing is a basic responsibility of any manager to ensure subordinates are coordinated, productive, and efficient.

- Producing. Producing is the ultimate revenue generator of all teams. Club managers may initially argue that providing no-charge services at the Club is a cost and not a revenue generator. However, they are only partially correct. Ultimately, no-charge services at the Club are part of a carefully constructed package of member amenities. Here we speak in the context of new member attraction (initiation fees, dues, and charges) or existing member retention (dues, and charges).

- Inspecting. Inspecting ensures that high quality has been maintained and that accurate records are kept. People may do what you expect; however, people will likely do what you inspect.

- Maintaining. Maintaining ensures that the infrastructure is in place so the team can work with maximum efficiency. An example of maintaining is an assistant manager making sure that the dining service team has enough china and silver inventory to make it through the New Year's Eve gala.

- Linking. Linking is the coordination and integration of all work roles to ensure maximum cooperation and interchange of ideas, expertise, and experience. While any team member may contribute to this function, it is logical that the GM will have the functional responsibility for linking at a club.

Work Preferences

While most people can function in almost any of the team roles, they are most comfortable in only a few of them. Since individuals are more motivated to perform functions they prefer, matching preferences and work functions can produce improved performance. The following list can help teams become aware of members' individual preferences.

- Amiables function well in advisor and maintainer roles. They like to make information available and give advice so others can make the decisions.

- Expressives often enjoy involvement in new developments outside the organization and bring back ideas that may challenge the existing ways of doing things. Consequently, they are effective in the innovating and promoting roles.

- Drivers may prefer developing and organizing roles. They look for ways to make ideas work in practice.

- Analyticals take pride in producing a product or service to a standard. They may enjoy doing detailed inspections by concentrating carefully on facts and figures to uncover variances or errors.

2.5. Mini Case: The Club Menus

I am slammed, exclaimed Dave Buck, food and beverage manager of Deerwood Country Club. *The GM has just dropped the menu project on me. She needs the breakfast, lunch, dinner, and special function menus revised, priced out, and ready to present to the social committee next week. The chef is trying to get ready for the member-guest tournament and the storeroom manager is on vacation. I will just get it done by myself.*

Discussion Question

If you were the general manager and knew that this was going to be Dave's strategy, how would you counsel him and why would you counsel him in that manner? Remember, the house and social committee is expecting the menus at next week's meeting!

Manager Response 1

Dave Buck has a problem and is making rookie mistakes by trying to do it all himself. As the GM, I would be concerned about me assigning such a major project to the F&B director if he did not have the necessary resources to do the job correctly. He should not revise menu content that the Chef will be held accountable for, without the Chef's knowledge. Dave cannot cost out any of the plates or buffets accurately since the purchasing agent was on vacation. This situation is further confounded by the Chef being too busy with the member guest tournament to help.

Dave could probably get it all done by working 18-hour days. While he would be getting issues off of his list, they will not be done correctly. He will be making assumptions without the proper information. He will also be making decisions for others who will have to live with the incompleteness and inaccuracies of those assumptions and decisions. Last, when the committee meets to review the work, they will likely be able to tell that the menus were thrown together. When the committee asks how the Chef feels about the menus, how will club management answer?

I would postpone the meeting until the following month after providing reasoning that management wanted the senior staff dedicated to the flawless execution of the member guest event and in order to give the menus the proper attention needed it is best if additional time is taken to review and approve menu adjustments.

The GM should make sure that Dave knows when to say *when*. A mark of an effective manager is one that knows when to say, *If you want this done right, this is the way that we should go about it.* I always ask my direct reports not to present me with a problem, unless they have a proposed solution. In this example, ideally the GM should not assign such an important task given the timing and obstacles.

Manager Response 2

Do team solutions make sense?

This is a relatively easy problem to rectify. Dave Buck does not realize that he is not alone on this project. He has a vast amount of resources to tap into with the wait staff and kitchen employees.

Dave should schedule a meeting of key wait staff employees, ones who have worked at the Club for many years and know and understand the membership. It is the wait staff that knows what the members eat and like because of their daily contact. Dave could get a long list of menu suggestions from the staff to start building the menus.

Dave should then solicit the help of the line cooks in the kitchen who prepare the meals for the members each day. It is the cooks who have a good sense as whether the members like food prepared a specific way, like spicy, gourmet, seasoned, or just simple, American grill food.

Not only would Dave be getting assistance from a great many of the employees, the employees will most likely prepare and service the food better because they will have taken ownership in the menu structure. They can say that they played a part in the process. Everyone wins.

I might also enlist the help of the accounting office to assist in pricing the menu items. Based on budgeted margins, the accounting department could help develop suggested selling prices to assist Dave.

Manager Response 3

Dave, you cannot do it all by yourself. In our business, it is delegate or die!

I would ask him to get the Chef involved. The Chef has much at stake in this scenario and should be eager to participate. Honestly, I do not know of any chef who would want this to happen to him or her.

The Chef or Sous Chef could probably provide any information missing from the purchasing manager. Or, Dave could contact the Club's purveyors for pricing. This would also probably result in the lowering of some prices. (It seems that when you do a price comparative survey, purveyors will lower prices where possible to keep your business!)

If these menus were already priced out, then the process would be much easier. They should be analyzed often, perhaps every three months to check on price fluctuations, availability, and the like.

I say all this, but the possibility remains that Dave can do it all by himself, and easily—provided that he does the necessary amount of consulting up front. Maybe he knows most of the answers already and can bang it out quickly. This is especially true if he has been working with his team for some time.

Ideally, no matter the amount of Dave's knowledge, it is important to have buy off from key players, such as the storeroom manager and the Chef.

Manager Response 4

Dave's solution to his menu challenge is not a good one for himself, his direct reports, or the Club. Pricing menu items is one thing; but revising items without the chef's input could have disastrous consequences.

No matter how busy the chef may be, Dave should take the chef aside and explain to him that he will have to live with the revisions. Almost any chef in his or her right mind will find the time to sit down with Dave to come up with menu items. No chef wants menu items rammed down, which is exactly what will happen if Dave goes it alone.

Dave should also realize that not involving the chef will breed resentment. Last, Dave is forgetting his role. He is the food and beverage manager, not the chef. It is the chef's job to create menus, not the food and beverage manager's job.

If Dave is doing the chef's job, then who is doing Dave's job? In Summary, Dave can easily crunch the numbers in the absence of the storeroom manager, but he should involve the chef in menu revisions.

Manager Response 5

If I were the General Manager and knew that Dave's strategy was that he alone would be preparing and pricing all the menus to be presented to the social committee in a week's time, I would strongly encourage him to seek help from other members of the staff, house committee, and or Board members. Creating a team of people would be much more effective to the positive outcome than Dave trying to do it all alone. Teams are often more successful than individuals in solving problems. In the club business, teamwork approaches have always been and still are a foundational part of the industry.

As a manager, I would be concerned about the accuracy and presentation of Dave's work to the social committee. I would tolerate nothing less than a first rate job that I could be proud of. Under no circumstances would Dave be excused for being short of help or because the short time frame permitted to complete the project did not allow him to do an accurate job.

The first thing Dave should do is assemble a team of people whom he sees as knowledgeable about the menus for breakfast, lunch, and dinner, as well as special functions. Once the team is in place, he can take a cooperative approach to getting the project completed accurately and on time.

He may consult with the wait staff and kitchen staff to get feedback about the current menus and the level of satisfaction from the members. Often, the wait staff and kitchen staff members have valuable input, as they are the ones who deal directly with the members on a daily basis.

The House Committee or Board could also be used to discuss pricing and quality. As members, they can represent the membership as to the level of quality they expect and how much they are willing to pay. They may also be able to share what other clubs or restaurants are doing to keep up with food trends.

Once Dave has the information he needs to put together his presentation, he could break the team up and have them work in smaller groups to prepare for his submission to the social committee.

Manager Response 6

Wow! To have the menus revised, costed and ready to present to the house and social committee during a busy period is tough, indeed. I would counsel our Superhero Dave and try to save him from himself.

The fact that he wants to do this by himself is ridiculous. He would not be able to do the menus justice in terms of thought and preparation. The key is first to attack the task. Is there a recipe database that is costed. If so, the needed changes could easily be slipped into the worksheet. Or, are the items coming from scratch and hand written? If this is the case, it will be tougher to input.

A process of teamwork and cooperation is needed that will flow through one person, the F&B, or the person presenting the menus. If the Chef writes the menus in conjunction with the F&B, then the Sous Chefs or lead line cooks could use this exercise as a valuable lesson down the road in costing and implementation. The system referred to in the text is called a brigade. The brigade system is a flow chart of hierarchy that dictates responsibilities and structure.

People at the bottom levels want to get to the top and are working their way through the brigade. This is a valuable fact that the underlings need to know to progress in their careers. This would be a great time for creating a learning environment. One of the advantages to our industry is that the barriers for entry and ascension into management are still relatively low.

Those who may not be formally educated, but who have desire and drive can still progress through the ranks.

I would begin the process by evaluating the menu with a key core of people. Cooks, a server, the Chef and the F&B Manager would collaborate on the effectiveness of the current menus and evaluate what needs to be changed. In this case, hopefully not too much would need to be done. Once the brainstorming process had yielded many ideas, which had been reduced down to a final menu, the recipes would be drawn. Once the recipes were drawn, then the costing would come into play. This is the most difficult stage. I would divide the menus among teams and cost from the same inventory. This is a laborious process, but for a team, it is simpler if broken down to its basic components. Time lines are paramount. The looming deadline keeps a good amount of pressure on to excel in efficiency. Once the forms are drafted, I would take another look before they are put into the final presentation stages. This will help ensure that nothing has been overlooked. This method would involve both team and individual works to produce the timely goal faster and more efficiently than by using the individualistic approach.

Manager Response 7

I would invite Dave Buck, the Food and Beverage Manager to my office for a heart-to-heart conversation. I would let him know that although we do need the menus for the social committee next week, that the menus really do fall within his responsibilities, and that I did not just drop them on him. I would also explain that menu rotations are done on a regular basis, and that he should remember that this is the time that we do menus each year. I would also remind him that he had a similar response last year to the same project.

I would then try to set his mind at ease, letting him know that, once again, this is not a project he should or can complete himself, but that it requires full cooperation from everyone. I would help him lay out the following list of tasks:

- Initial meeting with the Executive Chef, myself, Director of Catering and the F & B Director to decide on which menu items are being changed on the menu (not all items will be new, some will be revised, and some will stay the same).

- Let the Chef know the deadline and let him know when the menu changes are required.

- The menu changes will include cost cards, recipes, and descriptors to use on the menu.

- Once the Chef has submitted these items, the F & B Director should do the menu layout according to what he knows about menu layout in relation to contribution margin.

- The menu should then be typed by the F & B Administrative Assistant and then it should be proof-read by me, the Executive Chef and the Marketing Coordinator.

- Once the go-ahead is given for the menu, it should be printed in-house.

- The point of sale system needs to be updated with the new menu items and pricing.

- A training session should happen with the team members for the new menu items the morning of the Social Committee meeting, and then the new items should be prepared for the Social Committee.

- You should be set to go live with the menu the following day in the dining room.

Again, I would reiterate that *you eat an elephant one bite at a time* and that it is all about attitude. I would let him know that the attitude I am seeing in *The GM has just dropped the menu project on me...I will just get it done by myself* is not okay, and that his approach does not promote team work or getting the work done efficiently. I would also let him know that he does not have the expertise to make the menu changes by himself (recipes and menu choices), and in trying to do so would probably fail.

I would also prioritize the menus for him, letting him know that I want them done in this order:

- Dinner
- Lunch
- Breakfast
- Special Functions

This way, our members will see the changes first, and the banquets can roll right behind. Also, there is only so much food the Social Committee can taste, and if we did not have everything finished, and could produce the dinner, lunch, and breakfast menus, they should be quite happy with the tasting. Having said all of this, it is still my goal for Dave Buck to have all of the work complete for presentation to the Social Committee next week.

I would then let him know how valuable he is to the team, let him know that I know he can handle the oversight of this project, and let him know he has my support and that I will be able to help him in any areas he requires assistance.

Conclusion

The relationship between and among individuals and groups has been the source of inquiry for many centuries, and varying philosophical approaches for individual effort or for group process have been adopted in different regions. Americans are still considered by many to be individually independent, while the Japanese are renowned for their team approaches. Yet today's emphasis on group and team approaches in America is hardly a temporary response to Japanese success during recent decades. Many of the teamwork ideals supporting Japanese business are American concepts developed over decades of research and theorizing.

Many reasons exist for individuals to form into groups and teams, and these reasons have changed very little over the centuries. Still, some tasks appear to be managed better by individuals while other tasks are managed better by teams. In many cases, the very best individuals can produce superior results for relatively simple tasks. Empirical evidence suggests that group or team approaches result in superior results for complex tasks involving high creativity.

Many tasks involving significant division of labor are simply too voluminous for individual mastery. Success requires the collective resources of teams. More importantly, individuals need group affiliation and interaction for identity and purpose. As groups already exist within organizations, the threat of loss of productivity by individuals who feel ostracized by teams must be a major concern of managers who are intent upon increasing overall productivity.

Recent evidence suggests that use of team-based total quality management programs emphasizing employee involvement contribute significantly to superior performance and improved financial results. For example, quality service at Disney can be traced back to Disneyland's opening. The emphasis of their approach is simple: Make people happy. The company recognizes that it has an energetic, loyal audience with high expectations, and meeting those expectations requires more than just adherence to a policy manual (sound familiar?). Disney executives recognize that supervision of all employees at all times is not possible, so quality must be ingrained in the organization's culture. Moreover, Disney's secret to team-based quality management is no secret at all; it has built a business sharing the Disney philosophy with other organizations at Disney University in Orlando: Know your guests, empower your employees and treat them with care, build delivery systems to ensure quality service, and create a service theme so simple that it can be understood by everyone: *We create happiness by providing the finest in family entertainment.* As a result of its total quality orientation, Disney is has grown and prospered.

Anecdotal evidence suggests that a return to re-designed, traditional team approaches in the hospitality industry by some clubs also has resulted in increases in positive contributions to the bottom line. As perhaps the largest and single most people-intensive industry, the hospitality industry is standing at the threshold of a new era in team approaches promising improved efficiency, morale, and financial performance.

So what is the appropriate approach for the club manager interested in enhancing team work? Certainly credence must be given to some managers' opinions that much work is more easily performed by individuals than by teams. Top-performing managers will find themselves hampered by the extra time and compromise inherent in team processes—especially for projects that do not need significant division of labor. The issue is not one of deciding between embracing a team approach rather than an individual approach. Rather, it is one of becoming sufficiently familiar with the techniques and processes for managing teams to be able to decide knowledgeably about which circumstances are better addressed via the team approach and which should be dealt with individually.

Chapter 3

Phases in Team Development

This is the third of four major topics in the course Organizational Behavior: Team Processes in Private Clubs. So far, we have covered these two topics:

Goal setting: Managing yourself to manage others, and

Why teams are important.

In this third topic we will discuss the importance of understanding the phases in team development to one's success as a club manager.

A complete listing in order of the four topics covered in this book:

1. Goal setting: managing yourself to manage others,

2. Why teams are important,

3. Phases in team development, and

4. Decision making.

About This Topic

The Phases in Team Development Topic is divided into three lessons. Each lesson will take approximately 60-90 minutes to read and understand. Furthermore, each lesson will take another 60-90 minutes to envision ways in which one can apply the ideas presented in the text.

Note: I want to gratefully acknowledge the valuable contributions of Professor Florence Berger to this section.

Organization

The unifying and recurring stream used throughout this text is in providing readers with information that will allow them to become better and more effective managers in their positions. Each chapter topic begins with the introduction and discussion of theories, concepts, ideas, and best practices relative to the subject topic.

Following the presentation of theories and ideas, I have designed mini cases, which propose scenarios that can be solved, managed, and or mitigated using this new knowledge. The application exercises (the mini cases) are best solved using a combination of both new knowledge and past knowledge that has come from training, education, logic, and experience.

Finally, for each mini case, I have re-printed seven example answers from managers with whom I have worked in the past. I have found that readers benefit tremendously from having a variety of answer examples drawn from managers from all corners of the globe and each with different perspectives, educations, and backgrounds.

Competencies

1. Given an applied scenario, the student will be able to compare and contrast among the four phases in team development: Forming, Storming, Norming, and Performing. Taxonomy of Measurable Variables: Bloom: Evaluation. ACPHA: Emphasize.

2. Given a case, the student will be able to distinguish and explain in his or her own words the meaning of the four phases in team development. Taxonomy of Measurable Variables: Bloom: Analysis. ACPHA: Reinforce.

3. Given a real-club situation, the student will be able to measure team members' effectiveness in any of the four phases in team development. Taxonomy of Measurable Variables: Bloom: Evaluation. ACPHA: Emphasize.

4. Given a list of stages, the student will be able to judge among the four stages in team development and recognize the relationships among them. Taxonomy of Measurable Variables: Bloom: Evaluation. ACPHA: Emphasize.

Lesson 1

Introduction to Phases

Whether you are a club general manager, department manager, team leader, or team participant, it is helpful to understand the various phases of development your team will experience as it evolves. Simply stated, team development is the path a team takes over its life span toward the accomplishment of its main tasks (Gersick).

Most researchers studying theories about the life cycle phases of teams feel that each team, notwithstanding its individuality, goes through phases that fall into one of two broad categories. The recurring phase model suggests that certain aspects, themes, issues, or parts of the process regularly prevail during the life of the team but not necessarily in any consistent order or sequence. The sequential stage model suggests that certain aspects, themes, or parts dominate the discussions and that they do tend to follow a step order during the group's life.

Recurring Phases

Therapy Groups

Group development in therapy groups developed by Bion illustrates the recurring phases notion. Changes in these groups sometimes are described in terms of three prevailing, but not necessarily sequential, aspects or themes: 1) Leader dependency, 2) Pairing for emotional support, and 3) Fight-flight responses.

Interaction Process Analysis

The equilibrium model of Bales, called Interaction Process Analysis (IPA), delineates three major categories. 1) Socio-emotional or interpersonal phase, 2) Task, and 3) Control. Since its phases need not necessarily occur in a prescribed order, IPA is another example of a recurring phase model. The socio-emotional aspect refers to the inter-personal relating problems a group experiences. The task refers to the job of the group apart from personalities. Control includes communication about possible directions and actions the group can take.

Sequential Stages

The Four-Stage Process

Nelson and Quick describe a four-stage process of team development:

1. Mutual acceptance. In mutual acceptance, the group focuses on interpersonal relations such as trustworthiness, emotional comfort, and evaluative acceptance.
2. Decision making. During decision making, the focus turns to decisions related to the group's task at hand.
3. Motivation and commitment. In this stage, group member attention turns toward self and group motivation. Certain members begin initiating activity to ensure the group begins moving. Other members contribute by supporting, encouraging, and recognizing accomplishments. Still others may begin to establish work standards by which the team may evaluate its performance and members.
4. Control and sanctions. By the time it enters the final stage—control and sanctions—a group has become mature and

effective. It is in this stage that control is administered through the use of positive and negative reward.

Life Cycle

Lacoursiere described groups as living organisms with life stages. They grow and are subjected to stresses, and either mature or die as a result of the stresses. A summary of Lacoursiere's life cycle of groups:

1. Orientation. When a group forms, its members tend to be highly committed to the group, but do not have the experience to work together efficiently. Members tend to be concerned about what the group is supposed to do and how they will fit in.

2. Dissatisfaction. At this stage, group members are more competent at working together; however, their initial enthusiasm has given way to disappointment with the day-to-day reality of being part of the group.

3. Resolution. If group members are able to reconcile their differences, the group moves to this stage of resolution. Group members continue to become more productive and morale improves.

4. Production. If group members continue to resolve conflicts and develop a workable structure for the group, their output and morale will continue to increase. In this stage, the group is effectively working as a team.

5. Termination. At some point, most groups must come to an end. If the group has successfully reached the production stage (Stage 4) before termination, group members will be sad. If the group ends before that stage, members are more likely to be relieved than sad.

Phases

Heinem and Jackson focus the results of their research from a decision-making perspective. They identify five stages including: Forming, storming, initial integration, total integration, and dissolution.

1. Forming. In the forming stage the group members become acquainted and learn to accept one another.

2. Storming. This is the period of high emotions as cliques and coalitions of subgroups may form. It is often accompanied by tensions.

3. Initial integration. In this stage group members begin to cooperate. Individual needs become less important than the good of the group.

4. Total integration. In total integration, the group becomes fully functioning. The primary concerns of the group at this stage are continuing to achieve results and adapting to change.

5. Dissolution. At some point, all groups dissolve. Temporary groups do so when they have accomplished their task. Permanent groups do so when their work is restructured or is no longer necessary.

Heinem and Jackson's phases of group development are similar to those of Lacoursiere's life cycle of groups. The first stages of both interpretations describe a time that group members come together and get to know each other. The second stages both describe periods of tumult. The third stages in each begin a healing period whereby group members start resolving their differences and focus on the task. In the fourth stages members work effectively as a team. In the final stages the team winds down its work.

Five Stages

Tuckman proposed five sequential stages from his research. That is, such distinguishable stages appear typically in order and recur throughout a group's five-stage development: Forming, storming, norming, performing, and disengagement. Because this model is one of the most recognizable and includes similarities with the others, we will use Tuckman's five stages as the basis for our analysis on team phases.

Forming

The time during which team relationships are budding is exciting and filled with positive expectations. During this early stage of development, referred to by Higgins as the forming stage, teams become acquainted; they begin to generate plans, formulate ideas and set goals, and learn about the objectives and tasks they are to accomplish. The outlook is positive. Members examine these issues in view of their own needs and the personal need satisfaction that may result from being on the team. Tuckman concluded that this is the phase in which team members test and feel their way along. It is likely that you will experience similar feelings as you become oriented to the task at hand and seek to understand the team mission.

Storming

The forming stage eventually gives way to a period punctuated by high emotions including fears, anxieties, and dissatisfaction that can lead to hostility and conflict between subgroups. Team members become uncomfortable with one another, since no discernible group structure exists. Tuckman refers to this behavior as *Storming* to describe intragroup (inside the team) conflict, the seemingly requisite amount of overt elbowing, and covert backbiting as frustration sets in. Teammates express emotional responses to one another and to their tasks' demands. Higgins writes that team members are uncertain of their relationships with other team members and may attempt to learn about each other during this stage. They are also uncertain about themselves and exhibit guardedness in revealing information about themselves. Vorrath discovered what he described as a mixture of curiosity and confusion. Tuckman found that during this early stage, members develop a dependence on each other. They may even seek out a scapegoat in a weak member (Vorrath) to help absorb some of the blame for the frustration and unpleasantness that develops.

Confusion is a normal part of team development. By understanding the early part of this highly defensive stage, you will be equipped to deal with issues more effectively and to help your team evolve toward a more productive and satisfying level.

3.1. Mini Case: The Beginning

This is a situation involving a team charged with resolving an internal communications problem at a country club located in Florida:

The Llenroc Country Club, a large, member-owned club located in Central Florida, has an internal problem communicating banquet arrangements effectively throughout the Club. 20 percent of the previous quarter's total banquet functions have received back-end monetary adjustments—all traced to late or undelivered changes sheets to banquet event orders (BEOs) issued by the banquet department.

Effective and timely updates are critical to the Club because of the interdisciplinary nature of multiple departments playing key roles in booking, planning for, and servicing banquets. For example, services in support of banquet functions must be scheduled and coordinated with other departments such as housekeeping, engineering, storeroom, kitchen, and valet parking. In addition, several departments utilize the ballroom and private dining rooms at various times of the year when seasonal surges demand. For example, the rooms division (the Club has 75 deluxe suites and 25 apartments) utilizes banquet space for social season house parties. The sales department uses areas of the ballroom for overflow space during executive conference season. The food and beverage department books banquets for outside groups visiting the Orlando area (not associated with sleeping rooms). The human resources department uses private dining rooms for employee training.

The banquet department comes under the direction of the food and beverage department. Assistant GM, Anne Still, invited Alice White, banquet coordinator; Barry Vitale, steward and storeroom manager; Chuck Reynolds, sales manager; and Debbie Johnson, banquet chef, to form an ad hoc team charged with the task of improving the banquet department's communications.

For clarification and reference:

Alice White is the banquet coordinator and reports to the director of catering.

Barry Vitale is the steward and storeroom manager and reports to the assistant GM.

Chuck Reynolds is a sales manager and reports to the assistant GM.

Debbie Johnson is the banquet chef and reports to the executive chef.

Shortly after being appointed, the group meets in the Club's conference room to begin the team process. None of the members is sure of how to go about their work. As they test and feel their way along, not much productive work is accomplished. They spend more time gossiping about parking spaces, discussing food prices in the employee cafeteria, and criticizing Chuck's overbearing attitude than on banquet communications. Each member feels a certain amount of anxiety. It becomes clear to the group that there exists dissatisfaction with the situation. *This is a waste of my time! I have real work to do; in fact, I am behind now as a result of having to meet with you guys,* says Alice in frustration. *You may have time to meet all day, but I have my regular coordinating responsibilities, too.*

Barry is anxious about the process and expresses his opinions in guarded fashion. *I have no idea why I was asked to be on this team* states Barry. *While I oversee purchasing and setup, I have never been asked what I think. You operations people usually just blow us off.* Furthermore, Barry is an inward-thinking person and does not interact well with others in a team setting.

Chuck demands clarification of the mission—along with expressing his opinion of what their project is about: *Will somebody tell me what this team junk is all about? We have always done fine without it before. I think Anne has been taking too many of those touchy-feely classes from CMAA. The problem seems simple; make sure that everyone gets change sheets and that'll be it.*

Debbie is concerned about the extra duty load, but is the most optimistic member in the group about the project. *Look, I have plenty to do, too. But we have a real chance to make a difference. Anne is going out on a limb by giving us the opportunity to help solve an operations nightmare.*

The more participants immerse themselves in the project, the more they realize the complexity of the issues and that they all have different opinions of the problem—both its origins and solutions. Barry shares his opinion: *This situation is really confusing to me. We thought that there was a quick and dirty answer to straighten things out; but the more we discuss it, the more it seems hopeless. Besides, who knows if we will ever be able to agree on a solution.*

Each member expresses feelings of self-doubt, uncertainty with their purpose, the selection process, even doubts about the possibility for positive interrelationships with each other. While there are strides forward, as they test and feel their way, they spend much time just trying to get members together and to communicate. No significant breakthroughs develop. The group struggles.

As meetings progress, hostility and conflict emerge as an emotional response to their task's demands. Alice had this to say about the process: *Look, I really feel awkward with what we are trying to do. We have been brainstorming issues. But I am conflicted by the feeling that I have to defend myself and my area of responsibility every time an issue is raised. Brainstorming is about getting issues and possible solutions out into the open. I am trying to represent observations from the banquet department.*

During one meeting, Barry observes a frustration with short notice from the sales department about a special order. *Chuck, you need to give us a break. You promised that executive group from Atlanta that you would have The Wall Street Journal delivered to their suites each morning, but you did not bother to tell us you needed them until the afternoon before their arrival. We really looked goofy trying to get things smoothed over for bell service.*

Rather than work through the issue, Chuck mounts an internal campaign to discredit Barry. *You are a jerk! I have to be out selling to make this place work. I cannot be bothered by your silly requests. You should know how to plan better and just have the paper dude on an on-call basis. You are always fouling up on special orders. I am tired of dealing with you.* The move to discredit Barry is not successful, but it takes its toll on relationships and wastes valuable time that might have been used to move the project forward. The group seems unfocused. The process lacks structure.

Along the way, Debbie emerges as the leader and begins to focus the team: *We have been working together for almost two weeks and all we do is bicker and waste time! I say we set some ground rules and focus on our purpose.* Barry agrees, and adds that if they can all just get it together and become oriented to the task, they can improve banquet communications significantly.

Chuck chides Barry, *Yeah; we should all just magically get along? Baby seals, peace, love. That is a childish way to think. But, despite your unrealistic outlook, we probably can make a difference in the way the department handles communications.* The mood and outlook swings toward positive as team members begin to settle-in, settle their differences, and realize their opportunity to make a positive difference for the Club.

Discussion Question

Have you faced a similar situation at your club as a group experienced the growing pains of becoming a team? Recall the specifics of that encounter. If you had been the team leader in this situation (the part represented by banquet chef, Debbie Johnson), what are some possible interpersonal steps you could have taken to have made this phase come together more smoothly?

For example:

- How could you have helped allay the team's initial fears and anxieties at the start?

- How would you have explained the team's mission?

- Would you have helped mitigate the team's hostilities and conflict, particularly those between Barry and Chuck? If so, how?

- Debbie emerged as the team leader rather than being appointed as the leader. Do you agree with that strategy? Why or why not?

Manager Response 1

I faced a similar situation at a previous club. We had a group of managers all pointing fingers every time something went wrong. I found that preparing everyone for the meeting was just as important as the meeting. Communication among everyone only helps. Effective communication never hurts the situation.

Debbie Johnson should communicate with everyone on a daily basis. She needs to understand the situations and where the other managers are coming from. I would explain to them that we are all here for the same purpose. If one department were to look bad, then we all would look bad. In the meetings, I would ask everyone to try not to take anything that was said personally.

Hostilities are going to exist between certain members of the team. I would try to eliminate the chance for miscommunication between Chuck and Barry. I would try to help each of them understand the other's points and situation. There is no need to point fingers; there is only the need to work together for the common goal.

Debbie needs to do a lot of this behind the scenes and not during the meetings. She should try to involve everyone in all of the proceedings. She should try to help ensure that all departments are aware of the different situations and points of view. As communication becomes more professional and effective among the group, they will have to have a better understanding of how each group is affected by the other.

Debbie emerging as the group leader is better than appointing a leader. The group has a life of its own. Allowing the leader to emerge is better for the group and will make it stronger.

To help allay the team's initial fears and anxieties at the start I would have met with each of the team members separately to try to find out their perception of the problem, how they are affected, and how they reacted to past situations. Letting each of them know that the team is there to help each of them with their situation and to solve the overall communication problem would be one of my most important goals.

I would have explained the team's mission by letting them know the annual monetary dollar amount relating to this communication problem. I would let them know that each department needs to continue to work together, and that we needed to come up with a better way to communicate change.

I would have helped mitigate the team's hostilities and conflict—particularly those between Barry and Chuck—by meeting with them separately, listening to their perspective, and re-stating our goals in terms of finding a solution instead of pointing out problems in other departments.

Manager Response 2

We faced a similar experience. The hourly employees felt that they were not allowed fair input regarding benefits and rules that directly affected them. While these decisions had been left up to the General Manager in the past, I felt that employees should have the opportunity to be heard. I helped them form an employee board. They held an election to fill five positions—a pre-determined number from each department. I volunteered to sit in on the group's first few meetings to help facilitate. This turned out to be a mistake.

The employees wanted to make decisions as a group, and with me there, they felt that I was the leader and thereby depended on me to keep the Board moving forward. They had many initial fears. They had no idea what they should do. I suggested that they elect a group leader, then list their goals, and then list all the outcomes (good or bad) that would help them accomplish those goals. This helped remove hostility among the departments when they became involved together to work on a common goal.

The decision to have them elect a leader was a good idea. Without a leader, employees were not able to control the meetings. They seemed to meet and adjourn, then go back to their offices or work areas in a foul mood because all they did was gripe about management and co-workers. The leader was able to help keep control of the meetings and focus on the agenda issues.

In the end, the employee board has proven to be successful. Employees have made decisions that I, alone, would not have made on their behalf. For example, when given all the information, they chose an insurance plan that was higher cost due to better benefits. They also decided that employees would buy their own uniforms. In the past, employees were abusing the free uniform policy and not taking care of their uniforms or personal appearance. Employees decided that by having everyone pay for his or her uniform made them take better care of their uniform. These are just a few decisions that they have made. They also help plan employee outings. A position on the employee board is now a coveted position.

Manager Response 3

Last spring, I put together a team to anticipate and deal with menu and service problems we had historically been experiencing during summer dining season. Terrace Dining, as we call it, runs from mid-June to the end of August. It is an extremely popular form of dining at our club as the tables are alfresco overlooking our golf course, pool, and equestrian facilities.

The team consisted of our Executive Chef, Sous Chef, Dining Room Manager, and Maitre d'. The problems revolve around lack of space and equipment limitations to service demand. The menu has had to be kept simple and the quality has been less than desirable. While no members were complaining, we knew that it was only a matter of time and something had to be done.

I decided to form the group to see what ideas we could come up with to improve the quality.

The Chef and Sous Chef presented an idea to introduce a Tapas Bar. This extensive appetizer bar would allow the chefs enough time to prepare the meals in our main kitchen and transport the food to the terrace. The main kitchen has all of the equipment necessary to produce the food quality that we were hoping for. When the menus for summer were presented to the group, they looked great. The dining room manager and Maitre d' responded with frustration, lack of support, and self-doubt. They had concerns regarding food transportation, delays in service, and difficulties of communication (since the main kitchen was two buildings away from the Terrace).

Once all team members focused on the benefit to the members and how great it would be to improve the quality of the food, the service issues were next to be addressed. The team began to deal with each issue jointly. Everyone in the group contributed ideas. The season was a huge success. Members raved about the quality of the food, the new menu, and the service. The fact that we all worked toward positive outcomes for the members helped keep us open to each others' suggestions and input.

Had I been the team leader in the mini case (Debbie Johnson, banquet manager), I would have done things differently.

To begin, I think it would have been more effective for her to address the realities of the various stages of group development: forming, storming, norming, performing and adjourning. It did not seem that there was ever time for forming. The group was not clear on why they were there or what they were doing. Expectations of the group were not positive. They spent more time gossiping and criticizing each other than dealing with the subject at hand. There was a tremendous amount of storming, almost to the detriment of the team. Had the group known that after forming, that storming is a normal part of the process, this could have eliminated some hurt feelings and frustration.

The GM should have appointed Debbie. She was the likely choice since she had the healthiest and most optimistic attitude toward the project. She, like everyone else, was concerned about the time commitment, but felt it would be worth the investment. Debbie could have presented the team's mission. She could have explained why each member's input was critical to the success of the project. She could have explained that improving the overall banquet communication would not only benefit the Club operations and all team members. Having this information, the team may not have experienced the frustration and hostility which was apparent between Chuck and Barry.

Although the situation did seem to work itself out by Debbie stepping up and bringing the group into focus, the group was lucky. Had no one taken the responsibility or if someone who was not well respected by the rest of the team took control it could have been a disaster. No progress would have been made.

Manager Response 4

The main problem is that the team starts off in a leaderless state. You, Dr. Merritt, have been careful to point out that new management thinking provides evidence that letting the team struggle to find its own leader is acceptable and even preferred at times. However, I would not allow the agonizing amount of time for this to emerge on its own. The process, in this case, eventually worked itself out as Debbie became the leader, so you are right over the long run. However, we must evaluate how much time is wasted. I have a low tolerance for process issues. If Debbie had been appointed as team leader from the beginning, a good deal of non productive time could have been avoided.

Debbie, as appointed leader, could have focused the team on its mission from the start, which was to improve banquet communications. All that time spent gossiping about parking spaces, food prices in the employees' cafeteria, and criticizing one another could have been avoided. I want to be fair, however, because you tell us in management workshops that team time spent on such trivialities is really time well spent in establishing team norms and that it helps make the team more productive over the long haul in helping them progress through the stages.

Initially, Debbie could have pulled the group together and painted the big picture. She could have explained the goal as impact: that effective banquet communications directly impacts everyone at the Club. The current system is flawed and it is up to the group to come up with improvements and modifications. Further, we are not here to blame anyone or any department. We are here to repair a process in a system that is not functioning properly, which will make all of our jobs easier. This would have gone a long way towards minimizing initial fears and anxiety.

The problem with Barry and Chuck is a tough issue. In a situation like this, the group leader must act as a peer mediator. It was obvious that there was intense personal animosity. There was no way the two would have worked things out without intervention. Therefore, the leader must act as a referee when they flare. The leader must be careful not to take sides and maintain his or her objectiveness. If this can be done, the team can move forward and will not digress or lose momentum.

Manager Response 5

I experienced a similar situation. When I arrived at my new club, there was little organization not much communication of function sheets changes, and employees having territorial wars over responsibility on a consistent basis. The team did not meet to discuss issues or conflicts. Therefore, hard feelings were the norm and teamwork was almost nonexistent.

Because the Club had been without a GM for a number of months prior to my arrival, no one had taken charge. Managers were running in different directions. When I arrived, I formed a committee of the staff to tackle the issues of providing consistent and correct event sheets. We also instituted weekly meetings to discuss the upcoming 10 days of future functions and resolve any outstanding issues. The goal was to create a process so that all departments involved received timely information, in a consistent format, so that the members and staff were pleased.

I appointed myself as the leader of the group and added the Catering Manager, Chef, and F & B Service Director. We met and discussed the issues step-by-step in chronological order. We addressed each department's issues, compromised when necessary, and formulated a plan that now is in place and works well.

As far as working with Debbie to improve her interpersonal relationships with those in the group, I suggest using the following tactics:

- Have Debbie act as more of a moderator at first to outline the issues.

- Debbie should not be the leader if she is too passionate to compromise to make a situation a win-win for everyone.

- Debbie should take feedback to discuss the situation in a problem solving manner.

This team is like many, they were formed, not given much direction on objectives, no one is appointed as the leader, then they start to stress and complain, finally some of them become realistic and professional and decide to work together (norming), and then start to perform their duties/assignments within the group.

They had understandable initial fears mostly due to the lack of an assigned leader. A leader would *lead* the group toward the goal, time frame, assignments and discussion in a logical manner to resolve the issues. A leader should define the mission to help formulate a comprehensive game plan from, or from the point of a function being booked to the details being distributed to the specific departments. I would have resolved the conflict between Barry and Chuck by defining their roles within the group and letting them know that their input was vital to the success of the group. I would then ask for their suggestions/issues and place them on a flip chart to review and resolve each one-by-one. I would have stated that these are situations which are solvable in other clubs—and that we could resolve them, as well. I would make the team members accountable to each other.

I would assign a leader in a conflict situation such as this because the issue is complex among many departments. With no assigned leader, either no one takes charge initially or the wrong person takes charge and additional conflict emerges. However, in other cases, you could not assign a leader and let that person emerge.

Manager Response 6

I have put together many teams. I was a Chef for 10 years and my main job was retrenchment and turnaround. In hotels, it was fast and furious: Stay or go, but get out of my way. You are either part of the problem or part of the solution. There was no middle ground. At our club, which is my first club experience, I had to be quick to turn things around, but I also had some time to do so. I had more talent and more reinforcement to aide in my cause. My kitchen was easy to assemble and assessment was quick and decisive with positive outcomes.

This time I had more employees left than I was used to having. First, I gathered the team and explained that I worked with them not them working for me, and the ultimate was that we worked for the members. Special orders were our specialty. The more work, the more the job security. It was positive reinforcement and leading by example. That was then.

Now that I have moved from the heart to the front, things are quite a bit different. I know the players and have much more insight into the problems, but no longer can do all of the work myself. I have no choice but to rely on others. Not a good situation for an ex Chef. So, I have learned to look to the employees, they knew my work ethic and I knew their capabilities. I had some quick decisions to make, got them in my sights, and pulled the trigger. I knew some long-term employees had to go for our club to move to the next level. Over time, these changes are working out well.

Involvement is the key to my management style. There is never a stupid question. If I do not know or have doubt, I ask. I lead and teach. I now have a competent and young team that has a great attitude. What they lack in experience they make up in willingness and positive attitude.

The team in the case needed a leader to have been appointed. The team was given the goal of improving communications. I am a stickler for structure and project management, so I would have been at the meeting to lend support for the appointed leader. Keeping an eye on the objective and focusing on process needed to be kept in check. Any time that sales, kitchen, and stewards get together, you can count on a couple of scuffles. The initial fears could have been alleviated by outlining the process, the leader, and the objective.

The team mission was to improve communications. Defining the goal was necessary. Periodic checks on the meetings would aide in the progression toward the goal. Who is driving the ship, anyway?

Hostilities are naturally going to exist. In this instance, I would try role reversal and cross training for a day. For Barry and Chuck, it would have been beneficial. Sometimes this is a great way to develop sensitivity.

Debbie emerged as the team leader purely out of desperation. The focus was gone; the group was a gang that was just going to self-destruct. I would rather have appointed a leader. Use both the individual and team approach.

The team muddled through. It seemed like a fairly typical F&B environment. The groundwork of forming and time to build relationships that are advantageous to the entire group were not met. I was taught in culinary school that teamwork is like a hand. The fingers are independent but cannot do certain tasks without the help of the others. Working as a team or an individual is still representative of a cohesive unit.

Manager Response 7

In this instance, if I had been the team leader, Debbie Johnson, I am not sure exactly what I would have done. I was not appointed as the leader, rather I emerged as the leader. Also, I would not have had the information available to me about groups, so I may not have had the information at my fingertips to be able to explain many of the processes.

Assistant Manager Ann Still should have brought the group together for the first time or two to explain why they were together, explain the monetary implications of the situation which explains the severity of it, and explain how we will all benefit from solving this situation.

Without this happening, a group of people are meeting that have no direction, which adds to the frustration. If this situation caused a 20 percent write-down in banquet sales, this is a huge problem, which requires that the big guns be brought out. This issue has to be analyzed in exact dollars and cents. Anyone who, at that point, does not get the idea of why the team has been formed, then probably does not get it and should not be part of this team or the larger, overall team. Sometimes you just need to step up and push the weak birds out of the nest.

The initial fears and anxieties could have easily been put to rest by Ann Still if she had taken some time at the first meeting when the group was formed to explain the purpose of the group, the reason that each of these people were picked to work within the group, the challenge ahead of them, the goal, and the timeline of achieving the goal. It would also be natural to have explained some of the bumps that may lay ahead, and explain about group process.

I would have explained the team's mission in terms of goal, timeline, and overall dollar value to a satisfactory result. I might even put this in terms of something win-win. By doing so, I would set up a bonus based on actual savings.

Because both Chuck and Barry report to the Assistant GM, Ann Still, I would have told both of them that they were out of line talking with each other this way. There is a level of disrespect being shown, particularly from Chuck, both to Barry and about Ann Still. I would have a talk with Ann Still to ask her to take the two of them off-line to have a discussion about their interactions with each other and their attitudes. The attitude showing in this group is likely showing in other areas of their work, but it is not Debbie Johnson's position, or within her scope of authority to really try to get Chuck and Barry on track (which is what they need) outside of the scope of this group.

I do not agree with Debbie emerging as the team leader. The leader should have been appointed. This would have given Debbie the organizational position power to be the leader, as she would be recognized as the leader by the Assistant GM. There would have been a more formal direct reporting as the leader to the Assistant GM. The team would also have jelled more effectively, as it would have had strong direction from the start. I believe in formalizing processes for better accountability.

Lesson 2

The Middle

Storming Begins to Calm

As team members begin to reveal their basic personalities and true behavior, they gravitate into cliques and coalitions of subgroups. This continuing storming stage is characterized by Higgins as a period of high emotions. Individual members begin to experiment with techniques of participating in team meetings (perhaps even to mouthing the right words), but their ties to previous negative values continue. Considerable negativism can be expected during this time of testing the limits, especially if members have had past negative experiences with others on the team. Members learn more about their expected objectives and roles and about how their needs may be satisfied.

Conflict may occur as members seek to have their individual agendas adopted by the team. The amount of storming varies considerably in teams. In some cases may be almost nonexistent; in others it may be quite highly charged. This process can be difficult; often, a great deal of tension is generated around revealing oneself and one's feelings about other members. Although team members start to recognize their own distinct problems Vorrath found that they cannot yet function as a truly positive team. While some decision making may occur here, more often this stage deals with team dynamics, as opposed to the accomplishment of tasks (Higgins).

As team members discover alternatives to their previous values and behavior, they are brought to the point where they must decide whether they really want to change their ways. Cliques and subgroups become more tenuous and crumble away, producing much anxiety. Hostility and polarization may be prevalent within the team or directed toward the leader by factions of the team.

Growth and Interaction Emerge

However, the middle stage ushers in the beginnings of a period of dynamic growth and team interaction. As members learn to accept each other, the team begins to function cooperatively. As the process moves along, this is the time that members begin to resolve conflicts and develop group norms. Gradually, Vorrath noted, a common sense of purpose develops among some of the team members. Those who have started to adopt the new team value system are bound with a strong sense of mutual solidarity and team identification. Members align and work together toward a realistic appraisal of what they can accomplish. Most individual needs become less important than the good of the team, and most hostility ceases.

Decision making occurs relative to the task, but maintenance of the team may be a more important consideration at this stage than task accomplishment. A sense of closeness and team purpose emerges. The ability to repair boundaries and move as a whole to meet oncoming challenges characterize what Lewin describes as being, *the middle period*.

Those who are unable or unwilling to accept new and non-delinquent roles may react antagonistically, struggling to regain negative influence. When they fail, they may withdraw, even to the point of leaving the team (Vorrath).

Maturity Develops

Stability and maturity develop as members become more comfortable with themselves, their teammates, and their defined mission. This is the phase in which interdependency and trust form. Such interaction fosters cohesion. The team becomes fully functioning. Members arrive at productive decisions. Members are well organized, concerned about the team and its results, and are able to deal with task accomplishment and conflict in rational and creative ways. The primary foci of the team at this stage, according to Higgins, is continuing to achieve results and adapting over time to changing conditions.

Norming

The process of norming is characterized by members establishing the rules of acceptable conduct (norms). Alternatives are chosen and agreed upon, policies set, and goals established. An awareness of deep structure in terms of shared values and vision ensues. Team members by now have formed a strong, cohesive, clique-free team that embodies a value system of mutual care and concern, which helps foster a positive peer culture (Vorrath).

Members develop new skills and accept their appropriate roles within the team. Communication transforms from discussion into dialogue. An open exchange of relevant interpretations of the task problem emerges (Tuckman). The team relies less on leadership and places considerable demands on its members to face their problems, to help one another, and to work eagerly on the problems of the more defensive new members that may join the team (Vorrath).

Performing

Over time, an increasing sense of togetherness and alignment help move the team closer toward their common goal. Performing, according to Hare, categorizes functional role relatedness as solutions develop and members carry out the work. Members become like spokes in a wheel, each play a vital role in contributing to the overall team's success through aligned individual effort and thereby toward team effort. Such alignment engenders synergy, which can be described as a situation when the result is greater than the sum of team members' individual contributions or capabilities.

3.2. Mini Case: The Middle

We return to our case example at the Llenroc Country Club. By now, the team is beginning to define and thereby understand their mission. While ideas begin to emerge, Chuck is increasingly forceful in his style of pushing ideas down on the group for acceptance: *I have the answer. Everyone should just do what I say. I am trained to be able to see the big picture. You people are a bunch of small thinkers. I will take care of everything.* The others are resentful of his tactics. Finally, a blow up occurs, which is the culmination of weeks of negative statements, tension, hurt feelings, and frustration. Tempers flare. Though unpleasant, this serves both as a valuable cleansing process and the beginnings of a healing process.

Debbie allows a few days for a cool-down period. At their next meeting, members agree to resolve conflicts and work together. It works; the blow-up has cleared the air and leads to a fresh and productive environment. Members acknowledge differences in background, beliefs, and values; and they agree to utilize such differences as strength through which to discover creative alternatives. Debbie opens the next meeting with the following statement: *I know that we have been through difficult and frustrating times these past several weeks. We all have our opinions and experiences from different backgrounds and from working in different areas at the Club. I propose that we acknowledge those differences and use them as strengths in solving the Club's communication problems. By working together, we can come up with creative solutions.* Team members agree.

Concurrently, the team develops a set of norms by which they will operate. Alice reads the list back to the team: *Here is how we have agreed to conduct future team meetings:*

- *Everyone will be punctual for meetings.*

- *No one may participate in a meeting unless fully-prepared.*

- *We will publish informal minutes and an updated Gantt chart to ensure timely progress toward interim goals. Monthly we will update Anne, the assistant general manager, regarding our progress.*

- *Any team member can call for a five-minute safe zone for the purpose of expressing an idea to the team without interruption.*

- *Any team member can call for a five-minute time out if discussion becomes too heated.*

- *Any member can call for a delay on any decision to allow for further discussion, consideration, or investigation.*

Assuming that everyone agrees with my interpretation of the notes, can we concentrate on our assignment instead of wasting time on private agendas and politics? Everyone nods in agreement.

As time progresses, the team begins to align in their thinking and to develop and build upon ideas in a cooperative manner. The team begins once again to realize that they can realistically accomplish their goal if they are willing to work together. Barry opens up and begins to contribute in the group setting. Chuck realizes that if he throws his ideas out on the table, others are able to develop his thoughts into workable solutions. *I thought you were a bunch of idiots. What I am beginning to see is that I miss a lot of the fine points by being so big-picture oriented.* By developing and using synergy, the group generates solutions, some of which are far more effective than those Chuck originally proposed.

Debbie senses that her role as team leader should allow for increased flexibility: *I am going to stop being the behavior police and assume that we can all work together in an open exchange as teammates and begin to form a cohesive bond that leads to interdependence and trust.* Sounds like something from the movie, To Sir With Love.

All members become more comfortable with themselves, their teammates, and the defined mission. The team agrees upon several innovations to the banquet communications that they will present to Anne for implementation. Barry reads from his notes: *Okay people, listen up. We have been working hard and long to come up with solutions that will make a huge difference in the way we communicate and coordinate at the Club. Here's what we've been working toward; see if I have captured the essence before I turn it all into a draft:*

- Plot space reservation time frames including the who, what, where, when, why, and how of bookings.

- Appointments of a specific job function, by Anne, within the catering department to book all banquet space, publish all communications regarding arrangements, and complete updates.

- Establish a bi-weekly schedule for publishing the event calendars, as well as tentative and confirmed bookings.

- Develop a color scheme for communications: yellow for weekly calendars, pink for original programs, red for changes, blue for forecasts.

- Designate specific areas and a filing system within each department wherein to post programs, communications, and updates.

- Write a set procedure for dating and initialing all updates.

- Submit recommendations (again, I have attached our recommendations) to Anne for timeframes for releasing space as available for other departments to reserve through the catering department.

Discussion Questions

1. Reflect back upon the case. Debbie allowed for a cool-down period after the big blow up. Would you have handled the situation any differently? Why or why not?

2. The team agreed to six norms by which they would operate. In this case, was it appropriate to come up with such a detailed list? Why or why not?

3. If you had persons such as Chuck and Barry on your team—or under your direct supervision—how would you communicate, coach, or counsel them individually? Would you use the same style with each of them?

Manager Response 1

1. As a normal process in team building, the storming stage continued between team members. This stage produces high emotion and a great deal of tension. Chuck was forceful and bullying in his style of trying to get the group to accept his ideas. The other members of the team grew increasingly resentful of his tactics and finally a blow up occurred.

Debbie allowed for a cool down period after the blow up before she addressed the group. I agree with cool down periods when issues become heated. I would not have handled the situation differently. If Debbie would have addressed the group immediately tensions and emotions would have been running high and the group would not have had the opportunity to reflect on the things that were said. Also, with Debbie hoping to eventually take less of a role as a leader and more as a team participant, it was important for her to let the team work out the issues on their own and come to conclusions without her. It was effective when Debbie explained that conflicts are bound to occur when different personalities and diverse backgrounds working together. She blamed no one and encouraged the differences of the individuals to act as idea generators. No one felt as they had done anything wrong and the group progressed nicely to the middle stage where dynamic growth and team interaction emerged.

2. The team members aligned and began working together toward accomplishment. The six norms by which they would operate were necessary at this stage of development. Team members put the list together collectively, which created a sense of closeness and team purpose. The details in the list sound like they are addressing some concerns or frustrations team members had throughout the process regarding lateness, lack of preparation, and communication. These norms were helpful in the process for this team.

3. Barry and Chuck each play a vital role in contributing to the overall team's success. Barry needs to be encouraged to participate. Debbie's explaining that *different* ideas are *not* wrong ideas, would encourage someone like Barry to be more open in discussion. Everyone has a contribution to make in the overall growth of the team. That message needs to be clear to all team members. Chuck, although aggressive, has a lot to contribute to the group, as well. Once beyond the arrogance, you will discover creative ideas that can help in the planning process. By sharing ideas, all team members will become more comfortable with themselves, each other, and their mission.

Manager Response 2

Debbie did the right thing by calling for a cooling off period. She had little other choice if she was to pull this off successfully. The group was on the brink of exploding. The environment was counterproductive and it was interfering with the group's ability to move forward. Everyone needed a break to regain composure. Even Debbie needed a break. Being group leader in a situation such as this one is indeed stressful. Assuming that Debbie did not wish to start dismissing people from the group, this break was her only reasonable alternative.

The group's six norms are specific and helpful. The group needed to develop norms which would allow the group to move forward, even if things would intensify once again. They have done an admirable job of building in contingencies to handle just about anything.

Chuck and Barry are very different. Chuck is opinionated. He leaps before he looks. Sometimes it is difficult to get the attention of people like this. Barry is quite different. He is an inward thinking person who seems to be insecure. He will require a great deal of confidence building. He will need encouragement. He will avoid the team concept preferring to retreat if allowed.

Manager Response 3

I would not have handled the situation differently. Cooler heads prevail and at times strong opinions, if allowed to become personal and negative, can become heated exchanges. Heated exchanges, once gone corrosive, hamper team progress.

It was appropriate to get into the details of the issue, as there were strong opinions as to the outcome. No one seemed to be able to agree on the big picture, much less the fine points. By finalizing a standard operating procedure in step-by-step fashion, helped everyone to get working together to achieve the larger goal.

Chuck needs a strong person to manage him. His direct supervisor would have to be strong willed, competent, and effective to gain Chuck's trust and loyalty. Chuck is probably is a good big picture person and he can probably sell effectively. His dominant personality can aid him in the convincing aspects during the sales process. However, this strength can turn sour quickly when working with someone who is less competitive. Words like bullying, overbearing, obnoxious, and mean-spirited come to mind. There is no room for this level of nastiness in a team environment.

Barry, being somewhat shy and introspective, needs a supervisor who will listen and who can ask questions that will draw out responses from him. He has valuable ideas and solutions to problems, but feels that his role is small and non-participative when compared to someone as strong and outspoken as Chuck. His supervisor would have to encourage him to believe that his position is worthwhile and point out his positive impact on the operational side of the Club's business.

The similar aspects of managerial style that I would use with both of them are confidence, trust, and understanding. Recognizing the positive contributions of strong and less able team members help deliver effective team outcomes for the Club.

Manager Response 4

The cool-down period was a good idea for the people individually. However, at the Club, time is money. If this process took away from the team being able to meet to move forward to get an earlier solution to stop the losses sooner, then it was wrong to wait. Debbie has her challenges set out for her as group leader, dealing with some of the people on the team, particularly Chuck.

It was appropriate for the team to arrive at the six norms by which they would operate. This established an agreed upon set of expectations for the entire group. It also got everyone focused on the same goal and in agreement with each other—at least on these basic principles. These are all easy criteria to measure. It is easy to observe if everyone comes to the meeting on time or not, for example.

Because both Chuck and Barry report to the Assistant GM, there is some requirement for this person to step forward and speak with each of them. In Chuck's case, he needs an ego-deflating pill. Unfortunately, his ability and his confidence are not at the same level, which is dangerous for the organization. It is necessary for his confidence to match his ability, and his confidence is far greater than his actual ability. As the Assistant GM, I would give him a detailed look. Many of the problems are stemming from his area, and much of the problem could well be stemming from his ability, his attitude and his *put-his-mouth-in-motion-before-putting-his-brain-in-gear* approach. As well, he has an offensive approach. As the sales manager, what approach does he take with the members? I would be concerned about him alienating more than just the group members.

Ann needs to speak with Barry as well. From the comments, it appears as though Barry is a victim in the process and is always happened upon, rather than taking personal responsibility. There seem to be a number of excuses offered up, rather than concrete answers. Barry also seems to have confidence and self-esteem issues, which Chuck has not been contributing to in a positive way.

If I happened to be the Assistant Manager, I would probably have a talk with the General Manager about the people that were in place at the Club and examine this at length to see if we are happy with the people that are currently carrying out the duties for us at the Club.

Manager Response 5

By allowing a few days for a cooling down period, Debbie gave each member time to reflect on their actions. Hopefully, this will give each member the opportunity to think clearer and not react emotionally. I believe this gives each member to see the other side of the discussion. Debbie left just the right amount of time between meetings. Too much time between meetings and the group would likely lose track of its direction.

By coming up with the parameters for group norms, Debbie helped to level the playing field. She gave each member in the group a chance to feel that they have control in any given situation. With all that the group went through to get to this stage, she did the right thing in getting into this amount of detail.

If I had Chuck and Barry under my direct supervision, I would have had discussions with each of them outside of their group meetings. I would have treated them both fairly, but differently. I would have asked both of them for their patience and to work with me to help make this work to everyone's satisfaction.

Chuck, as the sales manager, probably has better people skills and he should understand why we were having this group meeting. He should be able to see the big picture—that I need everyone working together. Chuck should understand why Barry needs information on a timely basis.

I would also try to have Barry understand the job that Chuck is responsible for. I am sure that the change orders initiated by Chuck come directly from the customers/members. When Barry understands this, maybe he will empathize with Chuck and help to find a way to solve the problems.

By making them both part of the team, we would have less finger pointing, and more working together to achieve the desired goal.

Manager Response 6

Debbie handled the blow up in an appropriate manner. She had to allow tempers to cool in order to bring focus back to the group. If she returned to the meetings too quickly, she would have run the risk of the group disbanding.

The detailed list was correct, as well. To get everyone moving toward the desired mindset and back to the group's purpose there needed to be rules and guidelines. These also made the group more cohesive by building from having them let go of the individual agendas and concentrating on the overall goal.

Chuck and Barry are not unusual characters in our business. They play a role that if stoked and encouraged in a positive way, can yield high productivity. I would talk to them separately and then bring them together. They both focus on an individualistic way of doing things and do not appreciate the power and benefits of teamwork. Ideally, bringing them together would help build a team that could exist beyond the established infrastructure of group norms and develop into a highly evolved and productive team unit. Once the storming had passed, goals were more easily attained.

Manager Response 7

It depends! We can read a case scenario, but to actually *make* the decision, one needs to not only listen to people and gauge reaction, but also *feel* the situation.

After being a bit beat up, sometimes the best course is for a leader to be forceful and urge the team to adopt a positive, constructive, and fair mindset. At other times, like Debbie did in this case, the wounds of self destruction must heal over time. The chance for the group to harmonize naturally, without external influence, will result in a stronger, long-term, successful relationship.

My thought is that when you have a team of peer individuals with a naturally appointed leader, it would depend on the team dynamics if I were to suggest to that leader to take charge. My gut reaction is twofold. First is that Debbie executed the decision wisely, by giving the group a chance to heal. I have been a part of both situations before and the psychology of team dynamics is an amazing situation that brings to the surface a plethora of emotions. At times, nothing seems to make sense—except a time out. If however, the team can rebuild on its own, the effect will truly be inspiring. If the team was having difficulty with the healing process, it might need to be the GM who steps in—if only for a brief moment—to assist getting the group back on track.

The detailed list of norms.

The detailed list is appropriate. Sensing is a major positive quality for a successful team leader to possess. In this case, the list would help the team to re-establish trust. A foundation must exist for the team to not only interact, but feel comfortable in doing so. Each member of the team must feel that they can contribute based on grounds that make them feel protected, safe and comfortable.

If the list is too dramatic and detailed there will be a natural realization that a few of the items are extraneous and if the group is gelling well, they will toss out the unwanted guidelines. If the details are too cumbersome and the group is not in agreement, there will probably be another fallout or power struggle that the group will have to endure. Additional challenges are not necessarily negative; they just slow down the process.

Communicate, coach, or counsel Chuck and Barry.

Chuck and Barry are quite different individuals, albeit with some similarities. Chuck, being the more forceful, big-pictured person would be managed differently than Barry, the one who needs to be urged to speak in the group setting.

Chuck would need to see that his big picture concepts, as beneficial as they are, need to be complemented by the details of focused thinkers, in order to complete the process. The conversation with Chuck might get loud and might end with him leaving thinking the process is a waste of time. However, as he reflects on the meeting that might have just happened, he will experience the *a-ha effect* as some call it. The latter meaning, a-ha, now I understand what the big and small picture discussion means.

For Barry, we might need to emphasize his contributions in the form of importance, self-worth, and confidence in order to ensure that he knows how much his ideas count and how the group will be better with his input. Barry would need to hear examples of his past contributions and situations to see how and why he should forge ahead. Barry needs to see that his ideas will make the group better and how the Club will benefit, as well.

Lesson 3

Disengagement

Eventually, all teams dissolve. Temporary or ad hoc teams dissolve when their function is performed or accomplished. An example of a temporary or ad hoc team would be a committee formed to plan and execute the Club's 100th anniversary celebration. That committee would cease to exist after the celebration. Permanent teams dissolve when work is drastically restructured or, for some other reason, the work of the team is no longer necessary. An example of a permanent team dissolving might be the Club deciding to completely outsource the grounds maintenance and landscaping function, which had been a division within the Golf Course and Grounds Maintenance Department.

In an on-going team, the preceding stages would be similar when new members are admitted. This is especially true when enough new members are added to a team within a short time span so as to dilute the *understood and accepted ways of doing things*. New members would have to be accepted by and accept the team (forming); and they would have to learn to work out their needs and interpersonal relations (storming). The team would eventually begin to function in an integrated fashion as reconstituted (norming); then it should eventually mature and become highly productive (performing).

Knowing these stages, the team leader can take actions to ensure that the team progresses toward total integration. For example, the leader may be especially nurturing during the forming and storming stages to those who feel uncertain about their need satisfaction. Similarly, the leader may find it necessary to practice conflict resolution in these stages and to focus attention on objectives. Later, the leader may delegate more power to members or use other techniques to keep the team adapting and performing.

Disengagement

The end is the period of disengagement and adjournment. It is a time concerned with sadness, good-byes, and self evaluation. This final phase can be a difficult and emotional period for team members, inducing feelings of anxiety as members begin to think about life outside of the team.

Moreover, the final phase can produce positive effects as well, including those such as self satisfaction for a job well done. Feelings such as these go beyond monetary or other external rewards. Furthermore, team members can develop positive feelings for the leader, especially when the team process is successful and the project task goes well.

3.3. Mini Case: The End

We return to the Llenroc Country Club case one final time. The closeness of working together has Alice, Barry, Chuck, and Debbie fretful about the team's disengagement. Alice sums up their feelings: *We have all become close. I would not have believed that at first. Funny the way things work. I have an appreciation for elements of the Club that I never thought much about before this experience. Frankly, I am bummed that it is time for us to disband.*

Chuck admits a vulnerability to the team in stating that self evaluation points out many positive experiences from this team experience. He states: *I have found that there are, indeed, other ways, besides mine. Over this period, I have become aware of a number of painful shortcomings that I never held still long enough to think about before now. It is embarrassing. I am working to change the ways that I interact with others. I feel like a big bully!*

Barry points out feelings of self-satisfaction with his newly found group communication skills: *I had always been an outsider looking in. This experience has helped me see that I have something worthwhile to offer. Guess it is all part of it being okay to be different nowadays. When I was growing up, I never realized that taped glasses and pocket protectors would one day be considered cool.*

The team grew close emotionally as a result of their successful work project. Since team members work in different areas of the Club, they have come to appreciate the non-competitive nature of their relationships, the ability to share with each other without fear of reprisal. While it was difficult to balance project demands with regular job duties, the team acknowledges tremendous positive effects of their becoming more knowledgeable concerning the Club's overall inter-workings.

All members develop positive feelings for their leader. They reflect that Debbie helped guide them through their rough formative stage. Furthermore, they realize that the fact they were able to achieve a collective sense of accomplishment was due to her considerable ability to help guide the team through an arduous yet productive project. Debbie feels a sense of satisfaction, too. She oversees a staff of eight non-managerial employees in the kitchen. However, this was her first opportunity to manage others at the manager level: *It was an awesome experience! Dealing with peers is far different than dealing with those whose payroll you approve. It helped that I was used to working with an array of different people and personalities; but it still did not prepare me for the intensity of the peer team process.*

Each member expresses feelings of anxiety as they visualize life outside the team. This is a difficult and emotional period punctuated by sadness and good-byes. They vow to keep in touch.

Discussion Questions

1. Using the lesson text as a guide, what would have been the likely scenario if this team had been asked to become on-going instead of temporary and thereby accept a new task and three new team members?

2. If you were in Debbie's position as team leader and the assistant general manager asked you to head another task force (a temporary team project), what would be your reaction? Why would that be your reaction? Would you negotiate any issues before accepting such an assignment? If so, what?

Manager Response 1

If the team was asked to become on-going instead of temporary and were assigned a new task and new members, things would be very different from their current status. New members would have to be accepted into the group. Given the dynamics of the group and how far they have come both personally and professionally, the process of team building would perhaps be easier for them this time. Debbie has learned how to be an effective team leader, Chuck has recognized his shortcomings and accepts suggestions, and Barry feels that his contributions are worthwhile. This time, needs and interpersonal relations can be worked out and the team will come together, mature quickly, and work efficiently.

If I were Debbie and asked by the assistant general manager to head up another temporary task force, I would be delighted to do so under certain circumstances. To begin, the assistant general manager would have to make it known to the group that I am the team leader. Leaving it to chance in the last project was almost a disaster and could have caused the project to fail. Being appointed the team leader from the beginning could lead to more open communication regarding team building. I could explain the stages of team development, which would eliminate unknowns and reduce the anxiety of the team players. The reason I would do it again gladly is that the experience was rewarding both personally and professionally. Debbie developed positive relationships and a better understanding of her co-workers. Debbie learned about her peers and improved relationships. It was rewarding for her to be responsible for the group's success. Each person in the group admired her for her knowledge, hard work, and dedication—what a positive shot to her self confidence!

Manager Response 2

To make a dramatic change in team members would have been almost like starting from scratch. The new team members would have a difficult time fitting in with the current team members who have grown close. If the existing team could stay on permanently to help solve other inter-departmental problems, the team would work more efficiently. I would prefer to keep the bulk of the existing members and add only one or two new members to the team. An advantage of keeping key on-going team members is the knowledge that is retained and the influence of existing team norms on new members.

I would be happy to take on another task force. With the experience I had just gained, I would be even more effective. This would increase my usefulness at the Club and hopefully would result in more exposure, additional influence, a promotion, and or maybe even a raise. I would not negotiate any issues as deal killers. However, my strong preference would be to retain as many existing team members as possible.

Manager Response 3

It would be likely that the team would have matured even more and gone on to be a powerful team. They worked hard and had many obstacles in the forming, storming and norming parts of development. However, when they reached the performing part, they were starting to click as a team. If they had accepted a new task and three new team members, they would have moved back to the forming part for a while. It is unclear to me if three would be leaving and three new ones would be coming or there would be an addition of three to the team. If three would be replaced, the team would definitely go back to the forming stage and could likely experience much of what it already went through. If the three were an addition to the group, there would be some storming, no doubt, but according to the norms that were already in place for this group. The norms may change over time as the three new people acclimatize themselves on to the team.

If the new task had been taken on by the initial team, it would be likely that they would be able to handle the task quickly and effectively. They will probably still be able to do this. However, now the new team members will cause new challenges, but challenges that will be easy to overcome for a group that has been through so much.

If I was in Debbie's position as the team leader, I would be excited about the challenge. The fact that I was asked to head this up would make me feel special. Also, that fact that I was asked as part of my duties (regardless of how I might truly feel about this), I would do my best to lead this team to another successful accomplishment. Issues that I would try to negotiate ahead of time would be attitudinal issues. If I were to get another Chuck-type on the team, I would want to have authority to deal with him or her one-on-one, or I would want that person's supervisor to be supportive of me to any challenges I was having with the group. I would, of course, keep track of my accomplishments and at review time, I would be clear to point out the work that I had done as team-leader and hope that it paid off in a monetary and or promotion way, as well.

Manager Response 4

The team is asked to continue its work by accepting a new task and three new team members. Would this new team be able to function as one cohesive unit? Not without making fundamental changes. The new members would begin the group process on a different page. So once again we would go through some degree of forming, storming, norming, performing, and disengagement.

The organizational staging may not be as intense as before in that several members on the team are now on the same page and think as one cohesive unit. However, one would be naive to think that the new members would just jump right in and follow the lead of the existing members.

Debbie found the experience quite meaningful and she learned a great deal from it. However, an additional team leadership role? Whatever the answer, she should have the opportunity to earn more money by taking on the additional responsibilities. She is being expected to perform additional duties as team leader. She should be compensated for her skills. If the Club increases her duties and responsibilities, which they are doing, they should find a way to pay her more for her efforts. Pay could come in the form of salary, benefits, title, power, prestige, promotion, comp. time, or some other creative format. It does not always have to be dollars.

Manager Response 5

If the group was asked to be ongoing and new tasks and members were assigned, many of the growing pains would be eliminated, or at least minimized. The new members would have to deal with the same stages that the group did from its inception. The new members would have to gain acceptance from the others and buy into the group's procedures before optimal productivity could take place. The transition would undoubtedly be smoother, having had many team members already having been through the process before.

Before heading up another task force for the assistant general manager, I would ask to have the ground rules set up front. I would want to make sure that the new project would not take away from the productivity of the other group, and I would want my authority spelled out, to help ease the team stage transitions as much as possible.

Manager Response 6

The team would continue to thrive and bring new members into the *team way* quickly. The new members, especially if they come into the team as singles, would have a tough time breaking up the establishment due to the turmoil that the group has already overcome and the subsequent closeness that exists.

If I were Debbie I would want a short break, but I would look forward to the challenge of taking on the responsibilities of a new team. Provided that there are parameters and a clearer goal set, I would be better prepared for the leader position because of having gone through a tough team role just prior. If I were to be fed to the dogs again, I would not be too happy in trusting Anne further.

Debbie did do a fine job and should be commended. She should be asked to head another team, and take it as positive recognition of her leadership abilities with the last team.

Manager Response 7

I assumed that the question is being posed after the group had finished the first exercise. People react differently to something when they know it is only for a short while. Although saddened at their departure, they might have mixed emotions if being told they were to be together for an indefinite period of time.

However, this team would not only do well, but the lessons learned would be that much more dramatic, if the chemistry of introducing new team members was good. If the new members were easily accepted, the current team members would feel positive as they could apply the lessons learned from their previous experience to the new members (helping the new additions get through the team process). Accepting new team members is a difficult process. Individual team dynamics are unique and the ability to accept new members depends upon the team.

If I were asked to head another team.

Debbie did a great job, but it was also due in part to the makeup of that specific team. Just because you are good with one team does not ensure success with another. However, as Debbie, she would be flattered. If she is being asked to head up another team, then she must have potential. If I were Debbie and my position within the Club allowed to me to focus on my main responsibilities, as well as head up a particular short-term task force, I would accept the challenge eagerly. Debbie would want to agree to head task force number two. This would be a great way to move toward advancement and get a chance to improve her leadership and communication skills.

The situation, size, and scope of the task force would determine whether any other negotiations should occur. For example, if the task requires extra work and time, how would Debbie obtain extra compensation for her time? If Debbie had a proven track record after completing a few task force missions, then she might be in a better position to negotiate for increased compensation. Compensation however, might not be the only type of negotiation. Debbie might ask for full leadership, or a certain degree of autonomy.

High-Performance Teams

In the preceding section, the primary aim was to familiarize you with the various phases in team development—ones that all teams experience in their quests to become functioning, effective, and rewarding both for the team members and clubs. However, it is my hope that you and your team can progress even further into a realm rarely experienced in team life. The result is creating high-performance teams.

Chances are that you have only had a few opportunities, if any, to experience the exhilaration and satisfaction that can come from being a member of a high-performance team. If you have succeeded in accomplishing this phenomenon, you have likely looked back and tried to figure ways to re-capture the elements that made it so productive. If you have never experienced a team effort that truly became vital, absorbing, and high performing, it is likely that you have heard about them and have wondered how to go about facilitating such an undertaking at your club.

Characteristics unique to high-performance teams:

- The usual social and intellectual inhibitions are relaxed. Team members are treated as peers.

- There exists an atmosphere of ultra high dedication to accomplishing the team task.

- Dedication to the task increases by the amount of challenge involved. The more unusual or difficult the task, the stronger the resolve.

- Team members develop creative alternatives and ideas in their search for a successful outcome.

- Team members express their ideas and observations strongly. No one holds back on their concerns. Freewheeling discussions are more the rule than the exception.

- Team members volunteer to take on additional work in trying to find the right solutions.

- Communication is open. Members turn their efforts more toward solving the task than worrying about hurting each others' feelings.

While high-performance teams have distinctly positive characteristics, formation of such groups is not without downsides. For example, team members can become isolated from other teams and often function as separate entities. High-performance teams dislike interruptions from the outside. Newcomers are not welcomed to their teams. The intensity that arises due to the depth of involvement often leads to burnout. High-performance team members are often treated as super stars within their clubs, which can cause resentment between and among others.

High-performance teams organize along two general structures: a) As close personal relationships are important among team members, high-performance teams are usually small in size, typically ranging from 3 to 10 members and b) high-performance teams are almost always relatively short lived. This short life is especially true when turnover occurs.

There are certain internal conditions that need to be in place in order for high-performance teams to succeed. First, tightly-organized club managers tend to stifle high-performance teams in their desire to institutionalize processes through the HR department. Often, more entrepreneurial club leaders have more success in creating and nurturing high-performance teams because they do not have as much concern as bureaucratic managers do in treating everyone the same. Bureaucracy inhibits spontaneity, which is an important ingredient for high-performance team success.

There are two external conditions that need to be in place in order for high-performance teams to flourish: short deadlines and capable competitors. Both of these factors will generate high levels of energy and dedication. Short deadlines keep high-performance teams sharp and effective. (Consider the efficiency of the AM setup team in Golf Course Maintenance in mowing greens, cutting cups, and setting and aligning tees. All of this work needs to be done ahead of the early morning golfers.) Capable competitors provide incentive to high-performance teams to outperform the competition. (Consider two assembly lines in a Honda factory. Each high-performance team strives to outperform the other in terms of production and continuous quality improvement.)

Is your club in a position to foster high-performance teams? Organizational structures of clubs are facing many of the same pressures as corporations for quick and responsive adaptations to the environment becoming essential for long-term success.

Chapter 4

Decision Making

This is the fourth of four major topics in the course Organizational Behavior: Team Processes in Private Clubs. So far, we have covered the following topics:

Goal setting: Managing yourself to manage teams,

Why teams are important, and

Phases in team development.

In this fourth and final topic we will discuss the importance of decision making to one's success as a club manager.

About This Topic

The Team Decision Making Topic is divided into nine lessons. Each lesson will take approximately 30-45 minutes to read and understand. Furthermore, each lesson will take another 30-45 minutes to envision ways in which one can apply the ideas presented in the text.

Note: I want to gratefully acknowledge the valuable contributions of Professor Florence Berger to this section.

Organization

The unifying and recurring stream used throughout this text is in providing readers with information that will allow them to become better and more effective managers in their positions. Each chapter topic begins with the introduction and discussion of theories, concepts, ideas, and best practices relative to the subject topic.

Following the presentation of theories and ideas, I have designed mini cases, which propose scenarios that can be solved, managed, and or mitigated using this new knowledge. The application exercises (the mini cases) are best solved using a combination of both new knowledge and past knowledge that has come from training, education, logic, and experience.

Finally, for each mini case, I have re-printed seven example answers from managers with whom I have worked in the past. I have found that readers benefit tremendously from having a variety of answer examples drawn from managers from all corners of the globe and each with different perspectives, educations, and backgrounds.

Competencies

1. Identify the two primary models of decision making in an organization: The Classical Theory model and the Behavioral Theory model. In your own words, be able to argue the fundamental differences between the foci of the two approaches. Taxonomy of Measurable Variables: Bloom: Evaluation. ACPHA: Emphasize.

2. Using the memory hints listed below, interpret six advantages of team decision making over individual decision making:

    - Greater sum of knowledge

    - Better understanding of decision

    - Increased commitment to decision

- Broader search effort
- Risk is balanced
- Constituency representation

Taxonomy of Measurable Variables: Bloom: Evaluation. ACPHA: Emphasize.

3. Given the following list of concepts and ideas, differentiate their meaning in terms of the problems associated with team decision making:

    - Groupthink
    - Dominating personalities
    - That teams typically require more time to come to decisions than do individuals
    - Risky decisions
    - Poor communication skills
    - Forcing outcomes: Pounding square pegs into round holes
    - Rushing due to time pressure forcing a premature evaluation of ideas

Taxonomy of Measurable Variables: Bloom: Analysis. ACPHA: Reinforce.

4. Referring to the Vroom and Yetton model, formulate a plan using three factors that should be considered when deciding whether to make a decision alone or to involve others in the process. Taxonomy of Measurable Variables: Bloom: Synthesis. ACPHA: Emphasize.

5. Given a scenario calling for techniques fostering an open exchange of ideas, interpret in your own words the fundamental ideas behind following terms:

- Interacting techniques: Brainstorming and Storyboarding
- The Nominal Group Technique
- The Delphi Technique

Taxonomy of Measurable Variables: Bloom: Application. ACPHA: Reinforce.

6. Given the following structured forms of decision making, restate in your own words their meaning and how they may be beneficial:

    - Dialectical Inquiry
    - The Stepladder
    - Voting
    - Consensus Mapping
    - The Garbage Can
    - Procedural Rationality

Taxonomy of Measurable Variables: Bloom: Comprehension. ACPHA: Introduce.

7. Given the following unstructured form of decision making, construct a scenario in your own words an example of its meaning and how it may be beneficial:

    - Consensus

Taxonomy of Measurable Variables: Bloom: Synthesis. ACPHA: Emphasize.

Lesson 1

Team Decision Making

Teams spend much of their time reviewing and acting on problems they face. As such, it is common to hear some teams spoken of as decisive. It is also common to hear other teams spoken of as wishy-washy. That is why your team's chances for success are helped if you can make the right decisions in the areas you control and submit sound recommendations when requested by your boss (Hersey and Blanchard).

To be an effective member of a team it is critical to understand the team decision making process. The satisfactory team decision process is characterized by a large number of inputs from each individual member upon which other members may build. It is therefore a series of interrelated sub-decisions leading to a final overall decision (Hirokawa).

Advantages of Group Decision Making

The advantages of group decision making versus individual decision making:

- The team's closeness to the problem.

- The larger number of ideas generated due to brainstorming.

- The team's ability to build upon and thereby modify a singular solution (Higgins).

The Process

Decision making in an organization seems to occur according to two principal models: the classical and the behavioral. Fundamental differences: The classical decision theory model revolves around a highly rational, systematic, and comprehensive perspective. The Behavioral Theory of decision making focuses a more realistic and workable approach on the psychological and interpersonal aspects of decision making (Higgins).

Classical Theory was for many years believed to be *the way* decisions were actually made. However, more recent studies of decision making show that the behavioral approach is the more realistic of the two. People do not always make decisions in a strictly rational manner. Psychological and interpersonal factors greatly affect the process.

Classical Theory

Classical Theory assumes that decision making is (or should be) a rational process whereby decision makers seek out and choose the course of action that is most likely to maximize the attainment of their goals and objectives. According to Classical Theory, the decision-making process can be broken down into a series of sequential steps:

Discern a Problem or Opportunity. The decision-making process can begin either of two ways. First, a decision maker may perceive the existence of a problem—something that is not going well and that requires action. For example, a golf course superintendent may notice that absenteeism and turnover among the employees have been increasing to the point that adequate staff is not always available to complete work assignments on schedule and productivity is declining. A second possible trigger to the decision-making process is the perception of a unique opportunity that may have presented itself and that should be taken advantage of. For example, a country club manager may discover that a neighboring beach club is planning to close, opening up opportunities for the manager's organization to expand its own operations in that location. It is the perception of problems and opportunities, not their actual existence, which gets the decision-making process started. Problems and opportunities may exist all around us, but if they are not perceived and noticed, they do not initiate the decision-making process.

Formulate Goals and Objectives. Once a problem or opportunity has been identified, the decision maker must clearly identify the goals and objectives that a good decision should achieve. For example, if a golf professional is experiencing a lack of satisfaction and fulfillment with his or her current job, the pro's goals for the decision-making process might be to identify, obtain, and accept a new job that is most likely to maximize his or her future satisfaction, development, and feelings of accomplishment at another club or resort. The golf superintendent concerned about declining productivity and increased turnover might set goals of identifying and implementing changes in the work system that are most likely to result in increased productivity and reduced employee turnover.

Produce Alternatives. Once goals and objectives have been set, the decision maker then generates alternative courses of action that might result in goal attainment. This is the stage in the decision-making process that requires the greatest component of creativity and imagination. Ideally, the decision maker should seek to generate as many alternatives as possible and should try to ensure that the set of alternatives is relatively diverse. In this way the decision maker increases the likelihood that some good potential alternatives will not be excluded from further consideration in the decision-making process. For example, the golf superintendent concerned about high rates of absenteeism and turnover should consider changing the pay and reward systems, changing the design of work for employees, changing the leadership styles of supervisors, changing the methods of work assignments and scheduling, and so on. Restricting the consideration of alternatives to changes in the pay system, for example, might result in many potentially effective courses of action not being considered in the decision-making process.

Collect Information. The alternatives that have been gathered must be systematically evaluated. However, before evaluation can proceed, information must be gathered regarding each of the alternatives and their likely consequences. More specifically, the decision maker must seek to learn as much as possible regarding the likelihood that each alternative will result in the achievement of the goals and objectives being sought. For example, the golf professional who is dissatisfied with his or her current job must gather a great deal of information regarding other jobs that might be available. Information is required on what specific opportunities are available at other clubs, how those clubs treat their employees, what the person's long-term prospects might be at each club, and so on.

Assess the Alternatives. Once all available information has been collected regarding all of the alternatives under consideration, the decision maker must use that information to evaluate the alternatives in a systematic fashion. This requires the decision maker to employ some technique that permits all of the information collected regarding each of the alternatives to be analyzed and compared. The outcome of this evaluation process should then be a rank ordering of the alternatives from best to worst according to their likelihood of leading to the attainment of the goals and objectives of the decision maker. For example, the golf course superintendent dealing with the problem of increased absenteeism and turnover must systematically evaluate all of the consequences anticipated to follow each course of action under consideration. If changes in the pay system were made, what improvements would be expected in absenteeism and turnover at what increased payroll costs? If changes in job design were implemented, how disruptive would they be and how much improvement could be expected?

Select the Best Alternative. This step should be quite straightforward if the evaluation of alternatives has been conducted comprehensively and systematically. The decision maker simply chooses the alternative that the evaluation process has indicated to be most desirable. Problems may arise at this stage, however, if the evaluation process leads to the conclusion that two or more alternatives appear equally likely to be best. For example, a graduating hospitality student may have thought she always wanted to work for Los Angeles Country Club. At the conclusion of the interviewing process she simultaneously receives offers from Los Angeles Country Club and Sawgrass Country Club. No matter how much information she gathers or how much careful evaluation of alternatives she does, it may remain almost impossible to tell which of the two offers would be best for her.

Implement. Although, strictly speaking, the decision-making process has ended once a decision regarding the best alternative has been reached, it is also true that the decision-making process is no more than a mental exercise if the chosen course of action is not implemented. Further, issues of implementation are frequently important factors in the choice of an alternative in the previous stages. After a great deal of thought and analysis, the golf course superintendent concerned about high absenteeism and turnover may have decided that job redesign was the best solution to the problem. While his decision may be a good one, he still has much work ahead if that decision is to be implemented effectively.

Evaluate Effectiveness. The decision-making cycle should not end until the decision maker judges the extent to which the chosen alternative has succeeded in solving the initial problem and achieving the goals identified at the outset of the process. If such evaluation indicates success, then the decision-making cycle is concluded. However, if the chosen alternative has not solved the problem or achieved stated objectives, then the decision maker must recycle through the decision-making process to generate a new alternative. If, after implementing job enrichment, absenteeism and turnover decline to acceptable levels, the golf course superintendent can feel satisfied that a decision has resulted in the problem being effectively solved. If, however, absenteeism and turnover remain at high levels, the superintendent must go back to the alternative-generating phase and attempt to arrive at a new course of action.

The decision-making process can be divided into three major phases. The first phase includes framing the problem or opportunity, or, determining exactly what the decision maker faces and the objectives to be accomplished. The second phase requires the generation of ideas, alternatives, and information. The final phase requires a systematic analysis reduction of the information and alternatives down to a single choice of what will be pursued and implemented.

Assumptions

Classical Theory of decision making assumes that decision making follows the above series of steps and makes certain strong assumptions regarding what happens at various stages in the process. Here is a list of some of Classical Theory's critical assumptions as proposed by Higgins:

1. Goals and objectives are obvious and straightforward. Classical Theory does not address itself to situations in which goals are unclear, in disagreement, or in conflict with one another.

2. All alternatives are considered. The existence of the problem is recognized, its nature has been identified, and all possible courses of action are considered. According to Classical Theory, decision makers must generate and evaluate all possible courses of action. Decision making is thus an exhaustive (and probably exhausting) process in which no potential solution to a problem is excluded from consideration.

3. All consequences are considered. The consequences of implementing each alternative are certain, or a probability can be assigned.

4. Perfect information is freely available. It is assumed that decision makers either possess or can obtain perfect information regarding the value of every available outcome.

5. Decision makers search for the best alternative. Criteria for the best decision are known and agreed upon and decision makers will choose the best alternative.

6. Decision makers are rational thinkers. They can assign values, order, and make the optimal decision. This rationality results in the decision maker always choosing the optimal course of action.

Assessment

Classical Theory has enjoyed a good deal of popularity partly because it appears to provide a good description of how people should go about making decisions. In addition, it provides specific guidance to decision makers regarding how to improve the quality of decision making. The Classical Theory position that decision making should proceed systematically through the series of steps is sound. Better decisions likely result when decision makers carefully analyze problems, evaluate multiple alternatives, and make systematic choices on the basis of their analyses.

The problem with Classical Theory lies in the assumptions it makes regarding how decision makers can or should deal with each of the steps in the decision-making process. The assumptions of Classical Theory are overstated and generally impossible to implement in practice. Arnold describes many of the shortcomings of Classical Theory's assumptions:

1. Goals and objectives are obvious and straightforward. In many real decision-making situations goals are not obvious or straightforward. For example, does the graduating hospitality student with two job offers in hand choose the job with the highest salary (monetary goal), the best career advancement prospects (development goal), or the most interesting initial work assignments (challenge and interest goal)? Similarly, does a club making decisions regarding changes in its strategy choose one that it hopes will maximize profit, total revenues, market share, long-term growth and stability, or does it choose a strategy that will minimize costs, reduce overhead, and decrease turnover? The decision maker must determine which of a multitude of goals (many of which may be conflicting) is most important to pursue or must formulate a complete goal that weights each of the possibly conflicting goals in terms of its relative importance.

2. All alternatives are considered. For all but the most trivial decisions it is naive to suggest that all alternatives can even be identified, much less considered. How realistic is it to suggest that a graduating hospitality student should consider and evaluate all possible potential employers and jobs before choosing to accept an offer? The ambiguity and complexity of organizational decisions make this assumption even more untenable in that context. The golf course superintendent seeking to reduce absenteeism and turnover has a massive number of potential solutions available to choose from, including any number of changes to the pay system, new approaches to job design, and changes in supervisory styles.

3. All consequences are considered. Just as it is likely impossible to generate all possible alternatives, it is impossible to anticipate and predict all possible outcome consequences of each alternative. The hospitality student choosing between two job offers cannot know for sure exactly what it will be like working for either organization.

Will all of the hoped-for opportunities at each club actually materialize? Will the graduating student get along well with his or her new boss? How will his or her co-workers feel about a new person coming into the department? The future is inherently uncertain and unpredictable, and no decision maker can ever be sure that all possible outcomes of a decision have been taken into account even probabilistically.

4. Perfect information is freely available. Information is not free, and only rarely is it even feasible to obtain perfect information regarding the ramifications of a course of action. Generating and evaluating alternatives takes time, energy, and resources. Thus, the process of obtaining information for use in decision making frequently has high costs. As a result, almost all decisions are based upon information that is to some extent inadequate and incomplete.

5. Decision makers search for the best alternative. Classical Theory assumes that decision makers have a tremendous mental capacity both for remembering and storing huge quantities of information and for processing that information in order to assess which available alternative is the optimal one. Over time, this assumption has been discounted in view of the functional realities of decision making. Managers consider information from past experience, what others offer in conversation, and perhaps what some amount of research may uncover. Beyond that managers add in their rational and not-always-rational biases and preferences, make the decision, and move forward.

4.1. Mini Case: Electric Ethics

Julie Adams is the clubhouse manager at The Barbed Wire Country Club, a large member-owned club located in Texas. We now look in on an operations meeting she is leading with several department managers.

Julie: *We just received the latest electricity bill for the main clubhouse. While utility rates have not increased, the bill is up over 50 percent compared to the same period last year. We have a real problem that we must remedy. Last January we formulated goals and objectives in order to identify ways in which we could cut utility bills 10 percent. We all agreed that these methods were achievable. Unfortunately, we are woefully off target.*

Smitty, the chief engineer spoke up: *I am not sure that we produced enough ways that we could achieve our goal. For example, we were unable to anticipate that the weather would be this unseasonably hot. While our utility bill was up 50 percent last month, year-to-date figures are about the same since we saved quite a bit on heat during the cold months. What we really need to do is brainstorm some alternative methods for saving on electricity to meet our goal of a 10 percent overall reduction.*

Millard, one of the housekeepers had this to say: *I think we should consider adding by-pass switches to the HVAC system. Engineering had a great idea when we installed the computer system to control the heat and air-conditioning; but when food and beverage has a late event, I have to go into the utility room and manually turn the entire club-wide system back on so the ballroom does not become too hot or too cold. If we had those little egg-timer switches located above the thermostats, we could regulate the temperature in one room without firing-up the whole club.*

Or, we could just stop booking outside functions—or make sure events are over by 8:00 P.M. Then, we would save all kinds of money without having to go to the expense of adding timers, quipped Monhegan Lamanthsarrah, banquet supervisor. *Maybe we could close down altogether Monday through Wednesday; we could let the Club be dark.*

Everyone enjoys a good chuckle.

Okay, funny man, we get your point. Remember, what we are trying to do is eliminate waste, not cut down on service. Our original budget charge was to look for ways to trim unnecessary expenses, so we could hold the line on dues increases, stated Julie.

You are right, I'm sorry.

No problem. We should go back to Millard's suggestion. It sounds like a possibility.

Yes it is. As chief engineer, I can also look into reduced-wattage bulbs, more efficient system filters, re-balance the make-up air in the kitchen, and look into the possibility of tinting certain windows.

Now we are talking! Do it. Smitty, how much money do you need to get started implementing?

Julie, should we consider our alternatives? We are likely to spend $15,000 on these alternatives. I am not sure it will give us the payback we are looking for. Want me to run some numbers? Texas Power will give me all the information I need. I can get perfect information. We can run a regression model and predict how much money will be saved versus the investment required. We can maximize results.

Look, We are being evaluated on our ability to make our goals and objectives. I have decision authority to commit up to $5,000. You can spend the $15,000, but just make sure you fill out three purchase orders (for $5,000 each). Write it up so that it is clear that what you are buying will last for more than one year. Get them to bill you in three $5,000 increments. We can depreciate the $15,000 amount as a capital expense without it going into operations. Just do it. We must get back under control.

Discussion Questions

1. Discuss any positives you found with Julie's meeting with reference to Classical Theory.

2. If you were Julie's GM, what aspects of her plan would you find troublesome?

3. Using the steps described in the Classical Theory of decision making, what was missing in Julie's meeting and interchange?

- Discern a Problem or Opportunity,
- Formulate Goals and Objectives,
- Produce Alternatives,
- Collect Information,
- Assess the Alternatives,
- Select the Best Alternative,
- Implement the Decision, and
- Evaluate Decision Effectiveness.

Manager Response 1

The Classical Theory of decision making assumes that the problem is obvious. The problem identified in the mini case is that the electric bill for the main clubhouse has gone up over 50 percent and the utility rates have not increased.

Once the problems of increased utility costs have been identified, we must clearly define the goals and objectives that a good decision should achieve. Our goal should be to identify ways to reduce the use of electricity. To come up with ways to change current operations and implement changes in the workplace to conserve energy and be more conscious of energy waste.

Once goals and objectives have been set, it is time to generate alternative courses of action that might result in goal attainment. This process requires the greatest component of creativity and imagination. A reduction in electricity may be attainable by considering by-pass switches to the HVAC system. Another way to conserve would be to stop booking outside functions past 8:00 p.m. or close the Club Monday through Wednesday. Reduced wattage bulbs, more efficient system filters, re-balancing of make-up air in the kitchen, and looking into the possibility of tinting certain windows may also help.

Each of the alternatives must now be considered and evaluated. By-pass switches would be effectively located above the thermostats and each room could be effectively regulated independently of the Club. The cost associated with this solution would be minimal. To stop booking outside functions past 8 p.m. or to close the Club Monday through Wednesday to save money on electricity would reduce service to the membership and is not an option. The actual problem of energy waste would not be addressed by closing the Club. Looking into reduced wattage bulbs would also be a step in the right direction as well as more efficient system filters, re-balancing the make-up air in the kitchen, and tinting windows.

The consequences of these changes could be effective, but the cost to implement these changes may be too high to consider at this point. The end saving is not clear and the $15,000 investment spent to find out is not cost effective. The alternatives need to be ranked from best to worst. The most obvious decision would be to install the switches on the HVAC system. The switches would break the clubhouse into zones, only using energy in the rooms that are in operation. The cost associated with this installation is minimal. The other alternatives are either not practical or too expensive to consider.

The choice made to install the switches was in fact effective in solving the problem. This process of evaluating the decision for effectiveness is the final stage in Classical Theory. Had the decision to install switches not been effective, we should consider another alternative.

Julie should have allowed the brainstorming process to go on longer. She also did not rank and analyze the ideas. Each alternative was not evaluated nor were the likely consequences identified. Without considering the alternatives, Julie is rushing forward and gambling with $15,000.

I did find Julie's meeting positive in that once her initial ideas for energy savings did not generate the savings she hoped for, she returned to the group for more ideas and alternative solutions. She was on the right track, but she did not spend enough time on each of the stages to achieve the optimal results. She tossed out ideas before the group had the opportunity to analyze them. Regardless of how impractical an idea may have sounded, the Classical Theory does not eliminate possibilities. Julie's haste in making decisions will result in her returning to the brainstorming process. She will also be investing money that may be sunk, without generating the information necessary to reduce costs. While Julie struggles with the solution, energy costs will continue to be a financial drain on the Club.

Manager Response 2

Julie started off on the right track. However, she became derailed when she failed to collect information and assess alternatives.

As Julie's GM, I would be concerned that Julie had short-circuited the decision-making process. As a result, she may have not maximized savings for the Club. Over the long run, her haste may have cost the Club thousands of dollars in potential savings. Unfortunately, all-too-often, club managers are taking short cuts to get issues off of their to-do lists. The pressures of operations force this reality. While we must be aware of demonstrating urgency and responsiveness, it must not come at the expense of sloppiness and incompleteness. I look for managers who can think strategically over the long haul. While this process takes more time, I find that it sets in place positive outcomes over time for the Club.

Another issue concerns me. Julie seems to be working around the spirit of her signing authority—again, in haste to *get back under control*. She has concocted a work-around to get the process moving immediately. While I understand the realities of budget management, I do not agree with her method of implementation. Using this example, I would question her methods over the course of time. How often does she figure out creative solutions in other areas of management? She should have a conversation with the GM as to alternatives to best handle the issue of paying for energy-saving measures.

The steps process is described below:

Problem discerned: Electric bill showed a significant variance to budget for one month. Opportunity: There are a number of potential ways to save dollars on electricity.

Objective: The objective is to save dollars on electricity expenses.

Here is a list of some alternatives:

- Add a manual by-pass switch to the HVAC system.

- Install computer to control temperature and cycling, adjust or override manually as needed.

- Install individual (room or area) programmable thermostats.

- Replace existing light bulbs with lower wattage, energy saving bulbs.

- Use more efficient HVAC filters and ensure that they are changed every 30-60 days.

- Re-balance kitchen hoods and make-up air systems.

- Consider tinting windows to reduce energy demand.

Collect Information: After developing a list of alternatives, she should plan to research the alternatives on the basis of cost, availability, time to install, perceived effectiveness, etc.

Assess the Alternatives: After collecting information, she should utilize Texas Power to evaluate the effects of the alternatives and when they would pay for themselves through electric savings. If appropriate, she may wish to run a few small tests on her own—especially as it relates to acceptance by the membership and how it affects operations.

Select the Best Alternative: After assessing the info from Texas Power and her own tests at the Club, she should make the most effective decision as to what is most practical for the Club.

Implement: Take action right away to maximize potential savings. Keep accurate records to balance effectiveness with member and paid staff reaction. Keeping records will help start the process of evaluation, which is discussed next.

Evaluate: After the changes have been made, she should be sure to evaluate/monitor the monthly electric bills and member and paid staff comments.

Julie did not weigh all the options; she made a quick decision and did not consider her team's ideas. It appeared to start out well; she followed the first three steps of the classical theory. However, she did not take the time to collect information from Texas Power and her staff. Also, she did not assess the alternatives, so she could not know whether she made the most effective decision for the Club.

Manager Response 3

When one evaluates Julie's meeting and compares it to the classical theory of decision making, the meeting falls short in the area of producing alternatives. As Smitty states, *I am not sure that we produced enough ways that we could achieve our goal. For example, we did not anticipate that the weather would be this warm.* Since they failed to develop proper alternatives in their prior meeting, they are adjusting for the lack of foresight.

They also failed to collect information properly. They failed to make allowances for late food and beverage functions. Had they done so, they would have thought about the idea of adding egg timer switches to the thermostats to eliminate having to fire up the entire system during late events.

Julie has also not selected the best alternative. She should listen to the employee who states, *We are likely to spend $15,000.00 on these alternatives... Want me to run some numbers? Texas Power will give me all the information I need. I can get perfect information.*

That being said, she does do a fairly good job of pulling things together. Club managers are resourceful. She just is rushing and not thinking things through. If she slows the pace and listens more to the team, she will likely have better results.

As Julie's GM, I would be concerned about her inclination to not evaluate issues thoroughly. She also needs to do a more effective job in listening to the other members of the team. $15,000.00 is a lot of money to throw toward a problem. Her method of handling the expense is deceptive. When we are freewheeling to navigate issues, we should remind ourselves to use the *newsletter* test to check our method for handling a roadblock. The *newsletter* test simply asks the question, *Would I feel comfortable printing an explanation of what I am about to do on the cover of the Club newsletter?*

In summary, Julie should do a better job of listening to team members, think issues through more thoroughly, and use the *newsletter* test (questioning if you would be comfortable printing what you are about to do on the front page of the membership newsletter) for the way she intends to handle paying the $15,000.

Manager Response 4

The problem is that they are 50 percent usage over last year; the opportunity is to save at least 10 percent on costs associated with power, specifically electricity while not negatively affecting operations.

The goal is to save 10 percent. I do not see a specific timeline for this, other than as soon as possible. The method seems to be an organized, concentrated conservation program.

There are several alternatives outlined. Timers and thermostats seem to be the quickest, cheapest fix. I would install timers corresponding to the operational hours. I would add to the Manager's Opening and Closing Duties sheet their responsibility for turning off or on certain HVAC functions, lights, and equipment.

They have not collected any relevant information except the bill. The engineer is going to contact the provider and get additional information. Her decision to throw money at the problem may not be effective, as there is no formulated plan or data to support her theories.

The positives in the meeting mainly lie in producing alternatives. The engineer seemed to have good ideas and seemed motivated to solve the problem.

If I were Julie's GM, I would be concerned that she would use her fiscal decision-making powers in such a haphazard way. She is abusing the established procedure by instructing her staff to produce three purchase orders. She is also putting her staff in a difficult position with her ordering that be done. She has lost respect from her staff as a result of her willingness to work outside of the established bounds of ethics.

Manager Response 5

There seemed to be quite a bit missing in Julie's meeting and interchange. Using the steps of the classical theory of decision making, here is the situation:

- Discern a problem or opportunity. They knew exactly what the problem was and that they were focused correctly on the problem.

- Formulate goals and objectives. They formulated the goals and objectives and knew clearly what they wanted to accomplish.

- Produce alternatives. They did not produce enough alternatives. Brainstorming, without judging as they go, would have been a good approach. Asking for expert advice (from the power company) would have been another way to come up with alternatives.

- Collect information. More energy could and should have gone into this phase. One idea was presented and Julie decided to adopt it and move forward without enough information as to cost savings and other possible outcomes.

- Assess the alternatives. There was no assessment of alternatives. One course of action was chosen and Julie was moving forward on this.

- Select the best alternative. To select the best alternative, it is necessary to have a selection to choose from. It is necessary to evaluate alternatives based on soundness as well as overall benefit and cost to the Club and to the overall goal that is trying to be accomplished

- Implement the decision. The decision should be implemented based on the best alternative. Julie was walking on thin ice when she implemented a $15 thousand decision in three, $5 thousand phases, knowing that she was outside her limit. For her to share this with her team says that it is okay for them to stretch the rules, as well (the old *practice what you preach* principle). It would also be debatable if the solution would have been a capital item or a repair and maintenance item that would affect the bottom line on the operating statement.

The positives in Julie's meeting with reference to classical theory are that she did have the identification of the problem at hand, for the most part, and she presented the goal. I am not convinced, though that enough research was done to establish if it was an increase in kilowatt per hour or it was an increase in kilowatts used. This should all have been graphed as a way to try to analyze the problem. This was about as far as the positives ran with reference to using classical theory in her determination of an effective decision.

The aspects of the plan that I would find troublesome as Julie's GM would include these:

- Lack of overall investigation of the problem.

- She was jumping at the first, perhaps, logical solution to the situation.

- She was authorizing spending outside her spending limit, and her creative accounting approach. (How many other problems had she solved the same way?)

- Her overall knee-jerk reaction and the stress that was very apparent. She was planning a fix to this problem at all cost; and the fix that she was planning probably would cost more than it would save.

- She was appearing so stressed in the situation and thereby making poor decisions.

Manager Response 6

The classical approach is a rational approach that seeks out a simple method to maximize the goal and objectives. The goal was to decrease the electric bill by 10 percent. Last January the objectives and goals were decided, and agreed upon. What was missing in Julie's approach was the data gathering. She had a chance to get relevant information to aide in her decisions. Weighing cost versus savings would be a key evaluation in this case. She may be headed down the wrong path with her conclusion. The chance for perfect information does not come around often—and this chance seems good. Also, not evaluating the effectiveness of the decision can be detrimental to the project. She may go deeper into the hole.

Julie has decided on a clear-cut way to achieve the goal. However, this method may well get her fired. She identified the problem and brainstormed to develop ideas that are creative and plausible. Alternatives were produced, but the information gathering was lost. In assessing the alternatives she made a definitive decision and decided the course of action without listening to her teammates. Brainstorming and considering alternative suggestions to eventually gather information as to the effectiveness of the plan was partially completed. Answering the why, how, where, who, and what questions are key in completing the process. Following half of the steps doomed the process. There were chances for Julie to pursue better alternatives. She blew the chances and hurried through to a hasty decision.

If I were Julie's GM I would be concerned that it took a year to fix the problem. I would also be concerned that she wanted to use a quick fix that was not supported by research—and which could blow the budget. If she approved all of this prior to my knowledge, it would not be easy to undo, so I would have been extremely concerned about this, too. Finally, the way that she instructed the accounting office to pay for the expense is, at best, an ethical failure. She was intentionally going around the system. At worst, what she did should cost her the job.

Manager Response 7

We know that Julie's decision-making was not effective. The classical model of decision-making is based on a controlled, rational, and logical process. Julie's decision was a disaster. She will, no doubt, be looking for another job, soon.

It can be questioned whether Julie ever discovered the root of the problem. She may have been—and probably was—shortsighted, therefore only seeing the surface issues of the situation. As the engineer, Smitty referred to the fact that better or more perfect information was available by Texas Power to research the scenario and develop a much fuller model with other suggestions and alternating ideas. Instead, Julie fell into one of the Classical Model's myths that everyone partakes in a rationale decision-making process.

Formulate goals and objectives. Without fully researching all of the potential problems and opportunities, it becomes difficult to formulate goals and objectives. Julie has definitely skipped this part of the process. She might argue that the goals and objectives are clear: cut this year's utility costs by 10 percent based on last year's numbers. That might be the end objective, but there are many smaller goals or stepping stones that must be achieved to achieve victory.

Produce alternatives. This is another step that was skipped in the process by the leader of the team, and not the subordinates. Absolutely no alternative courses of action were identified in trying to seek goal attainment. Julie heard a combination of a few ideas, assumed they would help reach the end objective, and failed to look at items such as payback, initial costs, and other analysis elements. And we would be negligent to not bring up her ethics in approving a $15,000.00 cost versus the $5,000 that she is approved to give. The manner in which Julie handled that, as well as the perception from her other peers, is a lousy way to conduct business.

Collect information. No information was collected. Smitty tried, but Julie did not listen. This step proves invaluable anytime we are looking at high-priced, complicated, and difficult decisions.

Assess the alternatives. This step was not omitted. Alternatives were not discussed or even thought about. Nothing was ranked, reviewed, or discussed. This is poor planning and demonstrates an effective model of what not to do.

Select the best alternative. If no alternatives were reviewed, it is difficult to select any. Again, skipping a step will prove costly in the long run.

Implement the decision. Finally we see a step that was followed. However, it was flawed, since some of the prior steps are missing in the process. Julie is taking a gamble and she will be remembered, among her peers, for her poor process and unethical behavior. These are basic leadership failures. Julie will pay with her job.

Positives and negatives.

Julie was goal oriented from the big picture outlook, and in her eyes, she discerned the problem of being over budget. Her goals were clear: energy cost reduction. Her decision was implemented swiftly, which is a positive and negative. In the positive light, Julie did implement the decision, thereby making the exercise more than just a mental challenge.

In summarizing Julie's negative behaviors, the following steps were not touched upon:

- Discern the problem on both a macro and micro plane.
- Formulating total goals and objectives, not just reviewing the final step in a long process.
- No alternatives were produced.
- No information was collected.
- Obviously, alternatives were not assessed.
- There was no or minimal selection process.

As Julie's GM.

If I were Julie's GM, I would be troubled by the six negative factors just listed. Julie needs to review the decision making process, apply it to her actions, and then list what steps she did follow and explain why. Or, if she says that she knows the steps in the decision making process, she explain why they were not followed and then explain the poor decision making choices.

Not only did she not execute this process in the manner I would have desired and in the way that her team and the Club needed for her to have done so, but she was unethical, and a poor model for others to follow. The first issue would have been a learning experience for her. The last would have cost her the job.

Lesson 2

Behavioral Theory

One major problem with the classical view of decision making is that it assumes that decision makers have mental capacities for analysis and evaluation that vastly exceed those actually possessed by people. In addition, Davis found that neither computers nor smarter people are likely to be able to implement the Classical Theory approach to decision making in the face of the complexity of most real-world problems.

Given the difficulties and shortcomings of classical decision theory, we clearly need an approach to decision making that is (1) more likely to provide an accurate description of how individuals actually make decisions; and (2) more likely to provide realistic guidance to decision makers regarding how they should approach decision situations. Behavioral decision theory provides such an alternative approach.

The central ideas of behavioral decision theory recognize decision making often involves non-rational, social, and political processes. Decision makers must actually settle for something less than an ideal solution. Such ideas have been developed by Simon and his colleagues (Higgins).

Bounded Rationality. In response to this recognition of the complexity of most real-world problems and the seeming impossibility of actually implementing the Classical Theory approach to rational decision making, Simon and his colleagues developed the notion of bounded rationality (Trist).

The principle of bounded rationality posits that the human mind lacks the capacity for formulating and solving complex problems. Thus, bounded rationality implies these assumptions (Arnold):

1. Decisions are always based on an incomplete and inadequate comprehension of the situation.
2. Decision makers cannot generate all possible alternatives.
3. Alternatives are always evaluated incompletely since it is impossible to foresee and predict all possible outcomes.
4. The ultimate decision regarding which alternative to choose is based on weighing alternatives across a myriad of variables. It is almost always impossible to determine which alternative is the optimal one.

Satisficing. If everyone was always completely rational, individuals and organizations would make the best (or near-best) decisions. As a result, problems of organizing and managing organizations effectively would not exist to the extent they do in the real world. However, people, of course, are not always completely rational. Furthermore, people are not capable of gathering information and making decisions on the basis of all of the detailed and exhaustive analyses assumed by Classical Theory. Given this real-world situation, how then can they go about determining which alternative to choose when faced with a decision?

Simon has suggested that the key to understanding how people actually go about simplifying complicated decisions lies in the concept of *satisficing*. While the assumptions of Classical Theory suggest that a decision maker must continue to generate and evaluate alternatives until the best alternative has been identified, satisficing suggests that a decision maker continues to generate and evaluate alternatives until one alternative that is *good enough* to be acceptable is identified.

The advantages of satisficing as a basis for decision making (Arnold):

1. It does not require a decision maker to generate an exhaustive list of alternatives.
2. It recognizes the bounded rationality of people.
3. It provides a realistic description of how people make decisions.

Given the time, effort, and expense that must go into the process of generating and evaluating alternatives, satisficing keeps the decision-making process within manageable bounds and stops the process when an acceptable solution has been identified.

The Behavioral Model is based on the following assumptions (Higgins):

1. Objectives are often vague and not agreed upon.
2. Managers may not recognize that a problem exists.
3. Managers may not go through the identification process and therefore may solve the wrong problem.
4. Decision makers and problem solvers solve models apparent in their world. These models never encompass all the variables, facts, or relationships involved in the actual problem. Therefore, if and when rationality is applied, it is applied only to a part of the total problem.

Research at the University of Chicago reveals several biases in the construction of such models:

1. Poor framing. A European manager working in the United States may have received bids to refurbish the Club's clay courts. He recommends a French red clay product, when the courts are actually constructed with a Har-tru granular product, which is a synthetic clay of an entirely different composition.

2. Available evidence. A club manager from Seattle now working in Miami may make a decision to move an outdoor event indoors based on rain at 1:00 p.m., based on the most available evidence of past experience. While expedient, such a decision may not be made on the *best* evidence, especially to the disappointed guests arriving at 7:00 p.m. to a beautiful evening with having had no sign of showers for over five hours.

3. Anchoring on a piece of information. A manager moving from a young, progressive, developer-owned club in Southern California to rural North Carolina may make a huge mistake advising the Board that instituting a club-wide no-smoking policy would go smoothly.

4. Association of a solution with a past success. A private club Board's decision to maintain the jacket and tie requirement in the dining room based on tradition leads to serving only a handful of dining patrons on Saturday evenings.

5. Only a few of the possible alternatives are considered. The decision maker's knowledge of the situation is usually limited.

While the rational economic model is certainly one basis for decision making in organizations, the process is often anything but rational. It is also political, social, and satisficing (Arnold). What makes for the best decision is not always apparent. All decision makers must anticipate their own limitations and the constraints of the situation. They must also anticipate the political and social realities of not only the decision process but the implementation and control processes as well. Managers must recognize these constraints and work within them. They should also seek to improve the decision process and to reduce its limitations.

4.2. Mini Case: Renata's Plan

Renata Silverfield is director of human resources for Eagle's Eye Country Club, located in Smithfield, Montana. The country club is part of a high-end real estate development that will be developed over the next 10 years. Larry Weld, GM, has asked for Renata to help develop a strategic human resource plan that will help the Club achieve its strategic plan.

Larry, what should we do? I have been trying to help the various directors understand the importance of this process to the Club's future. The only one that seems to have any idea of what I am talking about is Fritzie Clemmons, the controller.

Tell me more, Renata.

Well, I know that you and the Board are trying to complete the economic model and decide when to sell the Club to the members, so I dug through some of my old HR and Statistics textbooks to put together a model that will show the Board that we know what we are doing. One is an additive value model; another predicts change based on three economic peaks; another uses Monte Carlo simulation, while yet another uses Markov analysis for forecasting internal supply. When I talk to these people about the importance of this process, they look at me with a glazed-over expression. It is as if they lack the capacity for formulating and solving complex problems. I want to get this down to a precise science for you.

Fritzie walks into the room and says, Hi guys. Renata, I have been thinking about your HR planning exercise and I have a couple of thoughts. Okay if I give you some impressions?

Fire away!

Well, remember that you are dealing with operations people. While we more represent the staff support side of the Club, most of the others are deeply involved with ongoing, revenue-producing hassles. I think we should keep that into focus and come up with something a bit less complicated. Remember, it was only a few years ago that we were able to get operations people to buy-in on being involved in HR issues at all. What I propose is that you take them through baby steps. When they get good with one concept, step them up to the next one... and so on. Sooner or later, one alternative will emerge that is acceptable to you and doable for them.

Good idea, Fritzie, thanks. What do you think I should do about Dave? Since he came to us (some gift) from the engineering and development side of the company, he cannot get it out of his mind that he should not make all the decisions that have to do with hiring and that HR should be the attendance police and the feel-good department. His model is based upon his experience in a hierarchically-constructed headquarters organization. He just does not get the fact that we are a flat, horizontal organization that values decentralization and empowerment. He makes decisions based on rules of thumb. For example, he thinks he needs to add one golf maintenance employee for every twenty golf members that join the Club!

I will work with him more. I think he will come around. He is just used to his engineering world, promises Larry. Furthermore, I think that I can finesse the Board. I have a good relationship with the executive committee. I think they will let us come up with a less technical method for the model.

Discussion Question

What is your experience with the scenario described in this mini case? Is it more or less similar to the way decisions are made at your club? Why or why not?

Manager Response 1

This situation is more familiar to me in member-owned clubs than in corporate-owned clubs. I worked in the corporate-owned world of club management for approximately 10 years until going to the member-owned side of the industry approximately 10 years ago. When I first arrived on the member-owned scene, I observed an old-school tendency toward autocratic leadership, and an overall lack of focus on and interest in HR issues. It was *my way or the highway* from the former GM's point of view. The department heads ran smaller fiefdoms in a similar manner.

We found ourselves in a situation similar to that of Renata. The newly-elected Board was comprised of successful and progressive business people. They wanted to develop a long-range plan with an emphasis on infrastructure. They felt that this was the proper way for us to accomplish our overall goals. By making much needed improvements to the back-of-the-house (facilities usually not seen by the members), the front-of-the-house could offer a much higher level of service to the membership and the overarching goals would be reached.

I, too, went about the project from a more corporate point of view than had been used in the past by the GM. As I met with department heads and supervisors to share the Board's vision, they looked at me as though I was from another planet and speaking a Martian language. What I discovered in that position was a lesson I still try to remember. Always approach your people on their level. When the focus changes in leadership, it is important to establish small steps that will lead to the completion of the projects. People come from many different levels of experience and trust and change take time. In some member-owned clubs, you may find a tendency more toward employees who have only held one job all of their working lives. Successful GMs have to be able to deal with employees one-on-one, on their level, and only after considering their experiences.

I would have the HR Director work with Dave (and I would reinforce the HR Director's message). The HR Director is the individual that must make it all come together and happen in this case. I would be willing to discuss alternative methods, but would allow that department head to achieve the objective.

Manager Response 2

This model is not quite what we deal with at our club, but I can certainly understand how they got there. First, there could have been clearer guidelines for her to follow to know what type of model to put together. She spent a lot of time researching the three different models, and each has merit in its own way. The effort to communicate these three models to employees, who have much different interests, is a frustrating experience.

It appears that the more competent people are in their functional areas (at the upper levels of management), the more difficult it is to manage them. It is a bit like *herding cats*! You want each person to have his or her own opinions and to be empowered and to act. However, when a strong personality trait comes through in a decision by a staff member, then you want to rein him or her in. Dave seems to be a bit this way. He appears to be good at what he does (although Fritzie does not give him much credit), but is set in his ways. To get him to think about anything but his particular area of responsibility will be a feat.

In our club, decisions are made based on the goal and the overall good of the Club. It if is a simple decision, we make it. But, when we agonize over something, we look at what the overall goal is and then how it will affect the Club both in the short and long term and then make the decision based on the information.

Manager Response 3

We recently went through the process of buying a new, integrated POS system for the Club that followed the case scenario to a certain extent. The current system needed to be replaced and we needed to find an acceptable replacement. *(Note to Dr. Merritt: We used the excellent guide to purchasing a POS template that you designed for the private club industry. Thank you very much for the valuable and no-cost resource that is available on your web site.)*

Well, the GM wanted nothing to do with the process, because he is not computer friendly. So it turned out to be the Chef, the Dining Room Manager, and me (the Clubhouse Manager) meeting with three different vendor companies. We listened to their presentations, watched their demonstrations, and received price quotes from each of them. After using your guide to help us manage the process and then meeting with the two other major department heads, we came to our conclusion.

Why we chose the system that we did, was based on what we found during the analysis as being the most compatible with what we liked personally and be the best fit for us as a club. Even though you had advised us to get a wide variety of future users (staff) involved in the process, we failed to do that because it was too time consuming. As it turned out, what we chose was not exactly what worked the best for the staff. It functions fairly well for the staff, thankfully. However, we concentrated our efforts on report production and programming features, instead of day-to-day ease of use and functionality. Strategically, we made a huge error in leaving out the people who would actually be using the system for entry.

Manager Response 4

The mini case described in this lesson is a similar to the way my club solves problems and makes decisions, as we use Behavioral Decision Theory. Behavioral Decision Theory recognizes that decision-making is often dominated by non-rational, social, and political processes and decision-makers must settle for something less than ideal.

The team at Eagles Eye Country Club is involved in a Real Estate Development plan over the next 10 years. Renata, who was asked to develop a strategic human resource plan, consulted old textbooks and came up with complex strategies. The directors whom she is trying to educate cannot comprehend her proposal. Fritzie Clemons has a better understanding of the approach necessary to be most effective and achieve the best results. Fritzie suggests the Behavioral Theory of approaching the directors with a series of small steps. Even though this has been a criticism of the Behavioral Theory approach, the process Renata has proposed will not overwhelm the team of directors. Dave's decision-making based on rules of thumb has also received criticism in that Behavioral Theory assumes managers will not evaluate alternatives according to criteria. It is believed that past experience is the basis for decision-making. Larry highlights a criticism of Behavioral Theory in the decision-making process. His attempt to finesse the Board highlights the effects of social relationships on the process. It shows how problem solvers must gain support of powerful individuals to ensure that their solutions are chosen and implemented.

Behavioral Theory, with its limitations, is a more realistic way of making decisions in organizations.

Manager Response 5

Their decision-making process is very similar to the one used at my club. Not only that, it resembles the process used at every other club where I have worked. The realities of the business and the need to decide issues and move forward suggest that it is normal for us to settle for something that we can all live with, but is less than ideal.

They are using data and standards from other organizations, which may not relate to their club and it may be outdated, as well.

The Engineer has clear notions of how things should be done. He probably was taught these concepts when he became a new manager and he is not accustomed to thinking in a creative manner.

Larry is playing the politics game. He feels the need to have a positive relationship with the influential decision-makers to enact decisions.

We are trying to find new alternatives and ways of thinking. I have a new Board that appears to be open to new suggestions and ways of doing things. I have to be careful not to make decisions based purely on my experience alone. I have a four-star hotel, high-end club background, and I am employed at a small, rural country club. Obviously, I have to change my mindset and ensure that the changes that I propose are appropriate for the Club and its members.

Dr. Merritt challenged about 200 of us in a workshop at world conference last year to test the alignment of the Board's vision by asking at a retreat, *if this club were an automobile, what kind would it be*? I quickly understood the wisdom of his challenge. What a great tool! While I thought our Board was fairly-well aligned in terms of vision, the answers to his question were all over the place. We had answers ranging from Chevrolet to Mercedes—and a lot of answers in between. Remember, these were all Board members! This simple question (which was posed by the President) created the basis for a two-day retreat, which ended in a degree of alignment by the Board that I have never seen before. We went away with a focused vision and an excellent direction for me to convey to the paid staff. We know the expectations of the Board. We have conveyed the vision to the members. We envision ourselves as being the best Buick-level club that we can possibly be in the marketplace. Hey, it may not be sexy, but it is honest. Further, and even more important, it is an amazing help to us in trying to define service, amenities, and dues levels. We are Hampton Inn level (dues fees, and charges). As such, we know that we cannot deliver Four Seasons level service. We know who we are strategically.

Manager Response 6

The experience I have with this scenario makes the memories all too real. I came from a large organization that was extremely tightly structured. Arriving at my new club, I quickly realized that I relied on my staff and two other people to sell functions. I was quick to jump on the blame wagon and felt like I was an alien speaking an unknown language when my staff did not understand my words and vision, and consequently did not get things right.

I just felt that there was one way—*my way*—to do business, and if people were not going about it in the *right* way, then it was up to me to either change them or try to work around them. Three years later I finally have begun to realize that opposition is not the way to go. Working with what you have and making it fit is the preferred method. When I was going through the different ways of decision-making I thought that classical was *the* way to think, methodically and rationally. But, factors and variables change. The more I see and learn, the more that I believe that there are many successful methods for and types of successful decision making. Much of its successful implementation lies in the personality and preference of the individual.

Similarities to the scenario can be found in our club. There is an established, vertical hierarchy (centralized); but most decisions are based on a flat, horizontal scale, which recognizes a de-centralized organization. Micro teams exist and working with those teams well is very beneficial to excellent outcomes for the members. The fact that decisions involve social, political, and satisficing elements is true beyond words. Every scenario demands a slightly different approach.

The teams that exist at our club are tightly knit and relatively calm. Everyone works well with each other and the big decisions are filtered through consultation with the GM. He, in turn, trusts us to make those decisions, but keeps the door open if we want to discuss it further or if we run into snags. We learn at the pace we want to learn. F&B, Golf, Tennis, Greens, and the Pool operations all depend on each other too much for us to waste time fighting. We would rather get busy solving the problem, then rip it apart and look at it from every angle and learn from our mistakes.

We have a great team.

Manager Response 7

This model makes several important points, which all point to the more realistic elements of the decision making model. This scenario brings in the central ideas of the Behavioral Theory of Decision Making, the sociopolitical and peer pressure concepts that affect the everyday relationships, and psychology of people. For example, we now are thrown into the stereotype of operations people and, more importantly, the operations mindset, versus that of the support side of the Club. This is a realistic challenge that occurs in great clubs during the decision-making processes.

My experience brings in a combination of the two counter cultures being behavioral based versus the classic model of decision-making. Ideally one's routine decisions are based on a combination of the two. The classic model is the decision foundation, the theoretically perfect (although we know it has faults) situation. However, despite its faults, and with the harsh realities of real world relationships, we naturally allow the classic model to be skewed by the natural interference of the behavioral model. We take theory and combine it with reality and hopefully have combined the best details of each model. Then, out of the blender comes the best human made decision (bounded rationality + theoretically correct classical model).

We assume that the General Manager knows what the best decision is for the Club. He mixes elements of that best decision with the quirks of his club, and the knowledge of the desires of the current Board, and the psychological relationship factors that exist in reality.

I am not claiming that the General Manager compromises his best decision just because of the political relationships that exist. However, it is those relationships that make the Club unique and lend to the historical composition and culture of the Club.

The General Manager makes that theoretical *best* decision and then tailors it to best fit his club and unique individual situation. That tailoring or customizing could be considered to be based on the Behavioral Model of Decision Making.

Lesson 3

Alternatives

In the two preceding lessons we have discussed the Classical Theory and the Behavioral Theory of decision making and some of the problems associated with each model. We will now focus on some of the decision making processes that can be used as alternatives to the Classical and Behavioral theories.

Do teams come up with more creative, imaginative ideas than individuals? The general answer to this question seems to be that it often depends upon the situation. The reasons that an individual approach may be better have to do with the tendency for teams to get into a rut in terms of how they think about problems, as well as the fear of criticism that may inhibit team members from expressing their ideas. In order to help reduce negative tendencies, teams should develop skills that foster an open interchange of ideas.

Three major types of decision making processes are: the Interacting group, the Nominal group, and the Delphi group. These groups are similar, yet distinct. Most teams are simple Interacting groups. The Nominal and Delphi groups are designed to overcome some of the problems Interacting groups encounter.

The Interacting Group

Interacting groups meet face-to-face with open interchange. They are usually unstructured, although many have an agenda and objectives. In creative situations, interactive group meetings usually begin with a statement of the problem to be addressed. Open discussion follows. Problem recognition, identification, the generation of alternatives, and choice processes are focal points of such teams. A simple majority usually controls the result (Higgins). Two highly productive, interactive, creative team processes are brainstorming and storyboarding.

Brainstorming. One well-known technique for stimulating creativity in teams is known as brainstorming. The purpose of brainstorming is to enhance creativity through team discussion. Certain procedural rules are enforced to permit all team members to express their ideas and to reduce critical evaluations that might inhibit creativity.

An example of an effective use of the brainstorming process would be a house and social committee brainstorming ideas for increasing covers during lunch.

Four rules in particular are central to the brainstorming process:

1. Criticism is forbidden. Ideas are to be generated, not evaluated. Negative feedback is only allowed after all alternatives have been generated.
2. Piggybacking or using others' ideas is encouraged. All ideas belong to the team.
3. Quantity of ideas is the key, not quality. Prioritizing, narrowing, and choosing will come later.
4. Freewheeling discussion is encouraged. No idea is to be considered too far-out.

These sessions have a leader and a recorder; the latter writes the ideas, usually on a board, where all participants can see them. Sessions last about thirty minutes. There are usually six to ten participants. Ideas are evaluated after brainstorming. Brainstorming is especially useful for generating alternative solutions.

Many organizations use brainstorming or a similar procedure in making team decisions. However, the popularity of the technique has resulted in a good deal of systematic evaluation of its impact on creativity. Most of that research has failed to support the claim that brainstorming can increase the creativity of a team making decisions.

Some studies suggest that individuals working alone and pooling their ideas can generate more ideas than the same people working together in brainstorming teams. These studies showed that when individuals work alone and subsequently pool their ideas, they produce on average nearly twice as many ideas as brainstorming teams do working together. However, while individuals may be better than teams in formulating new ideas, teams are better than individuals in developing and evaluating the ideas (Arnold).

Storyboarding. Storyboarding is a structured, but flexible brainstorming process that focuses on identifying major issues and then brainstorming each of them. Storyboarding allows for a complete picture (story) of the problem to be placed before participants, usually on some type of wallboard.

An example of an effective use of the storyboarding process would be a committee working with an architect who will be designing a complete remodeling of the mixed grill.

Storyboards have two thinking sessions. The first session is creative; the second is critical (Higgins). Basic brainstorming rules are followed in the creative thinking session. In the critical session, ideas are evaluated and the list of ideas is reduced. Storyboarding is good for analyzing a problem as well as generating alternatives. Implementation may also be an issue for a storyboard. A leader and recorder are used in a team that ranges from six to ten participants (Higgins).

The Nominal Group

Delbecq and Van de Ven originated the Nominal group technique, partly as a consequence of their dissatisfaction with interactive group processes (Higgins). A Nominal group is more structured than an interactive one. It intentionally eliminates much of the interpersonal exchange of the Interacting group. The primary purpose of this process is to eliminate dominance by one or a few people in the choice process. In fact, *nominal* refers to the fact that individuals are not allowed to communicate verbally.

An example of an effective use of the Nominal group technique might be a group of managers meeting at the annual conference to recommend a location and begin the general planning of an upcoming conference.

Nominal group technique follows four steps:

1. Team members write down their ideas of the problem.
2. Each idea is summarized so that all members can see them. No ideas are discussed until all are presented and recorded.
3. An open discussion of ideas follows to clarify ideas that members do not understand. No attack or defense is allowed.
4. Next, members vote (in secret) the top ideas in order of priority. The eventual decision of the Nominal group is the vote outcome.

The Delphi Technique

Dalkey developed the Delphi technique. It utilizes a series of questionnaires administered by a central group of individual experts who never meet together. As the respondents reply, their questionnaires are summarized. Then a new questionnaire based on their responses to the first one, is developed and sent to them. This process repeats until a team consensus on the problem is reached.

An example of an effective use of the Delphi technique would be a GM collecting ideas and input from other chapter GMs by email for a state-of-the-industry forecast and best practices presentation to be delivered at the CMAA annual conference.

Remember that the key to the Delphi technique is that the members never meet face-to-face.

The Delphi technique has four main applications:

1. Generating alternatives and forecasts.
2. Examining a situation for underlying assumptions or seeking additional information.
3. Discovering information that might lead to consensus.
4. Combining a broad array of expert opinions.

4.3. Mini Case: Use E-Mail

After a Board request, Norman Tallmadge, GM of the Long Key Club, located in the Florida Keys, is trying to decide whether his recommendation to the Board whether his recommendation to the Board will be to charge dues annually or by the month.

To help him gather input into this important decision, he has contacted 10 other GMs that are considered experts in operations at seasonal clubs. While none of them knows Norman—or each other—they have agreed to help him.

- Norman will create a questionnaire and e-mail it to the others.

- Based on responses, Norman will summarize the information and create yet a second questionnaire and e-mail it to the others.

- This process will continue until the team of experts reaches a team consensus on the problem of whether Norman's club should bill dues annually or monthly.

- Norman will present his recommendation to the Board.

Discussion Question

Referring to the three major types of decision-making teams: the Interacting group, the Nominal group, and the Delphi group, identify which technique was used and if another technique may have been more effective. Why?

Manager Response 1

Norman is using the Delphi technique to generate questionnaires, which will allow him to read what other managers already have in place at their clubs for monthly or annual dues. Norman is benchmarking—one of my favorite techniques to receive suggestions from other managers on a various operational questions.

Using these questionnaires, he will be able to determine what each club does with respect to dues. Additionally, and beyond *what* they do, a manager is able to learn the *why* they do what they do. This will allow the manager to research the answers to see if it matches his club's membership profile. This allows him to receive input and narrow the subject to specific questions that will help him make a decision, or present it to his Board. I would have used the same method, but would try to ensure that I was receiving information from similar clubs that had used this dues structure in the past or had recently changed to this method.

Manager Response 2

Norman Tallmadge utilized the Delphi group technique when he involved ten other club managers to help him solve his dues problem at the Long Key Club. He sent a series of questionnaires to a group of experts who never actually met (face-to-face) together. As the respondents replied, he summarized their replies and submitted subsequent questionnaires until a consensus was reached by the team.

Upon first reading this case study I thought that this very involved Delphi Group Procedure was overkill and that a Nominal Group Technique would be a more effective and less time consuming way to solve this dues billing problem. The eventual solution to the annual versus monthly billing dilemma can be only one of two alternatives—annual versus monthly. There is no great need to generate alternatives because they have already been defined. You want to know the reasons why another seasonal club would choose one over the other, their thought processes, whether you are overlooking anything, and if there are any hidden pitfalls associated with either solution.

A Nominal Group Technique would allow Norman to solicit from his panel of experts a written list of the reasons why their respective seasonal clubs bill their dues monthly or annually. He could then present, summarize and record these ideas with and for his financial committee, they could discuss these ideas to clarify them, and then the committee members could each secretly vote for one alternative or the other. The solution getting the greatest number of votes would be the decision of the committee. A thorough case could be made for each solution and the most logical alternative to the greatest number of voters would be the solution. It seems like a very logical and practical way to solve the problem.

The reason I am wavering on my initial decision of utilizing a Nominal Group Technique over a Delphi Group Technique is due to the fact that the latter procedure might allow for Norman Tallmadge to factor in demographics such as: size of club, average age of members, socioeconomic makeup of members, activities offered, budget of club, cash flow history of club, and other characteristics he deems relevant. As time went on, he could narrow his survey down to those clubs that are most similar to his. Along those same lines, the more pertinent information he can gather the better his chance of making a proper decision. If time is not a factor and your panel of experts do not mind answering numerous surveys, then Delphi Group Technique might be more informative in reaching a decision.

Manager Response 3

Norman is using a Delphi Group technique to come up with solutions to his question. He has definitely picked the best technique for the development of possible solutions. Since he is using the Internet and none of the managers know Norman or know each other, this seems to be the most streamlined approach towards generation possible solutions.

The other two techniques would involve way too much exchange of information back and forth. Managers do not have time for this. The Delphi technique is well suited for the efficient use of time and lends itself extremely well for Internet communication.

Manager Response 4

He is using the Delphi group technique, which relies on written communication without contributing parties ever meeting together in face-to-face discussion.

Ideally, the Nominal group technique would be more effective and expedient. This method would help expose potential problems with either decision during the open discussion.

He may need to use the Delphi technique because of geographical restrictions.

Manager Response 5

Based on the obvious method of utilizing a questionnaire and no face-to-face interaction, he is using the Delphi method. He is considering the input of a credible series of experts who in the end will have never met together as a group (at least for this purpose). This is the method I would have chosen.

However another method could be considered. A Nominal group of managers would eventually, after having met come up with a probable similar response to using the Delphi approach. The downside of this would be if he included members, if they voice their opinion and thus feel as if they had a vote, and you end up taking action other than they suggest they might feel as though they were ignored.

Manager Response 6

Norman is using the Delphi approach. He cannot use an interactive approach without meeting face-to-face. However, brainstorming would be helpful. The brainstorming of ideas from experts that can piggyback off each other's ideas would be helpful. Time would be a concern.

The Nominal approach could work by way of the internet and a conference call. But the need for secrecy in this case is not an issue. Expression of ideas is beneficial in this case. His approach has met all the criteria for the Delphi approach, and it is the logical choice. The expert opinions, consensus of information, underlying assumptions, and the generation of alternatives are all important facets of the approach.

The only thing that I would have done differently was that once I had the information, I would share it with the membership. After all, they are the ones paying the dues. Gathering information is important. What you do with the information after accumulation that is even more important.

Manager Response 7

In the mini case, the decision making process that was used was the Delphi Technique, which is a series of questionnaires administered by a central individual to experts who never meet face-to-face.

With regard to best practice.

The Delphi technique was used, as it is convenient and easy to administer in regard to the discussion boards that are prevalent on CMAA's website. In order to get the same talent in a room for a brainstorming session might cost thousands of dollars, flying people in from all over the world.

The other techniques could be just as beneficial if the other people involved were at Norman's disposal. However, the other benefit to Norman's choice is the flexibility in time. Norman can email them at 2:00 in the morning or at whatever time he is available. The same is true for the group in terms of responding on their own time, even if within a set deadline.

Lesson 4

Structured Decision Making

Why Use Structure?

Examples of structured forms of decision making include parliamentary procedure, alternative examination procedure, and information search procedure. When a team uses such methodical decision-making methods, it adheres to a highly systematic decision making process. Teams that use structured techniques are less likely to fall into the groupthink trap, since structured techniques promote constructive criticism, nonconformity, and open-mindedness within the decision making team. Without adequate decision procedures, highly cohesive teams will make poor decisions (Neck).

Expert-based technique is an alternative to structured technique. Experts make the decisions. When a team works on well-structured tasks, structured techniques usually lead to more effective decisions than do expert-based techniques (Priem).

In the paragraphs that follow you will become familiar with several of the more popular and effective forms of structured decision making.

Dialectical Inquiry

The first step of the dialectical inquiry process involves the division of the major team into two subgroups. The first subgroup independently develops recommendations for the problem, lists the assumptions on which these recommendations are based, and then presents these recommendations and assumptions to the second subgroup. Next, the second subgroup develops new assumptions that are counter to those presented by the first subgroup, then develops new recommendations from these new assumptions, finally presenting these counter assumptions and new recommendations to the first subgroup. The last step comprises both groups debating until they can agree upon a set of assumptions; these assumptions are worked on by the entire team to come up with the team's final recommendation.

The Stepladder

The Stepladder Technique improves team communication and decision making by ensuring that every member contributes to the decision making process. The process is delineated as follows:

Stage 1: Two team members (the initial core group) work together on a problem.

Stage 2: A third team member joins the core group and presents his/her preliminary solutions for the same problem.

Stage 3: The fourth team member joins the core group and presents his/her preliminary solutions.

Stage 4: The four members discuss until they come to a final group decision.

The number of stages increases or decreases, depending on the number of members. The structure can change to accommodate larger teams. For example, two members can enter each respective stage instead of one.

There are several prerequisites to be implemented to ensure the success of the Stepladder Technique. First, before each team member enters the group, they must be given the team's task and sufficient time to think about the problem. Second, the entering member must present his/her preliminary solutions before hearing the core group's preliminary solution. This constant verbalization and reiteration of team members' ideas will increase comprehension, understanding, and retention of information. Third, after each additional member joins the core group, the team needs sufficient time to discuss the problem. Fourth, the team should not come to a final decision until the entire team has formed.

Rogelberg's Stepladder Technique prevents team deficiencies in five ways.

1. The technique facilitates communication by all members.

2. Because members can no longer hide behind others' contributions, the technique cuts down on social loafing. A study found that stepladder team members work significantly harder on their task than their counterparts in conventional groups.

3. The constant addition of a new person generates new ideas and possibly some helpful controversy. Disagreement that arises in a structured setting fosters critical thinking. Teams that freely evaluate ideas and confront controversy come to better decisions.

4. The structure's communication mandate gives members the opportunity to reveal their knowledge. If a particular member makes his or her special expertise known, the team will typically allow more time for that person to express ideas and concerns, which contribute to higher decision quality.

5. By continuously refining decisions, the team will come to a higher quality decision.

The Stepladder Technique is most useful when the decision to be made is easily definable and has not been subdivided. In addition, the technique is most practical when each piece of key information is known by at least two people. Finally, when simultaneous participation is not a prerequisite and the process is not being conducted under urgent time pressure, the Stepladder Technique allows for team development through multiple steps.

There are, however, some limitations to the Stepladder Technique. First, members need equal status, or all members must be assigned randomly to entry positions. Second, the technique needs to be modified to fit the number of team members.

The Stepladder Technique has exhibited considerable success when implemented into the team decision making process. For example, Rogelberg found that teams that have used this approach were highly satisfied with the structure, felt that everyone agreed with the team solution, felt their solution was high in quality, and felt comfortable with the climate produced by the technique. Furthermore, the study found that stepladder teams produced significantly higher quality decisions than did conventional teams, surpassing the quality of their best individual decisions 56 percent of the time.

Voting

This is a goal-based decision making framework based on an interpersonal model. The leader's goals include both personal goals and adopted goals for team relationships; however, the leader must resolve conflict by making tradeoffs. Priorities drive the decision process.

The Vote Model process of decision making initially begins with a member submitting a suggestion or proposal through the appropriate committee to the Board. Such a proposal may be specific, such as funding for a child care program, or abstract such as the fairness of the Club's officer election procedures. Stances on the issues have representative sides who argue the proposal's pros and cons. The consequences of voting for or against a given proposal are further analyzed (usually by the

Club staff) and assigned a priority. Finally, depending upon the nature of the proposal, either the Board or the stockholding members vote the proposal in or out.

There are nine principles to the Vote Model of decision making:

1. Decision tradeoffs. Because a member has many goals and limited resources, he/she cannot realistically achieve all goals. In the effort to achieve some goals, members will have to make tradeoffs, compromises, and sacrifices.

2. Goal decomposition. Members can choose which goals to pursue first by breaking goals down into their original elements.

3. Principle of importance. The importance of a goal is proportional to the resources that the agent is willing to expend in pursuit of that goal.

4. Resource decomposition. Resources are also decomposed into primitive elements to use to compare and reason.

5. Cognitive resources. Members can allocate cognitive resources, such as attention and memory, in the pursuit of goals.

6. Cooperating agents. Members interact with other members through interpersonal relationships.

7. Principle of interpersonal goals. Adopted goals are processed uniformly as individual goals, with a priority determined by the importance of the relationship.

8. Organizational relationships. The principle of interpersonal goals may be extended to include goals adopted from institutions and organizations.

9. Goal-based decision making. An alternative to quantitative decision analysis is a model of decision making based on an agent's goals.

Lesson 5

Structured Decision Making (Continued)

Consensus Mapping

Consensus mapping is an approach that helps structure ideas into interrelated sets. This technique is conducted in small teams of five to nine participants. The approach is appropriate for complex problems by focusing the team's attention on interrelationships, sequences, and structure. Finally, consensus mapping helps a team with differing perspectives arrive at a shared image of a problem and an agreeable solution through in-depth discussion.

Consensus mapping assumes that a team has already generated a list of ideas, clarified the meaning of those ideas and conducted a preliminary evaluation (e.g., ratings or prioritization).

According to Boroush, there are two key steps to Consensus Mapping:

1. The team identifies and classifies the key parts of the problem. Once this classification has been agreed on, the individual items can be re-prioritized by using numerical ratings.

2. The team now creates a drawing to visually display the interrelationships and time dependencies among the categories. The team should not exclude ideas or design the overall structure to a specific end.

The benefit of Consensus Mapping is that the key results of the discussion are automatically documented. This is not generally the case in ordinary casual conversation.

Procedural Rationality

Given the reality of bounded rationality and satisficing, and the impossibility of making optimal decisions in the sense implied by classical decision theory, what should decision makers do to ensure that they are making the best possible decisions within the constraints inherent in all real decision situations? In order to deal with this question, Simon introduced the concept of procedural rationality. Procedural rationality states that since it is impossible for decision makers ever to ensure that they have made the optimal rational decision, they should instead turn their attention to the design of methods, or procedures for decision making that will be most likely to generate the best possible decisions within the constraints of human judgment and insight. Such rational procedures need to be designed in such a way that they capitalize on the strengths of human beings as problem solvers and decision makers. These strengths appear to lie not in any capacity to generate, process, and analyze huge amounts of information, but in the ability to employ insight and experience in identifying a small number of promising alternatives for further exploration and analysis (Simon).

The concept of *successive limited comparison* is an example of a method of decision making that incorporates the principle of procedural rationality. This method of decision making does not require total agreement on objectives, exhaustive analysis of all possible alternatives and outcomes, or determination of the optimal alternative. Instead, the approach views decision making as a process of successively comparing alternative courses of action until the team arrives at an alternative they can agree upon.

Instead of proposing an exhaustive analysis of many possible courses of action, the method of successive limited comparisons (as its name suggests) involves a drastically limited analytical process that ignores many alternatives and many important outcomes. It requires teams to consider only alternatives that are very similar to the current state of affairs, to focus analysis only upon differences between the current state and the alternative under consideration, and to ignore all outcomes of any alternative that are outside their own sphere of interest and concern. In this way the complexity of the decision-making process is brought within the feasible physical and mental bounds of decision makers.

4.4. Mini Case: Out Of Order

Conrad Jones is President of River Rock Country Club, located in Green Springs, Arkansas. At the Club annual meeting, he is presenting the concept of the need to replace the antiquated, point-to-point irrigation system on the golf course at a total cost of $250,000. The club does not have a reserve for replacement; therefore, the funding for such a capital improvement will be funded by the 100 stock-holding members. We look in on President Jones as one of the founding members of the Club levels an attack against the project:

Mr. Falsworth, your comment may be relevant, but it is out of order. Please wait until it is time for questions and comments.

Look Conrad, I have been a member of this club since before you were born. If you think I am going to wait until you have finished your diatribe about the reasons we should vote for a new irrigation system—to the tune of $250,000—you are out of your mind.

Mr. Falsworth, your comments are out of order. Please wait until it is time for questions and comments.

Conrad, you may be the President of this club, but that does not mean that you can railroad us into an on-going assessment. I demand that you hear me out. I demand that you hear what

I have to say. I was in law practice with your father for over 30 years. If he had any idea of the way you are running this club, he would turn over in his grave. I demand that you let me speak. I cannot sit here and listen to a bunch of bunk about why the Club needs to spend $250,000. Just lower the dues and we will get by with what we have.

Mr. Falsworth, you are out of order. If you cannot wait until it is time for questions and comments, I will have to ask you to leave the meeting. Please do not make me call security to escort you out.

Discussion Question

Have you ever experienced a situation such as this at the Club? Given the material presented in the text, what are some of the major advantages to structured forms of decision making? What is your evaluation of the way in which Conrad Jones, the Club President handled the situation with Gilbert Falsworth? Given the situation, what (if anything) would you have done differently?

Manager Response 1

Capital projects are often funded by member assessment. At times, assessments must be voted in by a super majority (2/3rds voting in favor) for it to be approved making presentation to the members more difficult and much more thorough.

The case suggests advantages of structured forms of decision making. Consensus mapping helps a team with different perspectives arrive at a shared image of a problem and mutually agreeable solutions through in-depth discussion about interrelationships and synergy among items.

One benefit of consensus mapping is that key results of the discussion are documented. Procedural Rationality states that rational procedures need to be designed in such a way that they capitalize on the strengths of human beings as problem solvers and decision-makers. These strengths lie in the ability to employ insight and experience in identifying a small number of alternatives for further exploration and analysis.

Successive limited comparisons do not require total agreement on objectives, exhaustive analysis of all possible alternatives and outcomes, or determination of the optimal alternative. The approach views decision-making as a process of successful comparing alternative course of action until the team arrives at an alternative they can agree upon. It only considers alternatives similar to the current state of affairs and focuses on differences between the current state and the alternative under consideration.

Conrad Jones should have presented the Club members with similar alternatives to replacing the irrigation system on the golf course. He should have allowed the members to participate in the decision-making process, especially since he needed their support to be successful. The choice given to the membership should not have been whether to do the project or not. The presentation should have been a detailed presentation of alternatives, so he could not only prove to the members that he had carefully considered options, but that they would have a say in the final outcome. This was an example of poor execution on Conrad Jones' part.

Manager Response 2

I have been in several situations where members voice their opinion to the Board or President of the Board. In those situations, as in the instance described in the mini case, it is important to explain the reasons before a decision is made, or why a particular direction is being taken, after a thorough analysis of a situation. For instance, at a club where I worked a few years ago, I made a presentation to the Board recommending the investment of capital dollars into the pool complex to maintain the facilities and not lose the members who were utilizing the pool. I also made another presentation to the Board for renewal of the employees' health insurance. In both cases, we formed a group of employees and/or members and conducted sessions to help resolve the issue by investigating alternatives. Using formal groups allowed us to include those individuals whom the decision would affect and get a wide range of input/feedback. In each case, the presentations passed without further discussion, because we presented the step-by-step decision making process which explained how we arrived at our decision.

In this mini case whereby a member made it a point to inform the President that his ideas must be listened to is a fair request. Members—especially those who own part of the Club—need to be informed as to how a decision was made and what alternatives were considered to make the decision. If you are going to implement an assessment, members will want to know the decision making process of how the Board reached their findings. In this case, the President should have presented the problem along these lines: *Our irrigation system is out-of-date and does not operate reliably. We have spent $2 million on a renovation of our greens and tees and need to maintain this investment. Therefore, we need our water supply to be reliable. The current system is 40 years old and is unreliable.* Then the President could provide a synopsis of the step-by-step methods used to come to the decision of purchasing a $250,000 system. Again, if the President gives the rationale as to how the decision was made, what decision making process was used, who was involved, the research conducted, bids placed, and the overall game plan, then members would feel more reassured and justified in spending funds for the golf course irrigation system.

This mini case describes a golf course irrigation situation, but the process of ensuring that members know that their money is being spent wisely is an important tenet to remember in any situation. This time spent on detail and reassurance is especially important when it involves a possible assessment.

Manager Response 3

It can be assumed that Conrad has had previous meetings with the General Manager, the Golf Course Superintendent, the Golf Committee, the Green(s) Committee, the Long-Range Planning Committee, and the Finance Committee. These meetings should have been held to discuss the need for the new system, the method of payment of the new system, and any alternatives that may be used to cut expenses, or whether there may be viable alternatives to a new system.

Once the meeting began, I have also assumed that Conrad is prepared to discuss the alternatives mentioned above and their rationale. His presentation would conclude with the only feasible, logical, and long term economic solution for the Club.

Recalling past experience with similar circumstances, other members of the Club usually help calm someone like Mr. Falsworth. After the situation settles, members request the information as to the where, why, and how on the project, which has not already been provided. When questions have been answered, Mr. Jones has the opportunity to convey his request and allow the opportunity to vote.

Conrad Jones calling Mr. Falsworth to order and instructing him to wait would be the normal process. I do not, however, agree with threats to have him removed. Assuming that the members had not yet intervened, it seems more advisable to allow Mr. Falsworth to take the floor and vent. Jones should yield to Falsworth only after making it plain to the crowd that he is graciously conceding the floor. Jones should try to swing the crowd toward the rational instead of to the absurd.

Manager Response 4

I have never experienced a situation such as this at my club. Our annual meeting is conducted via proxy. If three members attend it is considered crowded. However, I have been present at other Board meetings and association meetings where conflicting viewpoints need to be expressed. In order for the process to go forward in a fair, equitable, and organized manner there must be ground rules. These ground rules or structured forms of decision making include parliamentary procedure, alternative examination procedure, and information search procedure. When a team or group utilizes such decision making, it adheres to a highly systematic decision making process. Structured techniques promote constructive criticism, non conformity, and open mindedness within the decision making team.

However, one must also consider that since it is impossible for decision makers to ensure that they have made the optimal rational decision, they should turn their attention to the design of methods or procedures for decision making that will be most likely to generate the best possible decisions within the constraints of human judgment and insight. By implementing and following a predetermined set of ground rules increases the chance of communication by all members that transforms disagreement into critical thinking. There is an opportunity for all people involved to express their views, listen to the views of others, and debate positions on the issues in a systematic and efficient way.

Conrad Jones handled the situation with Gilbert Falsworth in an appropriate manner. Conrad was polite and courteous when addressing Gilbert. He simply asked that Gilbert wait his turn and express his views on the irrigation installation at the appropriate time. At some point, it was necessary for Conrad to inform Gilbert that procedures had to be followed. If Conrad had not stuck to his guns, he would have risked losing control of the meeting. He had an obligation to all members attending the meeting to run it in an organized and efficient manner. I would not have done anything different.

Manager Response 5

It can be assumed that Conrad has had previous meetings with the General Manager, Greens and Grounds Superintendent, and the Golf Director. These meeting should have been held to discuss the need for the new system, the method of payment of the new system, and any alternatives that may be used to cut expenses or make alternatives to a new system. It should also be assumed that the membership has been made aware of the proposal in advance and that the paid staff has had the opportunity to analyze the positive and negative ramifications of the proposal.

Once the meeting began, I was also assuming, Conrad was prepared to discuss the alternatives mentioned above and their rational, arriving at the decision in the only feasible, logical, and long term economical manner.

Recalling past experience in similar circumstances, the members of the Club usually stand-up and help calm someone like Mr. Falsworth, or chastise him for being so cantankerous. After confrontations such as this have been cooled by the members, then they (the reasonable members) request further information regarding the where, why and how. It is likely that other members feel strongly, too, just not as loudly as Falsworth. After an explanation period, Conrad Jones has the opportunity to repeat his proposal and allow the opportunity for members to vote. It should be noted that a vote is inappropriate until everyone is informed. Much of this work should be done in advance, long before the annual meeting.

I agree with the first steps taken by Mr. Jones. Calling Falsworth to order and instructing him to wait would be the normal process. I do not, however, agree with threats to have him removed from the meeting. If the members had not quieted the rowdy member, it would have been advisable to allow Mr. Falsworth to vent. Mr. Falsworth would probably not have done a convincing job of making his case to the other members. I would have only given Mr. Falsworth the floor after making it clear that I was doing so in the spirit of openness. Trying to swing the crowd toward openness, rational thinking, and what is best for the Club is the high road and the way to accomplish club projects.

Manager Response 6

The major advantages to structured forms are that they yield higher results on complex problems and facilitate a team's focus to the situation at hand. Generation of higher quality and quantity of ideas that nets a higher consensus is what we strive for in clubs. Ideas are documented and are often spun off of to help create alternatives, and ultimately to make more educated decisions.

I have assumed that the guidelines were drawn for the participants before the meeting started. The way Mr. Jones conducted himself was admirable. He acted as the facilitator that held the floor. He was level headed and followed a structured course of action. By doing so, he kept control over the situation.

The member was indeed out of line. Conrad could have diffused the situation and let Falsworth tell his side, but it would have probably brought about a lengthy diatribe and filibuster. A similar situation happened at our club when a vote to approve a conceptual master plan was on the table. Tension was high. An assessment of $20, 000 was imminent. The timing and the finances were in line, the approval of the membership was a close vote. In the end, it was approved. There were many sub-groups of members expressing various scenarios and hoping to influence those who were undecided. The President diffused the situation by acting according to the bylaws and following the meeting structure.

The President, in demonstrating strong leadership, did the right thing for the Club. If in the same or similar situation, I hope that I could be as strong. I would express the desire that his voice be heard, but under the guidelines set forth by the Club.

If he then were still disruptive, I would have to cut him off. Their history definitely has some bearing on the matter in that he was starting a personal attack on Mr. Jones.

Manager Response 7

I have never witnessed a situation exactly like the one described. However, I have witnessed members acting out of order at these types of meetings. In the situations that I have encountered, the executive committee, who was directing the annual meeting, handled the situation well. Usually, a member of the committee would allow the member to finish his or her statement and then reply, in a strong yet polite tone, that stated the member was not speaking at the correct time. In other meetings I have attended, a member from the Sergeant at Arms Committee would speak to the member talking out of turn, if need be. I have never witnessed a meeting that has gotten more out of control than what I just described.

Major advantages to structured forms of decision making.

Structured decision making allows different teams of different make-up to follow the same decision making process. No matter the situation or the people, we can be assured that the process and guidelines adhered to are consistent through the organization, regardless of team, department, or area of responsibility within the Club. This is beneficial from the point of the GM and Board. Additionally, structured groups allow for greater capacity and better quality decisions. Other benefits allow for constructive criticism, non-conformity, and greater open-mindedness.

Evaluation of the way in which Conrad Jones, the Club President, handled the situation with Gilbert Falsworth.

It is not *what* the Club President said; it is *how* he said what he said. I am a believer in that you can tell anyone anything, but it is the way that you say it that makes the difference. Members want to be heard, especially one that is standing up at the annual meeting.

The club President seemed defensive in his reply, almost as if he was anticipating Mr. Falsworth to say something. An effective President should be aware of who may say what and be prepared for a worst case scenario discussion. However, the President should not elevate his tone and manner to that level as soon as the speaker speaks. Mr. Jones should have let Mr. Falsworth finish his comments and then stated something along these lines: *Mr. Falsworth, the committee and Board appreciate your thoughts and comments and we take all input seriously. However, following the agenda and standard annual meeting guidelines, we need to postpone taking comments from the floor until the appropriate time on the agenda. If you will please just hold your comments for a little while longer, we will give you ample time to state your concerns.*

Lesson 6

Unstructured Decision Making

Having discussed a variety of popular and effective structured forms of decision making, we now focus our attention on four highly-evolved forms of unstructured decision making. If we consider *true* leadership to be both science and art, structured decision making would fall on the science side of the ledger while unstructured decision making would belong on the art side of the ledger. Experienced leaders often consider these forms of unstructured decision some of their most effective tools in gaining influence and deciding issues.

Consensus

Consensus is an informal approach which encourages the expression of cognitive conflict among team members without providing an explicit structure for team interaction. The team is instructed to be suspicious of early agreement, to encourage each member to fully express his or her opinions, and to treat disagreement as a positive part of the decision-making process. The goal is to strive for consensus among all members, not to opt for a majority rule, coin flips or other techniques to reach recommendations (Priem).

Leader Prerogative

Even the most democratic organizations are likely to reserve some decisions for their designated leaders—shift supervisors, department managers, or the GM. In some cases where policy does not intrude, it may include issues such as assigning schedules, or making committee assignments. Teams or groups may also defer decisions to their leaders: *We will go along with what you think is best.*

Some organizations practice leader prerogative more than others. Managers are paid more because they have more responsibilities. If their departments make huge mistakes, it is often times the department managers that suffer the consequences. Managers are therefore given additional responsibilities of overriding their staffs' decisions.

Delegation, Referral, and Delay

Certain decisions a group deals with may be delegated to a subgroup such as a standing committee, an ad hoc committee, or an expert individual. This may be done democratically or autocratically, depending upon the organization and the nature of the issues involved.

Some clubs are so devised that certain decisions must be referred to special groups or teams. For example, a recommendation by the staff, to the GM, to the Board to re-build the greens, would likely be referred to the green(s) committee. In certain organizations there is even a committee on committees that must be consulted in special cases of overlap. In a club, such a committee would likely reside within the Board, perhaps in the executive committee. For example, a committee on committees may have to mitigate the conflicting demands of the golf committee recommendations for pin placements and greens height-of-cut for the upcoming member-guest tournament, and the green(s) committee and staff concerns for the agronomic results of such decisions.

Negotiation

Some decisions that involve divergent goals on the part of factions in a given group may necessitate compromises that are brought about by bargaining rather than some form of consensus seeking. *The union will back off on its wage demands if management will agree to provide staff uniforms.* Negotiations often call for third-party interventions: experts, consultants, lawyers, and mediators. These people try to help your group negotiate and reach a compromise. They do not typically make the decision. There are federal and state mediation services available when problems involve labor agreements. In the larger area of labor contracts, when bargaining breaks down, organizations face strikes, lockouts, and other forceful efforts to bring about good-faith agreement and bargaining.

When a work group and its leaders cannot solve day-to-day differences of opinion over work rules, contract interpretations, or perceptions of unfairness, many contracts provide for a grievance procedure that moves up the levels of higher authority if lower-level negotiation fails. When all bargaining attempts fail, some organizations have an arbitration clause in their agreement whereby the grieving parties agree on an arbitrator who hears the case and makes a binding decision.

4.5. Mini Case: The Swim Team

Lilly Walters is club manager at Ivory Belle Country Club located in New Orleans, Louisiana. The house and social committee has asked her to help them facilitate a consensus on use of the aquatic center. We join them after the meeting has started:

Lilly, we have the opportunity to build a Class-A, Junior-Olympic caliber swim team this summer, but we need the pool for a few extra hours during the day.

Mrs. Stewart, will you present your proposal?

Yes. Indeed I will. We need the pool from 7-9:30 AM for morning practice; from 9:30-10:30 for lessons and stroke clinics; and from 3:00-5:30 PM for afternoon practice. I do not think that will create a problem, will it?

Hi. My name is Wilma Fuddwhistle. I would like to ask a question. What do you propose to do with the Water Babies, the pool aerobics group for seniors that uses the pool every morning from 9:00-9:30 AM?

Hey, my name is Wally Grand. The masters swim club practices every day from 4:00-6:00 PM. What about us?

My name is Louis L'Enfant. I have been a member at this fine club for over 50 years. I like to have the opportunity to relax at the pool without all of these structured activities—just to sit in the Sun and have a cocktail. I cannot enjoy myself with all these kids and activities going on. I worked all my life to be able to enjoy my club. You are driving me away if I cannot relax. All of the other members feel that way, too. They asked me to come here today to represent their point of view. We do not yell and scream, but we are among the silent majority at the Club. Think about that before you make a poor decision.

Discussion Question

If you were in Lilly Walters' position as the GM how would you facilitate this meeting into a consensus? The Board of the Club has authorized you to help the committee come to a decision. You cannot pass the buck.

Manager Response 1

I see no way to make all of this result in an optimal arrangement for all constituencies involved. There are too many competing elements to make everything work smoothly. There are a few adjustments that can be made, however, which may result in it being tolerable.

It seems there is enough time in the day to reschedule the Water Babies to keep Wilma content and to shift some time to keep Wally and the Masters Swim Club happy. Mr. L'Enfant, on the other hand, might never be content. It seems as though adding more structured time to the pool hours, will be met with discontent by several of the members.

Someone needs to ask the question, *How important is it to have a Junior Olympic caliber team?*, and then weigh the necessary concessions against the importance of the answer.

A solution will emerge when parties continue discussion and see how much the groups are willing to compromise. Perhaps Mr. L'Enfant and his friends would be content if they were given a block of time, which could be counted upon as set. It would be a period they could always count on for relaxation by the pool. There is also a possibility that the Masters Swim Club could use a lane or two in the afternoon and share the pool.

If they all would be willing to give a bit, a compromise could emerge that would work for all involved.

Manager Response 2

Consensus is an informal approach that encourages the expression of cognitive conflict among team members without providing an explicit structure for team interaction. Members are encouraged to express opinions and treat disagreement as a positive part of the decision-making process.

If I were Lily, I would be striving for consensus among members. Each person's complaint would be considered and discussed at length. Each member would be encouraged to contribute his or her thoughts, no matter how negative the input may seem

The goal is to have a class A, Junior Olympic caliber swim team this summer with as little inconvenience to the members as possible. Allowing members to express their concerns involves them in the process and thereby increases the considerations we need to take when making a final decision.

The amount of time the swim team uses the pool may have to be compromised and some of the member demands will have to be met. On the other hand, some of the member time may have to be reduced to accommodate the swim team. Each side will have to work it out possibly giving up something to come up with an agreeable schedule for the summer.

Manager Response 3

It appears that Lilly is in a committee meeting where everyone has their own personal agenda.

With everyone worrying over their own issues, it may be advised to begin by drawing a time line and inserting the schedule of events that is already committed. By discussing the time line and working with the committee members, an attempt can be made to have some schedules shifted to include the extra added time requested, even if not at the time requested. Lily will need to first gain agreement that a Class-A, Junior-Olympic swim team is wanted by the committee. Then, the idea would be to try to develop a plan and time frame that will allow for all the activities.

Allow each member the opportunity to have his or her say on the swim team and to explain the reason as to why they are opposed. Encourage each opposing member to explain why the proposal will not work. We often find that by encouraging this discussion, individuals get the negatives out of the way and other members counter the negatives with a solution. Once each member has had his or her turn, we usually find a number of viable solutions.

Each member needs to be persuaded to cooperate during the initial period of implementation. In order for the plan to work, members must be willing to make adjustments. Mr. L'Enfant will be the type of member who will pose the biggest challenge. When a member states the words, *I have been a member for 50 years*; Lilly should become alerted to the difficulty of the task ahead.

Members can be persuaded to adopt schedules that can serve everyone's needs, they provide the solutions themselves by brainstorming, negotiating, and finding consensus. The 50 year member will probably try to find fault with everyone. However, the membership will handle him accordingly.

Lilly must use her leadership and persuasion skills to bring this issue to a resolution.

Manager Response 4

Lilly Walters has certainly got her work cut out for her. The good news is the meeting participants do not need much coaxing or encouragement to express their thoughts and desires for the use of the pool. It is also positive that the Board has authorized Lilly to help the committee come to a decision today, which empowers her to act more autocratically than normal, and to practice leader prerogative. The bad news is that there are many demands for the use of the pool, and a consensus decision might have to give way to bargaining. No matter the decision reached, not everyone is going to be completely satisfied. Each individual group will have to make concessions for the general welfare of the Club.

- Since Lilly is the GM, she is familiar with these fundamental elements of the Club: the mission statement and goals of the Ivory Belle Country Club
- A historical reference for past pool use
- Who represents whom and how many of the membership

- Who is asking for unreasonable time blocks
- The Board's inclination in this scenario
- The ramifications on operating procedures and budgets

For these and other reasons, Lilly Walters should take control of the meeting and put forward her best guesstimate of a workable schedule as a starting point for negotiation. She should be careful to give each representative a specified rotation and time limit to express their amended views and proceed. The committee members that are present, together with the representatives, must stay in that room until the bargaining is transformed into consensus. Given a starting point and even-tempered supervision, the group of representative stakeholders will do the right thing for the Club as a whole. If the group leaves that meeting in general agreement, then Lilly Walters will have done a great job in addressing this issue.

Manager Response 5

If I were Lilly, I would thank everyone for their feedback and then request a member from each organization (junior swim; junior group; members who like to relax without noise; etc.) to join me in a committee to formulate a game plan to try please everyone's group to the extent that we possibly could. I would lead the meeting by listing all the groups which use the pool, times requested, and demographics of each group. Then we would list the various schedules that would accommodate the groups. I would solicit suggestions/alternatives and collect all the data possible to make a decision. Although the Board wants the GM to handle the issue, I would still present to the Board my decision and how I came to my conclusion. I would list the step-by-step process that we used as a committee to make the new schedule. I would also publicize this process in the newsletter, so all members would be educated as to how the process and decision evolved for the betterment of the entire membership.

Manager Response 6

The problem is not uncommon. The Board does not want to look like the *bad guy* and thus passes the buck. As the paid executive of the Club there are a number of steps, which must be followed to help ensure a positive outcome. First, I would identify the problem. Second, get input from a wide number of members and staff. Third, make a preliminary decision. Fourth, float the possible decision. Fifth, consider input and adjust. Sixth, communicate the decision and set a timeframe for implementation. This process can go on for some time— especially since the decision is not going to satisfy everyone completely.

However logical and elegant the decision may seem, the fact that people are going to need to compromise, suggests the need for the manager to exercise a high degree of tact and diplomacy.

Manager Response 7

Delegation, referral, delay, decide—that would be my short list of to dos, if I were Lilly Walters. I would have the meeting begin as it did in the scenario. But, after it began to turn into a gripe session, I might make a suggestion to the two committee chairs. My suggestion would be that instead of having a joint committee meeting with so many attendees, that each group should go back to their respective committee.

Each committee would draft a list of benefits and disadvantages to having the swim team. Then, each committee would nominate two people to serve on the joint, ad-hoc committee formed to research and come to a solution about the use of the pool. However, before doing so, I would make sure that the entire group of people was supplied with basic information.

First, the bylaws of the Club and each committee would be presented. Assuming there is no pool or swim committee, maybe now is the time to form a standing subcommittee, or a new committee, depending on the nature and culture of the Club. Second, I would ensure that we had agreement as to the mission statement of the pool operation, or at least what is the focus of the pool operation. For example, is the pool operation for member and guest pleasure, to provide an alternative for the non-golfers, or is it more for sport usage and skill development for the youth of the Club membership? Several answers need to be reached or at least presented to the membership before deliberation can occur. As a GM, it is our job to manage the policies and rules set forth by the governing bodies of the Club. (The members should decide as to how the pool will be used, not the GM.) The GM will ensure that the group is fully informed to make the best decision possible with long term goals of the membership in mind.

As we know, even though we seemed to be pigeon-holed in this situation, when the manager is used as the scapegoat, the manager will be looking for a new job. Those that do not like the outcome, regardless of position, will blame the General Manager, if it surfaces that the GM is deciding club policy instead of executing policy. So, getting back to our process, I would then suggest that the two representatives from each committee serve on this new ad-hoc committee and, representing all issues under consideration, make a final decision and report back to the house and social committee chairs. The four members of the ad-hoc will present their findings to the two chairs and a decision will be made and presented to the House and Social Committees at their next meetings.

Results of this process include: decision made, the GM still being employed, a majority of people being happy, and we publicize the outcome as a trial year. We will have all compromised and made some children happy in the process.

Competing Motives

Team members have dual or competing motives since they act as both individuals and team members. Silver's two stage model illustrates this dualistic information exchange.

Stage 1: Individual members can lose status if they give information that they know will receive negative evaluation, especially if this negative evaluation comes from high status members. An individual will often give only information that allows him/her to maintain his/her status. This type of information exchange helps the individual, but it may hurt the team. (Consider a Working Women's Tennis Team member contributing to the Tennis Committee, which is essentially run by A-Team tennis players.)

Stage 2: The team member will take a chance and go beyond this minimum level of information exchange in order to contribute to team decision quality. The increment the member accepts is proportional to his or her status (consider the high status of the men's golf champion serving on the green[s] committee), and is the basis for the initiation of ideas and negative evaluations.

Silver posits that Information exchange happens under the following requisite conditions:

1. Members occupying positions in a team have some basis to judge their own relative status position.
2. Members are motivated to avoid status loss. The motive to avoid status loss is greater than the motive to gain status.
3. Members are motivated to contribute to the team objective.
4. Members expect that the amount and type of information they send will influence the amount and type of information that they will receive. Thus, they at least implicitly recognize the causal relationship between information initiation and evaluation by others.

Ideas and negative evaluations contribute the most to the quality of team decisions; however, sending both of these information types, according to Silver, is characterized by higher expected status costs than sending data, questions, or positive evaluations. Most information exchanges will be messages of low risk (such as data), whether or not the information contributes to the task. In an effort to maintain status, members will not initiate negative evaluations. High-status members will over receive positive evaluations.

In teams with large status differences between members and low commitment to team objectives by medium and low status members, there exist: 1) Numerous ideas and of negative evaluations; 2) High proportions of positive evaluations sent to high status members; 3) High proportions of non participators.

Teams will produce the highest quality decision when the ideas and negative evaluations occur in whatever becomes defined as an ideal proportion.

Lesson 7

Advantages of Team Decision Making

Does participation in team decision making increase the level of understanding and acceptance of team decisions among individual members? Does participation in team decision making increase members' commitment to executing team decisions? According to Higgins and O'Hair, the answer to these questions is generally yes.

Many times the team can provide a superior solution to that of an individual. Teams can bring a greater sum total of knowledge and information to bear on a problem. A single individual who makes a decision is constrained to rely on his or her own limited personal knowledge. When several people make a decision jointly, more information can be brought to bear on the issue.

For example, a manager may be trying to decide how to allocate funds for pay raises among entry-level subordinates in the building maintenance department. If the manager were to sit down alone to make the pay raise decisions, he or she would have only formal performance evaluations and some random anecdotal evidence about the performance of these employees. By meeting with the chief engineer and the employees' immediate supervisors to discuss worker evaluations, the manager could elicit much richer data about the employees' individual performances.

Team participation leads to a better understanding of the decision. For example, if the GM involves all levels of management in the budget process from the beginning, everyone is aware of the process as the iterations evolve. In the end, all levels of management have a better understanding of where they ended up with respect to everyone else.

People who participate in team decision making are more committed to the team's decisions than to those given by a manager.

Using our example of the Club budget process, by involving all managers, everyone has had their opportunity to present their requests and reasoning in the marshaling of resources process. While not all departments will be satisfied with the outcome, they will most certainly understand and thereby be more likely to support the decisions.

Teams help ensure a broader search effort. Individual decisions are strongly affected by personal values, beliefs, competencies, goals, and personalities which can unknowingly distort and bias outcomes (Bowditch). For example, if we are from marketing, we tend to focus primarily on the planning, promoting, advertising, and selling aspects of club decisions. If we are from finance, we focus mostly on the accounting and cash flow aspects of club decisions. If we are from food and beverage, we focus mainly on the logistics of production and service when we make decisions. When a decision has to be made that affects many parts of the Club, it is often useful to employ a team so that "blind spots" in the decision can be identified early and better solutions devised.

Risk is balanced. Individuals who are high-risk takers often fail. Teams moderate this desire. Teams also encourage the risk avoider to take more risks since fixing of blame is shared by all participants.

For example, the buyer in the golf pro shop may be a high risk taker. If all buying decisions were left to him, the pro shop may still have 57 pairs of men's pink and black Foot Joy golf shoes in stock from a poor purchasing decision made more than 10 years ago. On the other hand, the pro shop manager may be a risk avoider. If all buying decisions were left to her, the pro shop may still be buying only solid-colored golf shirts and khaki slacks. By combining forces and involving other staff members, too, the Club can benefit from the flair of the buyer, the conservatism of the shop manager, and the breadth of input from other members of the professional staff.

Teams offer the extra-task virtues of constituency representation, the sometimes pleasures of social interaction ...and in the end *may foster confidence in and commitment to whatever decision the team may reach* (Davis).

4.6. Mini Case: Sam's Scotches

Sam Veal, GM of Flaminghills Club, in Coyote Canyon, New Mexico, rounded the corner of the clubhouse, only to be stopped by Susan Witherspoon, food and beverage director.

Could I have a minute, Sam?

Sure, what is on your mind?

I am a bit confused. In yesterday's meeting, you decided that we should reduce the number of single-malt scotches from 15 down to three. What is the idea?

Well, it just seems to me that 15, very expensive scotches on a bar that only does $2,000 a week in sales is about 12 too many. No big deal. Just let your inventory work down.

Sam, if I can be honest, did it ever occur to you to ask me, or Pablo Gomez (lead bartender) or Jere Kramer (shift bartender) for some input before making that decision?

No. I am the GM.

Okay, Sam, we will take care of it.

Good. I expect for you to get it done efficiently.

Discussion Question

In this case, how could team input have helped Sam make a better decision?

Manager Response 1

Team input could have helped Sam make a better decision, because a team approach is capable of bringing a greater sum total of knowledge and information to bear on a problem. It is possible that eight different single malt scotches are regularly consumed by eight different Board members, three more are offered at premium catering events, four more are the favorites of four big spenders, and the fifteenth one is the pouring brand. Unless Sam is aware of this information through his management people, he risks making a decision that could negatively affect the satisfaction level of members at his club.

Sam is viewing this scenario from a financial perspective, and as a result, his individual decision making process is biased. He is probably making a sound theoretical decision based on inventory management principles, but that is a shortsighted view from a marketing standpoint. In all probability, this is a small club ($2,000/week in beverage sales) and should be able to cater to the individual tastes of the membership. The elimination of 80 percent of the single malt scotches without input from his team is analogous to driving blind and is likely to upset more than a few members who have gotten used to their private stock being available at the Club.

Sam's decree to *just run the inventory down* and the elimination of the team decision process is preventing the management team from better understanding his financially based decision. If Sam had been willing to interact with Susan, Pablo, and Jere he might have either reached a more effective decision or have been able to better educate the workers as to what he was trying to accomplish. This participation process would have also given Sam's colleagues a better opportunity to become committed to the eventual decision. Even if they did not totally agree with the decision, they could at least understand why that decision had been reached and consequently support it. By thrusting his decision down on the team, Sam has lessened the chances of full cooperation and successful implementation by his staff. Sam is not utilizing the insights his team members have to offer and may have some serious explaining to do down the road.

Manager Response 2

Sam has made a hasty decision based on logic alone. However, issues in clubs are not always dealt with most effectively by using logic alone.

The Food and Beverage director is 100 percent correct. Why did Sam not consult her, the lead bartender, and the shift bartender? There is a reason why 15 single-malt scotches are inventoried in the first place. Often times, certain members like particular brands. In a club, you try as best you can to accommodate all members' wants and needs. If Sam had met with his managers, he may have learned that by discontinuing 12 single-malt scotches may save him a few dollars in purchases but cost him $100,000.00 in headaches.

What is he going to do when the members who were drinking these now discontinued scotches can no longer sip their favorite brands? As Creedence Clearwater Revival used to sing, *I see a bad moon rising. I see trouble on the way.*

Without a doubt, getting input from his managers would have enabled Sam to make a more intelligent decision. This situation is headed toward the ditch.

Manager Response 3

There is, no doubt, animosity in not being included in the decision-making process. Not only is Susan upset, but Pablo and Jere are upset, as well. They should be upset. Sam pulled a power move that will not work in implementation.

Sam should not play the position card. People do not appreciate a power answer—even though they know, full well, that he is the boss. In fact, Sam's answer is not an answer at all. Instead, it is an insult. *I am the GM* does not need to be stated. People are aware of positions. And, a GM should reflect that status by be an effective leader. Part of being an effective leader is by being approachable and open around the staff.

Susan likely knows more about the operational side of the F&B department that does the GM. Also, the bartenders have a better grasp of the impact on the members by reducing the scotch offerings. They should have been involved from the beginning.

Sam has made the management thing more difficult than it has to be. For example, the negative member response to this policy will almost assuredly cause Sam to reverse the decision. Sam will lose credibility with the members and the staff.

Manager Response 4

Sam is making a decision based on the hard-core factual numbers side of management. There might actually be huge potential for greater single malt scotch sales. About to enter a new position myself, I am reminded that one must see why people are doing things the way that they are before trying to change the situation. The employees in this case have obviously come to be mired in this predicament for several reasons.

What Sam should do is first pose the questions to the group of people involved, including the greater food and beverage team. *Why do we have so many single malt scotches with so little sales? Can we increase the sales of these items? How do you as individuals think this can happen?* And then, as a group, *how can we make this happen at all?* For example, a brainstorming session followed by an assessment of ideas and selection of the best outcomes would help tremendously in making the correct decision about scotches.

By following this type of decision-making process, Sam will help to develop employees who feel more involved in and better about their work and the environment in which they produce. When the employees feel better, they will work harder and contribute more to the organization, as well as stand up favorably for the operation and its leaders more readily. Loyalty will be generated. Additionally, Sam might also tap into a fantastic outcome of increased sales, which will make everyone happier. And, as we know, success breeds success. By creating the type of an open decision-making culture, the Club will improve in more ways than Sam may ever know, if as a GM he continues to make line level operational decisions, and then forces these decisions downward on his employees.

The concept that Dr. Ed Merritt teaches in his workshops is referred to as *learned helplessness*. The idea is that if managers always push their decisions downward on employees, then the employees will not make their own decisions, as there is too much at risk of being wrong and being blamed. Instead, they will wait for answers and direction even to the most basic situations. The Club becomes paralyzed and the manager cannot understand why he or she can never get away from the Club without being called at home.

What we should be doing is encouraging our employees by getting them involved in the decision-making process at all levels. This is especially true since service is delivered to our members largely unsupervised. Therefore, we should strive for employees to be ready, willing, and able to make decisions which favor the member by applying the *golden rule*.

Manager Response 5

Team input could have made a positive difference in this instance. Sam could have had the controller look at inventory turnover facts and he could have shared those with the food and beverage department. This decision could have been taken to a higher level, whereby the mandate could have been to reduce overall liquor inventory, instead of singling out a particular category. Sam should not care about how many single-malt scotches he has. He should be more concerned with an overall reduction in inventory.

I am also concerned with the attitude of the bar staff and how the decision will be relayed to the members. If a single-malt scotch drinker comes in and the bartender does not have what he wants, we all know how this will be handled! Single-malt scotch drinkers are particular about their drinks. So, the General Manager has set himself up for all kinds of problems being linked to this decision.

Once again, the better way to have handled this issue would have been to discuss the situation with the food and beverage director and let her know that inventory needs to be reduced. Then Sam should leave it to her to discuss with her team and come up with a solution. This will establish buy-in from the team and will not include micro-management from the General Manager.

His, *I am the General Manager*, comment will also get him into trouble. He is correct, but, he should know that he needs lots more people working with him rather than against him! This type of statement and attitude puts the G.M. out there alone, and is a dangerous position for him.

Manager Response 6

I do not agree with Sam's tactics. Sam is trying to do everything himself—and it does not work in a club environment.

Susan, Pablo, and Jere all have a good reason to be upset about the way that this decision was pushed down on top of them without discussion.

If it were me I would do the same thing as Susan did, and follow Sam's direction, but I would talk with him later about the way he came up with his decision. Then, I would go back to the Pablo and Jere and ask them what they think of the idea and who drinks what. I would download sales from the POS on those scotches that he wanted removed and base my findings on the facts.

If Sam had asked the key employees what they thought, he may still have made the same decision. However, by making an informed, educated decision, he would then have a rational reason as to why when that one member demands to have his favorite scotch. The decision would be longer lasting, better informed, and followed more by the staff if they were involved. And, the GM could share the risk of the decision, too. The move that he made was very risky.

Manager Response 7

Using the team process would have made a significant positive impact on this decision. Sam, the manager, appears to know everything that there is to know and makes a decision without doing any analysis. If the goal was to reduce inventory, perhaps it could have been achieved by checking usage or by asking the bartender what sells and what does not. The Board of Board may be made up of single malt drinkers. Whose brand do we choose to eliminate? Maybe Sam needs to make that decision. But then, he needed to get the right information and do some analysis if he wanted to make an effective decision.

He needed to get the right people involved and review some reports. The Food & Beverage team would be able to help Sam make the right decision. In the end, the right answer may have been to cut back the number of single malts. However, that decision should have come after discussion and analysis.

Lesson 8

Challenges in Team Decision Making

Groupthink

In interactive teams, there is social pressure to conform. Sometimes these teams become guilty of what is known as *groupthink*, which can be defined as a dysfunctional process by which people begin to think alike and one where new ideas or ideas contrary to the group's ideas are not tolerated.

Janis described groupthink as a decline in mental efficiency, reality testing, and moral judgment that comes about as a result of in-group pressure. Group members sometimes tend to overlook critical elements of tasks because they do not wish to disagree with consensus. Such a tendency creates a strange paradox. Teams should permit a free exchange of ideas including misgivings about decisions. On the other hand, a pleasant atmosphere is comfortable and congenial. Members may sense that a minority opinion will upset this atmosphere. Effective team meetings are based on a pleasant interpersonal atmosphere. However, when a team's goal becomes one of solidarity and unanimity, whereby disputes are not tolerated, productivity will be undermined. We suggest that teams recognize this danger and consciously emphasize the free exchange of ideas and information.

Certain conditions favor the development of groupthink. One of the antecedents is high cohesiveness. Highly cohesive groups can tend to avoid conflicts and to expect conformity. Other antecedents include a directive leader, high levels of stress, group insulation from the outside, and a lack of procedures for developing and examining alternatives. Having responsibility for making highly consequential or controversial decisions and having limited time constraints to make such decisions can foster groupthink. When team members feel that they have only a limited amount of time to make a decision, they may rush through the process and make a hasty decision. These situations can cause other team members to prefer concurrence in decisions and to fail to evaluate the available information critically.

Janis offered these guidelines in helping to prevent Groupthink:

- Promote open discussion and feedback. Solicit input from conflicting viewpoints.

- Ensure the team leader does not state his or her position before the decision.

- Break the team into sub groups and work on the problem concurrently.

- Bring in outsiders to help work on the problem.

- Establish a *devil's advocate* (contrary) position to consistently question the group's standpoint.

- Pose as many different motivations and intentions as is possible.

- Guard against premature agreement. Upon reaching a consensus, encourage the group to re-think its position once again by examining alternatives. Formulate contingency plans for things going wrong.

- Avoid emotional reactions. Protect independent, critical thinking—whatever the pressures to conform. If tempers flare, delay agreement until cooler heads can prevail. Janis refers to this as a *second chance* meeting.

Vigilant Interaction

Interaction is a social instrument that members use to discuss and shape decisions. In the past, according to Hirokawa, it was believed that it was through group interaction that the true determinants of group decision performance were able to work effectively. Theorists now realize that interaction plays an active role in determining team decision outcomes themselves.

In Vigilant Interaction Theory, the manner in which group members *talk* about the problems, options, and consequences that face the team affects the way they *think* about those problems, options, and consequences. This thinking, in turn, ultimately determines the quality of final choices they make as a group. The team's critical thinking process influences the quality of the decision.

Emotions

High levels of emotion hinder the capacity to think clearly, fostering misunderstanding and faulty communication within the group. However, Guzzo found that the expression of affective reactions by team members during the decision making process is almost always unavoidable and at least some expression of personal feeling is essential to decision making. On the other hand a manager can help the team *feel* less pressed for time by delaying the expression of affect until *after* the team has generated a list of alternative solutions and ideas.

Stress

The process of choosing among alternatives whose outcomes can never be perfectly anticipated can generate psychological stress and conflict. The level of stress experienced can vary from the relatively minor (as in choosing a wine to accompany an entree) to the totally debilitating (as in deciding which career to pursue or which job to accept). However, some moderate level of stress seems essential to create the motivation for the decision maker to engage in analysis and choice among alternatives. If only a low level of stress is generated by the decision problem (as in choosing a wine to accompany an entree), then the decision maker may not invest the time, energy, and effort required in a rational decision-making procedure. If, however, a decision situation generates a high level of stress, the high stress level may impede the decision maker's ability to engage systematically and objectively in careful analysis and choice. Hence, Arnold found that effective decision making only occurs when stress levels are sufficiently high to motivate the decision maker to engage in the process, but not so high as to be debilitating for the decision maker.

According to the centralization of authority hypothesis, when a team is making a decision under stress, subordinates will transfer the responsibility of the decision to the leader, while the leader becomes less likely to accept input from subordinates. Driskell proposed the alternative hypothesis—that under stress, *all* team members become more receptive to information provided by others. The study found that status was a significant determinant of group interaction. As expected, low status team members were more likely to defer to the decision inputs of higher status team members, and higher status team members were less likely to defer to subordinate team members. Low status members became even more willing to defer to others when under stress. High status team members under stress became more receptive to the task inputs of their partners (increased receptivity under stress). This result is contrary to the centralization-of-authority hypothesis.

According to Driskell, teams can make better decisions under stress by utilizing these suggestions:

- Building team cooperation that involves high and low status members,

- Recognizing subordinate team members' deferential behavior is a cooperative team status process rather than an individual affliction, and

- Using realistic training that simulates the potential overload under stressful conditions.

4.7. Mini Case: Golf Spikes

Mike Patrick, a member of Bellview Golf Club, located in Montclair, Nebraska, stepped just inside the upstairs entry to the Club onto the slate floor without first removing his golf spikes. *I will only be a minute. I am already late for my tee time. I just want to drop off my payment.*

Please, Mr. Patrick, you cannot come in on the upstairs level without first removing your golf shoes, warned assistant manager, Armondo Fiolla.

I am late; I will only be a minute.

It was too late. After a second step, everyone watched as Mr. Patrick slipped and lost his footing. His feet went upward toward the ceiling and his head went downward toward the hard slate floor. Wham! Blood began oozing from both of Mr. Patrick's ears creating small puddles on the floor.

Quick, somebody go get Reggie (Williams, the GM).

Get some towels. What should we do?

Go get Caroline (Duffy, the director of golf), she took a first aid course.

Chef Max knows how to do first aid, too.

Reggie, Caroline, and Chef Max all arrived at the scene within five minutes.

Armando began to describe the accident. *I asked him not to come in. He had on his cleats.*

Well, what do you think?

I do not know what to think.

Looks pretty bad, what do you think?

I have never seen anything like this, I pass.

His head is bleeding. I think we are supposed to stop the bleeding.

Yeah, but he is not breathing. I think we should get him breathing first.

What do you think we should do?

Maybe call an ambulance.

That might upset the other members.

Maybe we should call his wife and ask her what to do?

Max, call the police and ask them what we should do.

The police immediately dispatched the rescue squad. Mr. Patrick died before the ambulance arrived.

Discussion Question

While this story sounds farfetched, it is loosely based on an actual incident that occurred at a club not long ago. The point of the mini case is to illustrate that team decision making is not always the appropriate method to utilize. If you had been in Armando Fiolla's position when Mr. Patrick first entered the building, how would you have handled the situation with regard to the following points?

- Mr. Patrick's insistence on leaving on his cleats?

- Assuming the slip and fall happened anyway, what would you have done differently?

Manager Response 1

If Armando had thought carefully, the entire incident may have been avoided. At my club, I do not use specific job descriptions. While different areas of responsibility perform different tasks, we all have the same general job description. That is: Do whatever it requires to take excellent care of the members. Use your best judgment to get the job done! Armando's initial approach was flawed. Instead of first focusing on taking care of the member, his initial focus was on enforcing a rule. If Armando had offered to take the payment to the office for the member, there would have been no need for the member to enter the lobby.

If Mr. Patrick refused to give him the payment, Armando should have explained to Mr. Patrick the possible danger of walking on the slate floor while wearing cleats.

Assuming that Mr. Patrick entered and fell anyway, Armando should have immediately touched 911 and started first aid. All that time wasted asking various people what to do may have doomed the injured member. I assume that the blow to the head was serious to the point where the bleeding was quite heavy. Armando should have realized immediately that the injury was an emergency situation. And, in an emergency, employees should be trained to instantly take action to stop the bleeding and check for breathing. This is no time for a group decision.

Manager Response 2

I would not conclude that Mr. Patrick insisted on leaving on his cleats. He barely had time to enter the building. I probably would not have told Mr. Patrick he could not come in wearing his cleats. When seeing a member bend established policy, I step in to ask if there is something I can do for them. This usually stops the member in their action and allows me to redirect his or her effort. Once Patrick made the statement that he was late for a tee time and wanted to drop off his bill, I would have walked closer toward him and asked if I could please take the bill for him. This would have helped to enforce the rule and perhaps would have helped keep the accident from occurring. If done properly, it also could have established a perception of exceeding his expectations in the line of service. There would have been no mention of a member breaking the rules, nor should there be, unless the member persisted.

This was a life threatening situation. A person has suffered a fall that appears to have been fatal. Something of this nature is evidence of a club's worst nightmare becoming true, a member has died at the Club. High levels of emotion made the decision making process become blurred. However, the situation required clear thinking. Under these types of circumstances there is no time to gather other members of the staff to hold a meeting about what should happen next. By summoning other staff members and acting in a democratic leader mode, the participation would have yielded slower results. All the participants felt the urgency to act immediately. Everyone present should go into emergency mode with the leader taking charge in an authoritarian style and assigning duties, such as notifying 911, rendering appropriate first aid, considering privacy issues for the victim, considering the visual distress that other members will notice, contacting family members, sending a guide outside to help the rescue team reach the victim as quickly as possible, detouring concerned members from gathering at the scene, etc.

Manager Response 3

Armondo, the Assistant Manager, tried to stop Mr. Patrick from entering the clubhouse with his cleats on. Mr. Patrick chose to disregard Armondo's warning. In a private club setting, there is little that one can do at that moment to enforce the rules if a member wants to disobey them. Had Armondo been negligent in trying to stop Mr. Patrick, he may have received criticism that Mr. Patrick's death resulted from his negligence.

Armondo did his job admirably. Once Mr. Patrick fell however, the incident was poorly handled. It was a poor choice to have a group form to come up with the decision on how to handle this situation. Having no strong person to take control to make quick, conscious decisions may have led to Mr. Patrick's death.

The group: Armondo, Reggie, Carol and Max took five minutes to gather and more time to evaluate and assess the situation. Precious time was wasted while the group tossed out possible decisions without one person speaking up and taking control. The Assistant Manager should have immediately dialed 911 for emergency service. He should have then sent for the General Manager who could have contacted the team members most capable of handling this emergency. If the Chef or other department heads had special training for immediate assistance then the General Manager should have gotten them to the scene as quickly as possible to stabilize Mr. Patrick, while waiting for emergency service.

Clearly, in this case, a group decision was not appropriate. Quick thinking and individual control may have saved the life of Mr. Patrick.

Manager Response 4

It does not seem that there was enough time for Armando to say anything further to Mr. Patrick. Armando asked Mr. Patrick not to come in; he did anyway.

Being Armando, I would have immediately instructed someone to phone Emergency Medical Services (911). I would have had the first person at the scene to complete this task. I would be specific in my instructions. I would then have told that person to go out to the street and wait for the ambulance (to help facilitate a quick response).

I would have asked the second person on the scene to find the Chef or Caroline, as they both are trained in first aid. If Armando knew first aid, he should have checked for bleeding and breathing. He then should have then begun the prioritized list of first aid functions including CPR.

A strong individual should have taken charge of the situation. This was not the time for buyoff from the operations team. This failure to take charge resulted in a worst-case scenario for the member and the Club.

Manager Response 5

Prior to the fall, Armando did all that he could to handle the situation. Our deceased friend, Mr. Patrick, was determined to drop off that payment envelope, in his golf cleats, no matter what. Over his dead body was he going to be that close to his goal and be denied. Armando was in a tough situation that club employees face every day. It is one thing to empower employees to suggest policy to members and it is something else to physically restrain a member. For example, the Club cannot allow the bartender to serve a drink to an intoxicated person, but the Club cannot allow an employee to physically stop a member from entering the Club if the member is improperly dressed or in golf spikes. Management and line employees were not hired to be hall monitors or cafeteria police. Employees can only inform management of rule infractions and management can only pass this information on to the Board. It is not the function of the paid employees to enforce club rules. The members (on a peer-to-peer basis) must monitor themselves and allow the employees to focus on operations issues. Employees should point out policies and rules. If members insist on bending rules or disregarding policy, it is the staff's duty to inform, but the Board's function to discipline.

Unfortunately for our now dead member, Mr. Patrick, his insistence to disregard the warnings of the employee and overpower this weaker-position person proved to be very costly.

This is an example of how strong personalities can overpower others in a team or group setting. In this scenario, the socially stronger member pays the ultimate price for his domineering behavior. Members sometimes want rules to be in effect at their club for others and not themselves.

When an accident like this occurs, call 911 and find the nearest qualified person to administer first aid in the meantime. All Clubs should have a safety plan in place. Hopefully the team has practiced and that they would be able to perform effectively in saving a life.

Manager Response 6

In this instance, an individual decision is necessary. If I had seen blood coming from Mr. Patrick's head, immediately I would have directed the reception desk to press 911. In the case of an emergency, there is no time for conference; action should be quick and decisive.

Mr. Patrick was warned about the cleats, but not explained as to why. If he had been told that the slate was slippery, and he had a chance of falling, he would have—at least—exercised some degree of caution. Then, if he insisted on coming in, I would have gone to him and taken the payment from him myself.

This seemed like it could happen at a club. There is no doubt that under the circumstances I would have had the desk call 911 immediately. As to the first aid, that would depend on the situation and what I was able to do at the time. After the 911 call, then I would have called for help from any qualified member in the immediate area. Last, I would have sent one of the reception employees out to meet the ambulance.

Manager Response 7

As Armondo, I would have first told Mr. Patrick to be careful (explaining why) as those words would have stopped him in his tracks. Telling a member that he or she cannot do something is not effective in a club environment—the member is very likely one of the Club's owners. Then, when Mr. Patrick stated that he wanted to just drop off his payment, I would have suggested that I take his payment for him in order to help prevent his falling.

Fortunately or unfortunately, depending on how one views this particular case, I have faced similar accidents before. But even before knowing what to do, we knew how to approach an emergency. This is strategic. As soon as he fell and I saw bleeding from the head, I would have instructed that someone call 911 for a head injury on a male who was approximately 70 years of age. I then would have instructed one person to get the chef, another to get Caroline Duffy, and another to see if there was a physician somewhere inside the Club. I would then instruct someone to towels, another to meet or get someone to meet the ambulance at the front door or in the driveway depending on the setup of the Club. The other three acts that I would do would be to apply pressure to the head, clear the scene of onlookers, and have someone contact Mr. Patrick's wife.

A situation like this is one we hope people never have to face, but working at clubs, it is something we should expect to face. If we expect to encounter this type of emergency, we should plan for it in advance. Even if we do not put everyone through first aid training, we should at least teach the process of emergency response teams. A situation like this requires a team effort with a strong leader to marshal resources and provide clear directions, whereby people do not have to think. For example, *Fred, dial 911 and report that we have an injured male in his mid 70s that is bleeding from the head as the result of a slip and fall.* This is an ineffective example, *Fred, call someone for help.* By following the first set of directions, Fred does not need to think about who to call, at what number, and what to say.

Lesson 9

Deciding Alone or Using a Team

As beneficial as team participation can be, it is often used indiscriminately. Vroom and Yetton present several factors that must be considered when deciding whether to make a decision alone or to involve others in the process. Ettling summarized that team participation may be more appropriate than individual decision making in the following scenarios:

When the quality of the decision is critical. A group of people working on a decision reduces the possibility of error or omission in the judgment or reasoning processes. A team of individuals will have a greater pool of information to draw from when making the decision. Participation is more appropriate when a manager does not possess enough information to solve a problem alone. In these circumstances, the leader needs the expertise of subordinates to reach a high-quality decision. Participation is also more appropriate when the nature and the dimensions of the problem are unclear. Then, the team's help is needed to define the problem and to separate symptoms of the problem from the true problem.

When acceptance of the decision by other individuals or teams is necessary to implement the decision. Team members' involvement in the decision creates a sense of ownership. When team members are involved, they will work to ensure that the decision is implemented and carried out properly—especially when the decision or problem is important and relevant to them. On the other hand, team members can find extended consultation on matters of little relevance to them to be a waste of time.

When team members share the same goals and are trusted to carefully consider the decision. Individuals whose responsibilities will be greatly affected by the decision will likely take the decision seriously and put the appropriate time into making an optimal decision. Also, individuals who have successful track records in team decision making will be more trusted with a current decision (Locke). Furthermore, participation is more appropriate when subordinates share the leader's goals in solving a problem. If subordinates sense that the best solution might work against their own personal interest, the probability of reaching a good team decision is substantially lowered.

Barker found that individuals may be better suited to make decisions than are teams under the following circumstances:

When the individual has the information necessary to make a good decision. When an individual has the necessary information, it may be more effective to make the decision alone. The presence of confidential or sensitive information in the decision process may decrease the desirability of involving other individuals.

When there is an applicable solution that has worked well in the past. If a situation seems similar to an instance in the past where a decision has worked well, a similar solution may be utilized without the participation of others.

When there are time constraints. Strict time limits may make the inclusion of other individuals in the decision process less desirable. In such instances, an individual may be forced to make the decision alone. Caution must be taken, however, as the time factor can become a convenient excuse for the exclusion of others in decision making.

It is critical to ensure that team participation is essential to the task at hand. Participation in decision making should be utilized to allow knowledgeable individuals to contribute to a decision, to address conflicting views, or to gain new sources of expertise. On the other hand, when one individual has much greater knowledge on a subject than others, when there are serious time limits, or when individuals are able and wish to work alone, a non-participative approach will be more appropriate.

Higher Quality Outcomes

The utilization of teams fosters more input and the consideration of a wider range of values and opinions in consideration of a variety of alternatives. Davis found evidence that teams make fewer errors in judgment than do individuals. Another consideration is that some individuals may work harder individually than in a team. This can be especially prevalent if there is shared responsibility for the outcome, if the individuals believe their efforts are not essential, or if their motivation is low.

If a team performs a task that could be accomplished by one individual, the result will be merely the total of the outputs of the individuals. In such situations, team performance cannot exceed the performance of its strongest member. By contrast, in completing a task in which team effort is a necessity, team performance can exceed that of its strongest team member. Zaleznik and Moment identified this as the *assembly effect*, a situation in which a team is able to achieve collectively something which could not have been achieved by any member working alone or by a combination of individual efforts. Others refer to this type of high performance as *synergy*.

4.8. Mini Case: The Wedding Cake

Lucy Register, food and beverage director of Toolie Bay Yacht Club, in Geneva, Wisconsin, was faced with a dilemma: *Do I get the others involved, or do I make the decision myself?*

What decision, you ask? Consider these circumstances: The Waldorf bakery called to say that they had dropped the Johnson wedding cake. It is a total loss! With the reception starting in twenty minutes, there is no time to get another one delivered to the Club. Fortunately, there is an emergency, backup cake in the walk-in freezer, so the Johnsons will have a cake. The trouble is, of course, that it is not the cake they are expecting.

The question: Lucy is pondering whether to tell the family as they arrive, or bring out the cake and answer questions if anyone asks?

Discussion Question

Should Lucy confer with the chef, the dining room captain, and the Maitre d' before deciding what to do about the cake or should she make the decision herself?

Your answer choices:

- Take charge, tell the staff what will be done and assign task responsibilities.
- Take charge, involve key staff members and discuss alternatives, but maintain veto power over input.
- Consult with key staff members and perhaps the Johnson family before deciding and or taking action.
- Create some combination of the choices proposed or create your own solution to the situation.

In your answer, take a position (state clearly what you would do based on the answer choices listed) and then defend why this would be the appropriate course of action for the family, the successful and smooth performance of the reception function (as a whole), and the Club.

Manager Response 1

I would definitely involve the chef, the dining room captain and the maitre d' to make a team decision. Given the circumstances, a quality decision must be made and there can be no omission of reasoning or judgment in the process. By pooling their many years of expertise, the team will be in a more enlightened state to explore the options, rather than one individual with a single perspective. This is a judgment call and more input will increase the chances of dealing effectively with this problem.

Since they are all members of the Toolie Bay Yacht Club service team, and presumably have the shared goal of a successful wedding reception for the Johnson family, all the aforementioned players have a vested interest in the outcome of this dilemma. These employees all need to be on the same page and carry out the decision properly to better facilitate this catastrophe. The team's decision, and subsequent implementation, will greatly affect the Johnson's perception of how successful the wedding reception will be remembered. By getting a consensus on how to best proceed, the team is afforded an opportunity to take ownership of the problem, explore options, reach a unified consensus, and increase the chances of positively handling the challenge.

Manager Response 2

Lucy should absolutely get input from the Chef, the dining room captain, and the Maitre d'.

First, the quality of the decision is critical. And, a group of people working on a decision reduces the possibility of error or omission in the judgment or reasoning processes. This is definitely a critical decision. It would be beneficial to get the opinion of other team members as they may provide valuable insight as how Lucy should best handle the situation.

Second, all team members share the same goal. That is, to provide the reception guests with the best possible food and service. They are motivated to make sure things go properly and if there is a problem, such as a substitute cake for the wedding reception, the team members will work hard together to provide the best possible solution under the circumstances.

Manager Response 3

Team participation is more appropriate than individual decision making when the quality of the decision is critical. A group of people working on a decision reduces the possibility of error or omission in the judgment or reasoning process. Under this assumption, Lucy Register should be consulting with the chef, dining room captain, and maitre d' before deciding to tell the guests about the cake before the party or waiting to see what happens.

Team member involvement in the decision creates a sense of ownership. When team members are involved, they will work to help ensure that the decision is implemented and carried out properly. Lucy will need the support of these key employees to support her decision. She will need the cooperation of the chef and maitre d' to make the substitute cake presentation as smooth as possible for the guests.

When consulted from the beginning and being involved in the process of making the decision, it is more likely that a manager will get the cooperation from the staff. Also, individuals whose responsibilities will be greatly affected by the decision will likely take the decision seriously and put the appropriate time into making an optimal decision.

Manager Response 4

Lucy should make the decision herself. Also, she should inform the family of the issue as they arrive, take one or two of the family members into the kitchen, let them see the cake, reassure them that the issue will be handled in expert fashion, and make any changes possible with the Executive Chef, including providing a substitute cake (which is the likely scenario). The key to a successful outcome is letting the key family members see that their cake is a hopeless mess (so that they do not have unreasonable expectations), but reassuring them that the Chef will make a miracle happen. This situation actually happened to me a few years ago.

Lucy should make this decision because of the short time constraints. No other team members are involved with the outcome except the Chef, and Lucy has all of the information available at the time. There is no cake and there is no cake on the way. She can only act in one way, which is to produce a cake. She has two options with the presentation of the cake—repair or replace. However, there is no way to substitute a cake without people noticing. It is better to be up front and proactive about the situation. Effective reception management means no surprises for anyone.

Having an emergency wedding cake on-hand (stored in the freezer) is a small price for a club to pay, given the emotional importance to the member for a smooth outcome, as a cake is traditionally the most important symbol at a wedding reception. Having no cake is not an acceptable outcome. It is the responsibility of the Club to make a miracle happen!

Manager Response 5

This is an interesting scenario. In this case, I would use a combination of consulting and informing, but that is not one of the choices. I would confide in the Chef as the situation directly involves him or her. Can the Chef make the existing cake look anything like the original? What were the original flavors and what type of modifications can the chef make to accommodate those flavors. Also, the backup cake that is in the freezer, will it be ready by the time needed? As for the Captain and Maitre d', this is a tough call, but they should be more told the decision and then included in the outcome. Even though the Club is not at fault, one still has to be careful about the negative spin.

The only other twist is that it might also depend on how well the F&B Director knows the bride and the parents of the bride. Will they act hysterically and cause a scene, or are they more apt to be disappointed but understanding? My final answer based on current knowledge is to consult with the chef, and no one else, or given the choices of the answers listed above, not consult with anyone and make the decision as an individual.

Okay, now it is back to school and the world of theory. Based on Ettling's process, I would reverse my decision, as the criteria discussed below support a team process environment.

When the quality of the decision is critical, use team decision making. Is there no greater decision than for the bride's happiness and that of a defining moment such as the cake on her special day?

When acceptance of the decision by other individuals is necessary to implement the decision, use team decision making. Well, making the decision is only part of the issue. The other part is implementation. In this case, execution involves not only the chef, but also the captain and maitre d' as they are the front people who need to manage the bride, groom, and family's reaction to not getting the cake ordered.

When the team members share the same goals, use team decision making. One would hope all four personnel are on the same page, are working toward the same quality standards, and all take their responsibilities seriously.

Manager Response 6

Lucy has some quick thinking to do. She has a severe time constraint and has to make an individual decision that requires her to explain to the guests that the only option was to go with the backup cake.

She also should emphasize that she and her club had saved the day, because if she did not have the backup cake then there would be no good solution. As soon as the guests arrived, I would tell the family about the problem and the solution—that you have already made—to remedy the situation.

The involvement of the team members would be more along the line of information as to what we were going to do, and not *what do you think*? Informing each of the members of the team as to what had happened and what we were doing about the situation is a key element for effective communication during a special function—especially one that involves limited amounts of time, no good solution (since the cake is a custom feature), and high emotion (the wedding itself).

Manager Response 7

I would confer with the other supervisors working the event (Chef, Maitre d', and the Captain) to help ensure that we were on the same page regarding our course of action. Then, I would let the couple and the parents know what had happened to the cake and what we were going to do about the situation—produce a backup cake. I also would make sure that no matter who was at fault that the member did not have to pay for the cake. Honesty is the best policy in this case, because it is a special day for them and no one wants the cake fiasco overshadowing the event.

Bibliography

Ahrne, G. (1994). *Social organizations: Interaction inside, outside and between organizations*. London: Sage Publications.

Arnold, Hugh J. and Feldman, Daniel C. *Organizational Behavior*. McGraw-Hill, Inc. 1986.

Bales, R.F. and Strodtbeck, F.L. "Phases in Group Problem Solving," in *Group Dynamics: Research and Theory*, eds. Dorwin Cartwright and Alvin Zander. New York City: Harper & Row. 1960. PP. 624-638.

Barker, E. (1976). *The politics of Aristotle*. London: Oxford University Press.

Barker, Larry L., Cegala, Donald J., Kibler, Robert J., and Wahlers, Kathy J. 1979. *Groups In Process: An Interaction to Small Group Communication*. Prentice-Hall, Inc.: Englewood Cliffs, New Jersey.

Beach, L.R. (1983). "Muddling through: A response to Yates and Goldstein." *Organizational Behavior and Human Performance*, 31, 47-53.

Bion, W.R. *Experiences in Groups*. New York City: Basic Books. 1961.

Boroush, Mark, Stuart Hart, Gordon Enk and William Rornick. "Managing complexity."

Bowditch, James L. and Buono, Anthony F. *A Primer on Organizational Behavior*. New York City: John Wiley & Sons, 1985.

Burns, Greg. 1995. "The Secrets of team facilitation." *Training & Development*. June: 46-47.

Collective bargaining agreement between the New York City hotel and motel association and the hotel and restaurant workers of America, local 30. (1968).

Nelson, D.L. and J.C. Quick. *Organizational Behavior.* St. Paul, MN: West Publishing Company, 1997, pp. 255-256.

Davis, James H. 1992. "Some compelling intuitions about group consensus decisions, theoretical and empirical research, and interpersonal aggregation phenomena: Selected examples, 1950-1990." *Organizational Behavior and Human Decision Processes* (52): 3-38.

Davis, L.E. (1983). "Learnings for the design of new organizations." In Kolodny, H.F. & van Beinum, H. (Eds.) *The Quality Of Working Life And The 1980s.* New York: Praeger.

Driskell, James E. and Eduardo Salas. "Group Decision Making Under Stress." *Journal of Applied Psychology*, 1991, Vol.76, No.3, 473-478.

Earley, Christopher P, William Prest, and Pauline Wojnaroski. "Task Planning and Energy Expended: Exploration of How Goals Influence Performance." *Journal of Applied Psychology*, Vol.72, No.1, (1987), pp. 107-114.

Ettling, Jennifer T. and Arthur G. Jago. "Participation under conditions of conflict: More on the validity of the Vroom-Yetton model." *Journal of Management Studies*, 25:1 January 1988, 73-82.

Fisher, Aubrey B. 1990. *Small Group Decision Making: Communication and the Group Process.* McGraw Hill Publishing.

French, Wendell L. and Bell, Cecil H. (1990). *Organization development: Behavioral science interventions for organization improvement.* Englewood Cliffs, NJ: Prentice Hall.

Gardner, M., *The Annotated Alice: Alice's Adventures in Wonderland & Through the Looking Glass* (New York: Clarkson N. Potter, Inc., 1960), p. 88.

Gatewood, R. D., Taylor, R. R., and Ferrell, O. C., *Management Comprehension, Analysis, and Application.* (Burr Ridge, IL: Richard D. Irwin, Inc., 1995).

Gatewood, R. D., Taylor, R. R., and Ferrell, O. C., *Management Comprehension, Analysis, and Application.* (Burr Ridge, IL: Richard D. Irwin, Inc., 1995).

Gellatly, Ian R. and John P. Meyer. "The Effects of Goal Difficulty on Physiological Arousal, Cognition, and Task Performance." *Journal of Applied Psychology*, Vol.77, No.5, (1992), pp. 694-704.

Gersick, Connie J. G. 1988. "Time and Transition in Work Teams: Toward a New Model of Group Development." *Academy of Management Journal* (3), no. 1: 9-41.

Gilliland, Stephen W. and Ronald S. Lamis. "Quality and Quantity Goals in a Complex Decision Task: Strategies and Outcomes." *Journal of Applied Psychology*, Vol.77, No.5, (1992), pp. 672-681.

Guzzo, Richard A. and James A. Waters. "The expression of affect and the performance of decision-making groups." *Journal of Applied Psychology*, 1982, Vol.67, No.1, 67-74.

Hare, A. Paul. 1992. *Groups, Teams, and Social Interaction: Theories and Applications.* New York: Praeger.

Heinem, J. Steven and Eugene Jackson. "A Model of Task Group Development in Complex Organization and a Strategy of Implementation," *Academy of Management Review* (October 1976), pp. 98-111.

Hersey, P. and Blanchard, Kenneth H. 1988. *Management of Organizational Behavior: Utilizing Human Resources*, 5th Edition. Englewood Cliffs, New Jersey: Prentice Hall.

Higgins, James M. (1991). *The Management Challenge.* New York City: Macmillan Publishing Co.

Hinkin, Timothy, ed. (1995). *Human behavior in organizations.* New York: McGraw-Hill Primis.

Hirokawa, Randy Y., Rost, Kathryn M. 1992. "Effective group decision making in organizations." *Management Communication Quarterly* (5), no. 3: 267-288.

Janis, Irving L. and Mann, L. (1977). *Decision Making.* New York: The Free Press.

Janis, Irving L. (1982). *Victims of Groupthink.* Boston: Houghton Mifflin.

Johnson, Rick. (1991, September/October). A strategy for style. *The Journal of Business Strategy:* 38-43.

Katzenback, Jon R. and Smith, Douglas K. (1993). *The Wisdom of teams.* New York City: HarperCollins.

Lacoursiere, R.B. (1980) *The Life Cycle of Groups: Group Development Stage Theory.* New York City: Human Service Press.

Latham, Gary P. and Edwin A. Locke. "Self-Regulation Through Goal Setting." *Organizational Behavior and Human Decision Processes*, 50, (1991), pp. 212-247.

Latham, Gary P. and Edwin A. Locke. "Self-Regulation Through Goal Setting." *Organizational Behavior and Human Decision Processes*, 50, (1991), pp. 212-247.

Lewin, David and Steven Schecter. "Four Factors Lower Disability Rates." *Personnel Journal*, November 1995, p.14-16.

Likert, Rensis. (1961). *New patterns of management.* New York City: McGraw-Hill.

Locke, E. A. and Latham, G. P. *A Theory of Goal Setting and Task Performance* (Englewood Cliffs, NJ: Prentice Hall, 1990).

Locke, E. A., Chah, D., Harrison, S., and Lustgarten, N. "Separating the Effects of Goal Specificity From Goal Level." *Organizational Behavior and Human Decision Making*, 43, (1989), pp. 270-287.

Locke, Edwin A. "The Determinants of Goal Commitment." *Academy of Management Review*, Vol.13, No.1, (1988), pp. 23-39.

Locke, Edwin A., Schweiger, David M, and Latham, Gary P. 1994. "Participation in decision making: When should it be used?" in Barry Allen Gold, *Exploring Organizational Behavior: Cases, Readings and Experiences*, Dryden Press, 251-261.

MacCrimmon, K.R. and Taylor, R.N. 1976. "Decision making and problem solving. In M.D. Dunnette (Ed.), *Handbook of Industrial and Organizational Psychology*. Chicago: Rand McNally.

Maier, Norman R. F. "Assets and Liabilities in Group Problem Solving: The Need for an Integrative Function." *Psychological Review*, Vol.74(4), (1967), pp.233-249.

March, James G. (1994). *A Primer on Decision Making*. New York: The Free Press.

Margerison, Charles and McCann, Dick. (1990). *Team management: Practical new approaches.* London: Mercury).

Margerison, Charles and McCann, Dick. (1989). "Managing high-performance teams." *Training & Development Journal* (43), no. 11, November.

Mathis, R. L. and Jackson, J. H. (1997). *Human Resource Management*. (St. Paul, MN: West Publishing Co., 1997).

Matthews, Linda M., Terence R. Mitchell, Jane George-Flavy, and Robert E. Wood. "Goal Selection in a Simulated Managerial Environment." *Group and Organization Management*, Vol.19, No.4, (December 1994), pp. 425-449.

McClelland, David. (1961). *The achieving society.* Princeton, NJ: Van Nostrand.

Mesch, Debra J., Jiing-Lih Farh, and Philip M. Podsakoff. "Effects of Feedback Signs on Group Goal Setting, Strategies, and Performance." *Group and Organization Management*, Vol.19, No.3, (September 1994), pp. 309-333.

Mitchell, Terence R. and William S. Silver. "Individual and Group Goals When Workers Are Interdependent: Effects on Task Strategies and Performance." *Journal of Applied Psychology*, Vol. 73, No. 2, (1990), pp. 185-193.

Morhman, S. A., Lawler III, E. E., and Ledford, Jr., G. E. (1996, January/February). Do employee involvement and TQM programs work? *Journal of quality and participation.*

Neck, Christopher P. and Gregory Moorhead. 1995. "Groupthink remodeled: The importance of leadership, time pressure, and methodical decision-making procedures." *Human Relations*, Vol.48, No.5.

Nelson, D. L. and Quick, J. C. (1995). *Organizational behavior: Foundations, realities and challenges.* Minneapolis: West Publishing.

O'Hair, D. and Friedrich, G. W. (1992). *Strategic Communication in Business and the Professions* (Boston: Houghton Mifflin Company, 1992).

Ostwald, M., trans. (1978). *Aristotle: Nicomachean ethics.* Indianapolis: Bobbs-Merrill.

Priem, Richard L., David A. Harrison and Nan Kanoff Muir. (1995). "Structured conflict and consensus outcomes in group decision making." *Journal of Management*, Vol.21, No.4, 691-710.

Rogelberg, Steven G. Janet L. Barnes and Charles A. Lowe. (1992). "The stepladder technique: An alternative group structure facilitating effective group decision making." *Journal of Applied Psychology*, Vol.77, No.5, 730-737.

Shalley, Christina E. "Effects of Productivity Goals, Creativity Goals, and Personal Discretion on Individual Creativity." *Journal of Applied Psychology*, Vol. 76, No.2, (1991), pp. 179-185.

Shaw, Marvin E. (1981). *Group Dynamics: The Psychology of Small Group Behavior*. Third Edition, New York: McGraw-Hill Book Company.

Silver, Steven D. (1995). "A dual-motive heuristic for member information initiation in group decision making: managing risk and commitment." *Decision Support Systems* 15, 83-97.

Simon, H.A. (1976). *Administrative Behavior* (3rd ed.) New York: The Free Press.

Stallworth, H. "Realistic goals help avoid burnout." *HR Magazine*, Vol. 35, 6, (June 1990), p. 171.

Strauss, L. and Cropsey, J. eds. (1972). *History of political philosophy*. Chicago: Rand McNally College Publishing.

Terpstra, David E. and Elizabeth J. Rozell. "The Relationship of Goal Setting to Organizational Profitability." *Group and Organization Management*. Vol. 19, No. 3, (September 1994), pp. 285-294.

Thompson, Jr., A. A. and Strickland III, A. J., *Strategic Management Concepts and Cases*. (Burr-Ridge, IL: Richard D. Irwin, Inc., 1995).

Trist, E.L. (1981). "The evolution of sociotechnical systems." In A. Van de Ven & R. Joyce (Eds.), *Organization design and performance*. New York: Wiley.

Tuckman, Bruce W. and Mary Ann C. Jensen. "Stages of Small-Group Development Revisited." *Group and Organization Studies*, December 1977, 2(4), 419-427.

Verderber, Rudolph. (1982). *Working Together: Fundamentals of Group Decision-making.* Wadsworth Publishing Company: Belmont, California.

Vorrath, Harry H. and Brendtro, Larry. *Positive Peer Culture.* Hawthorne, NY: Aldine de Gruyter, 1985.

Zander, Alvin, *The Purposes of Groups and Organizations.* (San Francisco: Jossey-Bass Publishers, 1985).

CPSIA information can be obtained at www.ICGtesting.com
Printed in the USA
LVOW091042220612

287228LV00001B/8/P